Praise for *Living on Border of the Holy*

"You may not think of yourself as a priest and you may be in some doubt about what it means when others use the label. But by the time you have finished reading Bill Countryman's work you will have discovered that you are one. You will have learned something about the joys and perils of serving as one. And you will have captured a glimpse of what it means to live 'on the border of the Holy.'

"As a culture, we are more than a little lost. We are drawn to an encounter with the Holy, but we find it easy to shun its demands. We sporadically search for guidance, but we are suspicious of religion and religious leaders. . . Bill Countryman cuts through our malaise without being simplistic or obscure, grounding his vision in the larger priesthood of humanity."

—Frederick W. Schmidt
  Canon Educator, Washington National Cathedral, and author of
  A Still Small Voice: Women, Ordination, and the Church

"For anyone struggling with how to live in the thin places between heaven and earth, Dr. Countryman's brilliant book offers hope, companionship, and the fruits of years of experience. His theory of a 'fundamental human priesthood' gives us all a compassionate guide to follow as we enter the borderlands, and it should help end the division between clergy and laity. Countryman's human priesthood leads us into the future, where God calls us to be. This book could save the church.

—Nora Gallagher
  author of *Things Seen and Unseen: A Year Lived in Faith*

LIVING ON THE BORDER
OF THE HOLY

LIVING ON THE BORDER

of the Holy

Renewing
the Priesthood of All

L. William Countryman

MOREHOUSE PUBLISHING
HARRISBURG, PA

Morehouse Publishing
P.O. Box 1321
Harrisburg, PA 17105

Morehouse Publishing is a division of The Morehouse Group.

Printed in the United States of America

Cover art: Wolfgang Kaehler/Corbis.
Cover design by Corey Kent

Library of Congress Cataloging-in-Publication Data

Countryman, Louis William, 1941–
    Living on the border of the holy : renewing the priesthood of all
/ L. William Countryman.
            p.   cm.
    Includes bibliographical references (p.   ).
    ISBN 0-8192-1773-5 (paper)
    1. Priesthood, Universal. 2. Priesthood. 3. Episcopal Church—
Clergy. 4. Laity. I. Title.
BX5182.C68   1999
234—dc21   98–42777
                                                        CIP

for

Joe McInerney
gardener & priest

Contents

Preface

By "priest" I mean any person who lives in the dangerous, exhilarating, life-giving borderlands of human existence, where the everyday experience of life opens up to reveal glimpses of the HOLY—and not only lives there but comes to the aid of others who are living there. The HOLY that the priest encounters in the borderlands is none other than TRUTH, the TRUTH that underlies, permeates, upholds (and judges) us and our everyday world. It is remote and transcendent, and yet also as close and intimate as our own breath. The border where we encounter the HOLY is not just at the edge of our existence but, even more truly, at its center. There all of us must find ourselves sooner or later, and when we do we want a priest to engage us in a mutual ministry of support and encouragement, of interpretation and understanding. Without such priestly ministry, we are in danger of finding ourselves bewildered and cast adrift.

This priesthood belongs to all humanity. That is how we have been fashioned. In living it out, however, we find that we learn our priesthood and practice it in terms of a particular cultural and religious heritage. Priesthood is common to us all, yet it is lived out in myriad ways. Much of the guidance we get for our priesthood comes from religion, for humanity creates religion in an effort to hold onto some of what we have glimpsed in the borderlands with the HOLY. With religion we can construct a language of words and signs that will enable us to communicate these glimpses. Accordingly, to speak and think clearly about priesthood, we need to be constantly aware of how it is anchored in common human experience and also of how it is shaped in specific religious traditions. I write with particular reference to the Christian churches of the Western world. Many questions and problems about ministry have troubled churches in the latter part of the twentieth century. I hope to show how two distinct but related priesthoods coexist in the life of the church—the fundamental human priesthood and its sacramental counterpart, the priesthood of religion. When we understand their relationship, perhaps we can find a way through some of our present uncertainties and perplexities.

Priesthood (or "ministry," if you find that term more familiar and comfortable)* stands in the midst of a complex constellation of ideas, hopes, tensions, beliefs, and norms among Christians today. The ministry of the laity is often contrasted with the ministry of the ordained. The ordained are under a certain suspicion of misconduct. The whole purpose of ordination in a world that has become more democratic may not be obvious. Churches often have trouble defining exactly what they see as the responsibilities of the ordained. Lay people are equally uncertain about their own role. In addition, many churches are embroiled in prolonged struggles over whom to ordain, while church authorities and seminary faculties engage in ongoing debates about how to prepare them for their work.

I wish to call both those who are ordained and those who are not to a new appreciation of the fundamental priesthood they share with one another, with Christ, and indeed with all humanity. Only a return to the priestly character of all human existence can ground a renewal of our common priesthood. I wish also to propose a more thoroughly sacramental understanding of the priesthood of the ordained, which will root their work and identity in the fundamental priesthood of the whole people instead of in opposition to them. The ordained exist only in and for the priesthood of all; in turn, they bear a certain iconic significance for the larger priesthood. Recognizing this fact, I trust, will enable us to deal more effectively with some of our practical problems.

The present work, in attempting these tasks, crosses a number of the existing boundaries of theological thinking. This work touches on biblical studies, church history, history of religions, theology, practical theology, and spirituality. We are not used to having one book traverse all these terrains. Church polity has usually been kept safely away from spirituality, lest their interaction set off a chain reaction that would prove mutually destructive. Biblical scholars and theologians keep to their separate turfs and eye one another suspiciously. GOD knows that each of us has enough to do at home without trespassing on one another's territory, and I certainly have no illusion of having mastered all these fields.

---

* I prefer "priesthood" not only because it is part of my Anglican heritage, but because it carries with it a connotation of standing in the presence of the HOLY that is not perhaps quite so strongly felt in the word "ministry." Readers for whom the term "priesthood" is not comfortable or familiar, however, will find that if they mentally substitute "ministry" for it, they will not lose the main import of the ideas I am presenting here.

It may be that only the proverbial fool would rush into such a cross-disciplinary trek. If so, I plead guilty to foolishness, and hope that the reader will at least accept that it has been a faithful kind of folly. The examination is inspired less by the illicit pleasures of trespass than by a sense that we are exploring central issues in the life of faith today, and that none of the theological disciplines can handle these issues alone. If the present effort does not fully satisfy every reader (and I think I can guarantee that it will not), perhaps it will at least provoke wiser heads to do the job better.

I do not pretend to deal with all the issues raised for each separate discipline. I hope, rather, that my work may make up for its failure to plumb the depths of each by focusing the disciplines together on a set of common issues and ideas. Above all, I hope that you, the reader, may find in this work something that will support your own priestly ministry in the presence of the HOLY and in the priestly company of all humanity.

Part I

Rediscovering Priesthood

1

The Priesthood of Humanity

It might appear, at first sight, as if a book about the life of the church ought to begin with the church itself or, at least, with what is distinctive to the Christian tradition—with Jesus, perhaps, or the Bible. But we can never truly understand what is distinctively Christian without placing it in the broader context of human existence itself. The gospel was not spoken (and cannot be spoken) in a timeless or abstract way. It is always spoken to specific people, who hear it with human ears and human minds. The news GOD speaks to human beings can only be good news if it addresses and affirms our humanness, the very humanness with which GOD first endowed us in creation. There is no contradiction between gospel and creation. The gospel takes what is already intrinsic to us and fills and enhances and clarifies it. We cannot explore the life of the church, then, or the meaning of priesthood in and for the church without, at the same time, exploring the meaning of priesthood to us as human beings.

The first thing to say in our exploration of priesthood, then, is that priesthood is a fundamental and inescapable part of being human. All human beings, knowingly or not, minister as priests to one another. All of us, knowingly or not, receive priestly ministrations from one another. This is the first thing to say about priesthood because it is the most basic. Because it is basic, it is also fundamental and therefore useful. Unless we begin here, we are not likely to understand the confusions, uncertainties, and opportunities we have been encountering in the life of the church itself in recent years. We shall be in danger, in fact, of creating makeshift solutions to half-understood problems, easy answers to misleading questions, and temporary bandages for institutions that need to be healed from the ground up.

What, then, is priestly ministry? It is the ministry that introduces us to *arcana*—hidden things, secrets. In one sense, priestly ministry is the most ordinary thing imaginable. All our lives, we are repeatedly in the position of finding, revealing, explaining, and teaching—or, conversely, of being led, taught, and illuminated. Everyone is the priest of a mystery that someone else does not know: how to construct a budget, how to maneuver through the politics of the workplace, how to roast a turkey, how to win the affections of the girl or boy to whom one is attracted. The experience is so common that much of the time we do not notice it at all. We are all constantly serving others as priests of mysteries known to us and not to them. And we are constantly being served by those who know what we do not.

Some human work is priestly in a very obvious way: teaching, parenting, mentoring, coaching, the performing arts, the arts of statecraft. These make use of what we know to sustain human life or to initiate the young into adulthood or to hand on our cultural traditions. Other tasks involve a voyage into the unknown in order to bring back news for priestly use. Prayer is like this—the prayer of quiet listening and reflection. Scientific research is a journey into the unknown. So is the work of creative artists and all serious thinkers. But even in the most daily of our daily routines, the process of priestly service never ceases. It belongs to the very fabric of ordinary human interactions. We are constantly standing alongside someone else, giving or receiving some new understanding of the world before us, whether through direct interchange or through the more remote means of communication made possible by technology. To be human means to be engaged in priestly discourse—the unveiling of secrets.

These secrets are not, for the most part, kept hidden on purpose or as a way of excluding ordinary folk. Deliberately held secrets—the secrets of governments, of corporations, of cliques—are usually trivial in the long run. We keep such secrets mainly in order to present ourselves to the world as "insiders," and we reveal them for the same purpose or because they will gain us some immediate advantage. This kind of secrecy has little to do with priesthood. Insofar as it is priestly, it tends to manifest a malformed and misleading priesthood. A fascination with being an insider actually impedes the ministry of true priesthood, which is as much about revealing as about finding.[1]

The deepest arcana are secret because they are hard to know, hard to reveal, hard to learn. They can be known only by experiencing

---

1. Sometimes, as in the ancient mysteries, the arcana may be deliberately hidden in order to set the stage for an initiation, so that the force of the arcana, suddenly revealed, can explode into new consciousness for the initiate. But this practice is a recognition of the secret nature of the arcana and serves as a way of putting them to use mystagogically, not the fundamental reason why they are kept secret.

them.[2] Anything that can be fully conveyed in language, without remainder, is probably not of ultimate importance. The truly human knowledge is that which is obtained through living. If experience is passed on through language, the language is at most a map, a directional sign, a helpful guide to the experience itself. These arcana are secret, then, because they concern dimensions of human experience where language fails (or, often, where language multiplies to the point of becoming useless). Some things are known only through our direct involvement. You cannot know what it is to be in love until it happens to you. You cannot know what it is to stand, unprotected, in GOD's presence until you are there.

The deepest arcana take us beyond the realm of everyday things. There are secrets that are sufficiently rare, sufficiently difficult to grasp in our experience, that we barely have language to talk about them. When we speak of "the HOLY," for example, we have no way of being sure that all of us mean the same thing. All we can do is pay attention to one another, listen for the implications of what the other person is saying, and try to match the other's words with our own experience to see if they overlap. Some things—many things, actually—are secret by their very nature. They can be revealed only indirectly and partially. When our language about such things puts on an appearance of solidity and complete specificity, like that of words used for common daily objects, the language misleads us. It is when we stand in the very presence of this HOLY that cannot be clearly or simply expressed that we most truly recognize our priesthood for what it is.[3]

---

2. "The knowledge which constitutes eternal life is not a projected knowledge as of an external thing, but an experimental knowledge. We do not merely know about the Divine Relationships. That is only the dead form of knowledge which the intellect is capable of receiving. In spiritual life we know these Relationships by substantial identification in the Spirit of love." R. M. Benson, quoted by Martin L. Smith, "The Theological Vision of Father Benson," in Martin Smith, ed., *Benson of Cowley* (Cambridge, Mass.: Cowley Publications, 1983) 30–31.

3. By "the HOLY" I mean roughly what Rudolf Otto described using the term—or more specifically his conception of the HOLY as "nonrational." I cannot follow him in his concept of the HOLY as an a priori category, since this mingles elements of the HOLY (as I am using the term) with elements of the sacred (see below, chapter 2). I see the sacred as a category of religion and therefore externally related to the HOLY, not truly integrated with it. See Rudolf Otto, *The Idea of the Holy: An Inquiry into the Non-rational Factor in the Idea of the Divine and Its Relation to the Rational,* trans. John W. Harvey (New York: Oxford University Press, 1958) 1–40, 112–42.

This priesthood belongs to everyone. Every human being has some access to arcana that is given to no one else—at least, not in quite the same way. Every human being has a unique privilege of encounter with these arcana and therefore a unique priesthood. Everyone has a vocation leading them into a deeper acquaintance with GOD and so bringing them home to our true humanity in GOD's presence. Grounded in this experience, we find our priestly interactions flowering and bearing fruit in often unexpected ways.

"But wait!" someone may say. "Isn't this making it all too easy? Hasn't priesthood always been difficult? Haven't the religions taught us that priesthood is remote and inaccessible to the ordinary person, that only the privileged few can know what is hidden and show it to the many? Isn't GOD revealed only to the elect? Isn't this remote GOD to be known only through the long study of scripture and theology, of halakah and midrash, or through ascetic renunciation and mystical contemplation?" Without denying that such pursuits have their legitimate uses and that one may grow in wisdom and discernment with their help, we must still answer "No."

The encounter with the HIDDEN is a kind of fault line running through the middle of our lives; no one can escape its presence. The HIDDEN forms a border country that turns out to be, paradoxically, our native land. We all live with it, on it, in terms of it. We all have our unique experience of it. It is as near as breathing. The HIDDEN is inescapable. We can ignore it, with varying degrees of success, but it does not go away. It is part of who we as human beings are. This is where every priesthood begins.

The hidden reality of which I speak has many names. It may be called GOD, the DIVINE, the HOLY, the NUMINOUS. It may equally be called REALITY, LOVE, TRUTH, MEANING, WISDOM, LIFE, DIRECTION, WHOLENESS, HOME.[4] No one can make a complete list. Not one of these names will ever be entirely adequate by itself. If we use one to the exclusion of the others, our language may even become misleading.[5]

---

4. I have chosen to set names for the substance of the arcana in small capitals, both to help the reader relate them to one another as equivalents and also to remind us that they cannot be understood in an entirely literal way.

5. "We must use names because we are speaking about a God who is personal, not an 'it.' We speak to God as Father, Mother, Friend, Lover, because we are speaking to one who is closer to us than we are to ourselves, one who has in Jesus become one with us. Yet we also know that our speaking to God is not like speaking to a father, mother, lover, or friend, because we are speaking to one who utterly transcends all of those descriptions." James Griffiss, *Naming the Mystery: How Our Words Shape Prayer and Belief* (Cambridge, Mass.: Cowley Publications, 1990) 83.

We cannot name the HIDDEN REALITY in the way we name the objects of daily existence. If we attempt to do so, we create a fundamental error in apprehension. If we take "GOD" as a term pointing to something that coexists, on an equivalent level of reality, with "universe," "cat," "coin," "loaf of bread," or "daisy," then GOD is reduced to being one thing among many. But the GOD who stands at the inmost depths of the arcana is not one among many.[6] This GOD is both different from all else and yet deeply involved in all else. GOD is, in the language of the early Christian scriptures, *ho ón*, "the ONE WHO IS."[7] Apart from GOD, nothing. In and with GOD, everything.

GOD is deeply implicated in our lives, in every place and moment of human experience. Yet this presence of GOD does not mean that GOD is an object we can control, something to which we have access at will. The HOLY retains its freedom; it can be absent even in its presence. The HIDDEN TRUTH is equally near and equally far, equally hidden and equally revealed, equally accessible and equally removed from each of us. There is no way to get control of GOD, to make GOD remain accessible or perceptible or close, and thereby to turn the HOLY to our particular use. Quite the contrary, we recognize the HIDDEN, when we encounter it, because of its absolute priority over us in time, in being, in power, in creativity, in height and depth, in beauty, in grace. Encountering it, we both fear and love: fear because we see that we are so small and have so little control, love because it is the source of being, of life, of all good.

Despite our ancient human longing to pin GOD down, we cannot even confine the HOLY in a shrine or a rite, to wait there on our bidding. We should like to tie the DIVINE to some particular place or time so that, knowing its precise location, we could avoid it when we wish and summon it on our own terms, by our own choice. If we could do so, however, we would only succeed in removing the HOLY from where it really lives, deep inside all our experience, at the origin of all that exists. Ultimately, pinning GOD down is a futile and wrongheaded exercise. Religious shrines and rites have a substantial value, but it is not

---

6. To some extent, even the most ordinary words share in this complex relationship with their referents: "All names, whether of God or anything else, are interpretations of a reality that is ultimately hidden from us, and they all fall short of the reality they would name. For that reason they are sacramental; they direct us to the reality, but are not to be confused with it" (Griffiss, *Naming the Mystery*, 63).

7. Exodus 3:14, Septuagint.

the value of guaranteeing our access to the arcana on which all priest-hood rests. That access is always and only a gift—indeed, a self-giving—of GOD that may come upon us anywhere in our lives in the world. The most we can do is try to pay attention.

It can be helpful to imagine our human encounter with the HOLY as life in a border country. It is a country in which, at privileged moments of access, we find ourselves looking over from the everyday world into another, into a world that undergirds the everyday world, limits it, defines it, gives it coherence and meaning, drives it. Yet this hidden world is not *another* world, but the familiar world discovered afresh. It is the everyday world seen at new depth, with new compre-hension. It is like discovering that the small part of the iceberg we are familiar with is buoyed up by a much larger mass of ice beneath the surface. In the border country one discovers connections, roots, lim-its, *meaning*. To live there for a while is like having veils pulled away. In the long run we find that the border country is in fact the place we have always lived, but it is seen in a new and clearer light.

It may take an exceptional moment or event to pull the veils back for us. But, paradoxically, such a moment reveals that the border between the everyday and hidden worlds is found everywhere, even in the most ordinary moments of life.[8] The poet Fredegond Shove could speak of such a moment as a "transformation." And yet, the moment was not remote or alien:

> No iceberg floating at the pole; no mark
> Of glittering, perfect consciousness, nor dark
> And mystic root of riddles; . . .
>   not at all strange,
> Not set beyond the common, human range;

---

8. "I would say that most of the time we are for all practical purposes withdrawn from that sharpness of being, and only at rare intervals does one suddenly realize the distinctive tension of being alive. It is as if a machine were just quietly turning over, when suddenly it speeds up with almost unbearable acceleration and the pitch of its whine becomes almost excruciating to the hearing." Ralph Harper, *On Pres-ence: Variations and Reflections* (Philadelphia: Trinity Press International, 1991) 93–94.

Possible in the steep, quotidian stream,
Possible in a dream. . . .[9]

Some "peak experience," unexpected and disruptive, may be necessary to wake us up, but it is far from being the only moment when we live on the border with the HOLY. Once awakened, we begin to see the TRANSCENDENT in the ordinary and to recognize that the dullest circumstances may be unexpectedly shot through with fire.[10]

The discoveries we make in the arcane border country focus around two things: finitude and connections. These, after all, are the two most basic conditions of human existence. We are finite—bounded and limited in many ways, most obviously by the ultimate boundary we call death, but also by any number of other factors external and internal to us. We are limited by the existence of other human beings, by space and time, by culture and history, by education or its lack, by disease. We are also bounded by the limits of our abilities, by the strength or weakness of our bodies or our intellects or our souls, by the difficulty we find in doing what we believe to be right, by our struggle for and against truthfulness, by sickness, by death.

In the borderlands, we become inescapably aware of our own smallness and incompleteness. In the half-awake world of everyday life, we may encounter the bounded quality of our lives only as isolated moments of guilt or fear or as that moral anxiety (often quite secularized and deprived of its real meaning) that pervades modern middle-class Western culture. In the border country, these moments of incompleteness or uncertainty prove to be aspects of something larger, grounded in the single reality of finitude as a fundamental defining fact of human exis-

---

9. Fredegond Shove, "Revelation," in *Poems* (Cambridge: Cambridge University Press, 1956) 20.

10. "Attention to the ordinary tends to be in conflict with contemporary experience with its emphasis on the dramatic, the violent, and the shocking. . . . The sacred character of the ordinary things of life is prominent in [Barbara] Pym's novels. It will continue to be so in contemporary life within and outside the church because the ordinary permeates all human experience. No human life is devoid of the ordinary, and any attempt to dispense with it is a move in the direction of meaninglessness and non-being." Belinda Bede, "A 'kinder, gentler' Anglican Church: The Novels of Barbara Pym," *Anglican Theological Review* 75 (1993): 395–96.

tence. Our presence here is not always pleasant, but it is truthful and therefore strengthening.[11]

Equally fundamental to our existence is the fact of connection. However narrowly our finite boundaries are drawn about us, no one can in fact be human in isolation. Human existence is always social, even for the hermit.[12] It is social not only in relation to other human beings, but in relation to the entire world in which we live and to the arcane REALITY which undergirds it.[13] To be human means to be in interaction with other beings. If one is deprived of the usual opportunities for communication, one will resort to whatever can be found—to remembered encounters, to the hope of being restored to one's friends and family, to imagined companionship, or to communion with the world of nature or of spirits. In the borderlands, this need for connection is revealed as something more than a string of

---

11. "Ironically, or perhaps very appropriately, it is a harder side of nature that often grounds me. Nature is not only beautiful and bountiful; at times it is devastatingly destructive, and at others, exquisitely indifferent. We can't blackmail nature. We can't wheedle or cajole it into perpetuating illusions we hold about ourselves. . . . Nature's indifference leaves us quietly to face our own truth, while in constancy it stands at our side. Its very indifference creates an environment at once unrelenting and gracious." Jean M. Blomquist, "Barefoot Basics: Yearning and Learning to Stand on Holy Ground," *Weavings* 8/5 (September/October 1992): 11.

12. "[The] completeness of emphasis on first-hand solitary seeking, [the] one-by-one achievement of Eternity, has not in fact proved truly fruitful in the past. Where it seems to be fruitful, the solitude is illusory. Each great regenerator and revealer of Reality, each God-intoxicated soul achieving transcendence, owes something to its predecessors and contemporaries. All great spiritual achievement, like all great artistic achievement, however spontaneous it may seem to be, however much the fruit of a personal love and vision, is firmly rooted in the racial past. It fulfills rather than destroys. . . ." Evelyn Underhill, *The Life of the Spirit and the Life of Today* (San Francisco: Harper & Row, 1986) 118–19.

13. This is the insight expressed in the Christian doctrine of the Trinity. "If God were alone, there would be solitude and concentration in unity and oneness. If God were two, a duality, Father and Son only, there would be separation (one being distinct from the other) and exclusions (one not being the other). But God is three, a Trinity, and being three avoids solitude, overcomes separation and surpasses exclusion. . . . Through being an open reality, this triune God also includes other differences; so the created universe enters into communion with the divine." Leonardo Boff, *Trinity and Society*, trans. Paul Burns (Maryknoll, N.Y.: Orbis Books, 1988) 3.

isolated needs and solutions. It is a basic, defining fact of our humanness.[14]

The border country, therefore, is a place of intense vitality. It does not draw us away from the everyday world as much as it plunges us deeper into a reality of which the everyday world is the surface.[15] It is a country of intense experience, not always pleasant. We may experience fear and dread, anger and desire in their full power. We are likely to encounter our own smallness and the limitations of our power in a way that proves, for a time at least, frightening. But we may also experience the love that binds heaven and earth together, which pervades and unites all things. We may find a kind of joy that can only be described, in the language of absurdity, as ecstasy, *ekstasis*, an emerging from and standing outside oneself. We may experience a peace that is not absence of distress but rather an intense, intimate, and fertile connection with oneself and one's world. Of such are the arcana made.[16]

No human being has, in principle, any better or surer access to this arcane border country than any other person. We all live equally near it, indeed within it, though perhaps without being aware of it. One person, through some accident of temperament or history, may become more attentive than another and may therefore come to be recognized

---

14. "Ultimate Reality confronts us in such a way that we are addressed. By being addressed we encounter One who is other to ourselves, but the otherness disclosed in this manner is one of communion and not separation." Christopher Morse, *Not Every Spirit: A Dogmatics of Christian Disbelief* (Valley Forge, Pa.: Trinity Press International, 1994) 91.

15. The border country connects the "surface" or ordinary reality with its deeper roots. We will imagine it best if we think of the border not as dividing "natural" from "supernatural" or "this world" from "the world to come" or even "creation" from "God," but rather as connecting the "everyday" with the "transcendent." The "transcendent" may as easily be "within" the everyday as beyond or under or over or next to or otherwise "outside" it.

16. "Our ministry [in the AIDS pandemic] is a theology of redemptive and sacrificial acts, expressing through deed—and through loss—what the Gospel proclaims in words. What we do, what we experience, and what we liberate others to do animates the new Law: We love God. And we love our neighbor. We are purified by our experience, and everything else is secondary. Our experience seems sometimes to be devoid of beauty, but it is never devoid of truth." Warren W. Buckingham III, opening plenary address for National Episcopal AIDS Coalition "Hope and Healing" Conference, Santa Monica, Calif., February 3, 1994.

as someone who knows the secrets and who can minister out of them; but this does not deny the priestly ministry of others. Indeed, without some ability to experience the secrets ourselves, we could not learn them from others. The secrets are never *taught*, in the sense that one can be taught, say, the names of plants. They are only experienced. But they require interpretation. There is always a process by which we begin to understand our experience and come to grips with it, and this process works best with the advice and support of those who know the arcana better than we do.

Even the best priest needs the service of others as priests. However long you live in the border country and however familiar you become with it, you will never pass beyond all need for priestly ministration from others. Since we are, by nature, finite beings, each of us limited by space and time, none of us will ever experience directly more than one life's worth of GOD, of TRUTH, of REALITY. What each of us comes to know are fragments of something immeasurably larger than we can grasp. My neighbor knows other fragments, which may well be the ones that make sense of my own. Therefore, I must turn to my neighbor in search of understanding, in search of the priestly ministries that can flow from that person's experience. And my neighbor will need to turn to others, too—perhaps to me.[17]

This is an ongoing, never-ending process that is characteristic of human life. As Gregory of Nyssa said long ago, human life is not directed toward a static goal. Heaven is an *epektasis*—not an arriving at GOD, but a continual process of stretching and being stretched out toward GOD.[18] The communion with the HOLY and with one another that characterizes priestly ministry is not only a means to some further end, but a participation in the goal itself. To be intimately connected

---

17. "[Charles Williams's] 'doctrine of substituted love' requires each of us to carry the burdens of others. . . . This may fly in the face of our very modern insistence— and pride—that we should do everything ourselves. To try to do everything our- selves, however, is to fly in the face of the laws of the universe, and it results in what Kierkegaard called 'sickness unto death.' [Gabriel] Marcel and Williams were convinced that only exchange or substitution can be a realistic antidote to despair. But first, 'you must be content to be helped,' and that is sometimes harder than to carry someone else's fear. And yet it can be done." Harper, *On Presence*, 44.

18. Gregory of Nyssa, *The Life of Moses*, trans. Abraham J. Malherbe and Everett Ferguson (New York: Paulist Press, 1978) 12–13. Cf. Rowan Williams, *Christian Spirituality: A Theological History from the New Testament to Luther and St. John of the Cross* (Atlanta: John Knox Press, 1979) 62–67.

with one another, to serve as priests to one another, together in the gracious presence of TRUTH, of REALITY, of the HOLY, of GOD—this is not only the way we grow in apprehension of the arcane border country; it is already, in itself, a taste of human life as it was meant to be from the beginning.

Each such experience enables me to risk further openness to the HOLY. Each such risk enables me to grow further in priesthood, so that I come to my own priestly ministrations with greater power and insight. There is more of me to participate in the ministry, more to give to the service of another, more to join in connection with the other. Yet what results, if one is paying attention, is not grandiosity, not a conviction of one's own excellence and importance. It is rather *enjoyment*, a deep openness that forswears grasping and control in favor of delight in GOD and one's neighbor, and in communion with them. For priesthood is not a thing in itself as much as it is a relation between beings.[19]

As I have already suggested, we experience the arcana in many forms. Some of them are of a kind that we commonly call "spiritual" or "mystical." We may even experience a union with the HOLY that seems almost to remove us entirely from the everyday world. At other times, however, our discoveries as we voyage further into TRUTH may seem quite "secular." The revelation may be political in its implications, like the vision of human dignity that prevented Rosa Parks from giving up her seat on the bus or the dream that drew Dr. Martin Luther King, Jr., into the struggle for civil rights. Or the revelation may take the characteristically twentieth-century Western form of self-discovery— the discovery, say, of hidden beliefs that have governed our behavior without our conscious awareness. One person discovers that he has never believed seriously in his own human worth and has merely been living out the expectations of others—of parents, perhaps, or of spouse. Another discovers that she has believed herself to be the only real human being in the world and has been living an entirely self-centered existence in which others have been reduced to tools or obstacles. Such a moment of personal insight is also a glimpse of some element of the hitherto hidden TRUTH.

19. "Perhaps [Gabriel] Marcel's single most important insight, more important than his distinction between problem and mystery, or his sense of being as presence and presence as mystery, is his insistence that what truly makes a person human is his or her capacity for being open to others." Harper, *On Presence*, 43.

Every moment of revelation is an encounter with TRUTH. It is said that the scientist who discovered the structure of the benzene molecule saw its hitherto indecipherable shape in a dream, in the form of a snake taking its tail in its mouth. This does not diminish the importance of his work in the laboratory or the careful attention to ordinary, everyday reality that such a discovery required. Without that work he would not have known what he was seeing. Yet, as is usual with great intellectual breakthroughs (paradigm shifts, as we have learned to call them), the solution came not only from hard work, but also as gift, as revelation. Every moment of discovery, every cry of "Aha!" or "Eureka!" represents an encounter with the HIDDEN HOLY.[20]

What all experiences of the arcana share is that they change our perspective and produce meaning where, before, there was confusion or misunderstanding. Human experience is far from being self-explanatory and is too rich for any a priori scheme to interpret it fully. The meaning of your life always has to be built on the spot. You may find some reusable planks from earlier buildings. Some existing plans may suit your needs. You may even find some prefabricated materials useful in the project. But meaning will still have to be built on the spot.[21] The true understanding and interpretation of life arises out of a conversation among ideas and world and people. The conversation involves both me, with my particular experience of my own life, and my neighbors, who experience the same reality from slightly different vantage points. This great, ongoing conversation is the exercise of priestly ministry.

My priests are not always people I have chosen or identified for myself as priests. Some of them may seem ill-equipped for the role. Some of them may even be my enemies. The only absolute qualification of a priest is insight, an insight that comes from some encounter

---

20. "Already in everyday human speech we sometimes hear someone say, 'That was a revelation for me.' . . . By that we mean that something surprising took place, something that broke through the experiences of everyday routine, and on closer inspection (for experience is also 'reason' and interpretation) that seemed to be 'news,' news in which we nevertheless recognize the deepest of ourselves. Here the new at the same time seemed to be the 'old familiar' which had not yet been expressed. . . ." Edward Schillebeeckx, *Church: The Human Story of God*, trans. John Bowden (New York: Crossroad, 1990) 22.

21. ". . . the Christian *perception* of the meaning of the offer of revelation comes about in a creative *giving* of meaning: in a new production of meaning or a re-reading of the Bible and the tradition of faith within constantly new situations of every kind." Schillebeeckx, *Church*, 44.

with the arcana, some time spent in awareness in the border country. Perhaps the person made a brief foray to the border country and no more. Perhaps someone may speak with insight while intending only to be cruel. Perhaps I may reveal to someone else a great truth that I do not really understand myself. There is nothing neat, tidy, or predictable about this process. Neophytes and slackers and the completely unwilling—as well as those who have grown old in faithful, attentive priesthood—may contribute something of value. One might not wish to rely primarily on the neophytes or slackers, but GOD is free to speak through any voice at all.

Even those elements of creation that do not have human voices—the physical environment, the animal world, or the angelic orders—may also contribute, speaking directly to soul and spirit without words. I will not deal with these nonhuman priesthoods in this book. Our primary priesthood is human and will be quite enough for one volume. But we share with the rest of the universe our creaturely status. We have much to give to one another and to learn from one another. There is much more that could be said on the subject of other beings as priests to us and of us as priests to them.[22]

Learning *about* religion, theology, or spirituality may strengthen one's priesthood, but it cannot substitute for the primary knowledge gleaned from one's own experience of the HOLY. That experience demands our own careful attention and also the wisdom of other priests to interpret it. Theology comes into its own when it is understood as a way to cultivate this process of interpretation. A person who lives faithfully and attentively in the border country may become a good priest without formal instruction. A learned theologian who avoids the border country will be a poor priest, no matter how much education he or she has.[23] The cultivation of attentiveness and the deepening

---

22. "Countless times nature has drawn me into itself. . . . It has reminded me over and over of the wonder and beauty of life and creation, as well as its power and fragility. . . . My sense of the Holy has always been rooted deeply in my relationship with the earth. Many, and perhaps most, of my early experiences of God—and many of my later ones as well—have mingled inextricably with the earth, with nature, with the holy ground of creation." Blomquist, "Barefoot Basics," 8–9.

23. "If ever humankind lived near the tree of the knowledge of good and evil and not near the tree of life, it is today. That is what Kierkegaard meant when he said that we know so much, have so much information, but have forgotten what it means to exist. It would be better to know less and to imagine more." Harper, *On Presence*, 106.

of understanding can make us better priests. And yet even the most indifferent human being will, at some time or other, hand on a stray insight that can turn someone's world around and make it new. So inevitable is our priestly ministry that it goes on, to some degree, even without our cooperation. How much more can it achieve with our cooperation?

The long-standing hope of all human spirituality is that we can learn to involve ourselves more effectively with the priestly dimensions of our lives. If so, this will occur by becoming more attentive and open to the REALITY that surrounds and upholds us. Sometimes, of course, the HOLY reaches out to us and calls us—even seizes us—through circumstances beyond our control. A great crisis or a great joy makes us suddenly aware that the world is much larger and deeper than we had supposed. Ultimately, the whole encounter in the border country is possible only to the degree that the HOLY is willing to meet us there.[24] Still, we can cultivate our attentiveness intentionally. We begin by cultivating humility. Humility does not mean some exaggerated demeaning of self, but a faithful, realistic, nondefensive appraisal of ourselves, of both our gifts and our weaknesses. Attentiveness also requires patience, a hopeful willingness to wait while the HOLY reveals itself, even if that seems to take far longer than we should wish. It calls for love—the love of the TRANSCENDENT that draws us onward, an answering love of our own from within, and a love for the neighbors who share this adventure with us. Attentiveness calls, above all, for a growing devotion to truth and a rejection of hypocrisy. Lies turn out to be like plugs in a conduit, damming the flow of the HOLY more effectively than any other barrier we can impose. Faithful humility, hopeful patience, love, integrity— these are the keys.

Even if we cultivate such virtues, however, there is no possibility of *mastering* this priesthood, only a hope that it may master us. One cannot by working at it make oneself the perfect priest. If you try, you will wind up focusing more on yourself than on the REALITY met in the arcana. Our experience of the HOLY always turns out to be conversational—always partly beyond our control. We cannot perfect priesthood by making ourselves perfect—even supposing this were possible—

---

24. " . . . the mysteries of God are the ways of God in getting through to us, in opening our eyes to face reality, in bringing us to faith, and hope, and love. . . . We can neither claim nor master these mysteries. They can only claim and master us." Morse, *Not Every Spirit*, 43.

because GOD's part in the conversation is not at our bidding.[25] No matter how advanced you may become in priesthood, the most penetrating, most astonishing insight may still be given to the seemingly unprepared person at your elbow. There is no program guaranteed to produce superior priests.[26]

With this reservation in mind, we can still make one basic observation about those who become exceptional priests. They often prove to be marginal, in some sense, to the mainstream of their society. This is only an observation, not a rule. There are certainly exceptions. Yet the person who is thoroughly at home in the everyday world probably finds less occasion to look beneath the surface. It is easier to take the world for granted when it flows smoothly and when you feel a clear sense of belonging. The person whirled in the eddies at the edge of the stream and battered, perhaps, against the rocks may be more ready to look at what is beneath the surface.[27]

The priestly value of marginality becomes manifest in a variety of ways. We have heard a good deal over the past few decades of "soul friends" or of "the wounded healer."[28] The phrases remind us that priestly ministry is not a gift from the strong to the weak, but rather a sharing between persons fundamentally equal. Indeed, this equality is

---

25. It may be that such perfection is not to be desired. The sculptor Stephen De Staebler has pointed out the value of our incompleteness: "It helps bridge the gulf when the other person or the image in the art is less complete. . . . We are who we are not so much because of what we have or are endowed with but because of what we are not endowed with." Quoted by Doug Adams, "De Staebler *Winged Figure* Installed at G.T.U. Library," *Arts* 6/3 (Summer 1994): 4. This is, in a sense, the negative statement of Paul's doctrine of gifts; we are defined not only by the gifts we receive from the SPIRIT, but by those we do not receive directly and must therefore depend on our neighbor for.

26. There is a significant irony in the Gospel of Mark that alludes to this reality. Jesus tells the disciples, "To you the mystery of GOD's kingdom is given, but for those people outside, all things turn out to be in riddles" (Mark 4:11). Yet from this point onward in Mark's Gospel, the disciples never really get anything right, and the moments of true insight all come to outsiders.

27. "Although there are many experiences of meaning in human life, nevertheless it is above all experiences of meaninglessness, of injustice and of innocent suffering that have a revelatory significance *par excellence*. . . . The authority of experiences therefore culminates in human stories of suffering." Schillebeeckx, *Church*, 28.

28. Kenneth Leech, *Soul Friends: The Practice of Christian Spirituality* (San Francisco: Harper & Row, 1977); Henri Nouwen, *The Wounded Healer: Ministry in Contemporary Society* (Garden City, N.Y.: Doubleday, 1972).

of the essence in priesthood. We stand beside one another sharing what we have found in the border country. Our weakness, more than our strength, reveals our mutual equality. Weakness drives us to the contemplation of a reality more encompassing and truer and more fundamental than the everyday, and then shows us that this revelation, granted in this way to us, must be granted in the same way to all. We understand that we cannot stand above anyone else in the presence of GOD, only alongside.

Another example of the value of marginality is the role of gay and lesbian people in the late twentieth century. As lesbians and gay men have come out of the closet, it becomes clear that there are far more of us in religious vocations than our percentage of the total population would lead one to expect. What brings us into such roles, often within religious institutions that are officially intolerant toward us even while they accept our contributions to their life? Some might argue that gay and lesbian people are simply more spiritual by "nature." But I think such an argument misses the point. It is not our strength but our marginalization in modern Western culture that compels us to pay attention to the deeper aspects of our human experience. Lesbians and gay men are not immune to the common temptation to pursue distraction instead of attentiveness. But whatever path we follow, we find ourselves living with a basic contradiction in everyday life, knowing that REALITY has shaped us in ways that the mainstream of our culture not only rejects, but even at times punishes. We have to ask questions that others do not have to ask.

People for whom the everyday world is not "working" have to do something about their experience of discontinuity. There are many possible responses, of which a conscious practice of priesthood is only one. Some marginalized people retreat into fantasy worlds, some into amusements and distractions, some into an excessive devotion to work or to serving others, some into the anesthetizing of their anxieties with drugs or into other kinds of hopelessness. Still others take the offensive in the hope either of changing a world that seems to have no place for them or of creating a world apart, where they will be freer to live as they think right. The priestly response does not necessarily sit in judgment on these other options. There are moments when each of them may be the best or even the only available choice for a given person.

But the person who takes up the priestly ministry in a conscious way is saying that the first order of business is neither to salve one's wounds nor to change the outer world, but to experience what is and to understand how one's experience of it is experience of the HOLY. By leading our lives, the lives we have been dealt by circumstance, on the boundary with the HIDDEN, we grow in understanding—an understanding which we can then share with others at the boundary. Priesthood begins with finding and continues with showing.[29] It is both reflective and active. Ultimately, it is in fact transformative, though we cannot always predict how it will transform us or the world around us.

Sometimes a person's priesthood is shaped and given its direction by circumstances one can only regret. In 1986, at a conference on AIDS at Grace Cathedral in San Francisco, I met Bill Irby, a gay man living with AIDS. He was doubly marginalized, both by his sexual orientation and by having AIDS—so often treated as disgraceful and unclean. He insisted on being open about both of aspects of his marginality, and he had the good fortune to work in a firm that was willing to accept that. Not long before the conference, the explosion of the space shuttle *Challenger* had reminded Americans how much life is beyond our control and how inescapable death finally is. After decades in which we had come to imagine that medical and other technologies were eradicating chance, we were appalled. We had forgotten how to deal with such realities.

When *Challenger* exploded, Bill found his coworkers turning to him. He was, after all, the only one among them who had already been brought face to face with the fact of his own mortality. He was living in that part of the borderlands called "sickness and death." People were practically lined up, he said, outside his office door, as if at a confessional, to hear what he might have to say about the unexpected limits of our lives. They hoped he might have found some wisdom that would help them deal with the shock of the unexpected disaster.

---

29. "To experience oneself as a human being is to feel life moving through one and claiming one as a part of it. It is like the moment of insight into a new idea or an aspect of truth. What initially is grasped by the mind and held there for meaning begins slowly or suddenly to hold the mind as if the mind itself is being thought by a vaster and greater Mind. It is like the thing that happens when you are trying to explain something to a child and you finally succeed in doing so. Then the child says, 'I see.' In that moment you are no longer there in fact. The barrier that stood between the child's comprehension of the idea and the idea itself has been removed. There is a flowing together, as if the child and the idea were alone in all the universe!" Howard Thurman, *The Luminous Darkness: A Personal Interpretation of the Anatomy of Segregation and the Ground of Hope* (New York: Harper & Row, 1965) 98.

I do not tell this story to suggest that such a priestly ministry is required or inevitable for those with terminal illness.[30] No, this was *his* particular priesthood, for which his illness had, as it turned out, prepared him. What was supremely painful and life-destroying in his own experience had turned out to be the means and occasion of his giving a priestly gift to others. Like him, any of us may find ourselves flung into a priesthood not of our choosing. But even if it is not so obviously and dramatically unwelcome, for all of us our priesthood is at least partly a product of who we are—of the lives we find ourselves living through accidents of birth and upbringing, temperament, education, and health.

While some of us are pushed into our priesthood by our everyday weaknesses and limitations, others may be drawn into it by a strong awareness of the arcana, an awareness that they cannot shake off and which summons them to serve the HOLY as priests. The pull of creativity, which is only partially under human control, has often drawn artists into priestly functions in our world. Indeed, for educated people in the modern West, the artist often ministers more effectively as priest than any religious functionary. Not all artists might wish to describe their work in these terms. Some abstractionists, for example, with their emphasis on pure line and color, might be uncomfortable with such language. Yet the public has found in the works of someone like Mark Rothko something of profoundly spiritual import. Sitting before his paintings, one has an uneasy and liberating sense of doors that lead further without leading away. They are compelling icons of the borderland.

Whether we are drawn or driven, then, whether our priesthood is shaped more by our marginality and our sufferings or by our gifts and longings, we become the priests that each of us, individually, alone can be. Our priesthood is a fulfillment of the potential that resides in the humanity of each of us. It is the experience of communion both with deepest REALITY and with one another.

But perhaps I am creating an impression that priesthood has to do only with great events or extraordinary gifts—with the exceptional rather than the ordinary dimensions of our lives. Nothing could be fur-

---

30. On the extraordinary depth of priesthood that AIDS has often elicited from those whom it effects, directly or through their loved ones, see Richard P. Hardy, *Knowing the God of Compassion: Spirituality and Persons Living with AIDS* (Ottawa: Novalis, 1993).

ther from the truth. As I have already suggested, priesthood is a pattern of human life acted out daily in the most ordinary ways. Parenting, for example, is a priesthood in which the parent reveals to the child the hopes and values that shape an inner center to our seemingly miscellaneous experience. Childhood, too, is a priesthood, for the child still sees things that adults have learned not to see, and the child will often show the parent a thing or two that the parent had long forgotten. It is this capacity in the child that Thomas Traherne and William Wordsworth emphasized in their differing ways.[31]

Mentors are also priests, sharing their experience of REALITY in a way intended for the good of the person they advise. We find that the perspective of our mentors, related to ours and yet distinct, reveals new dimensions to our own half-understood experience. Listeners, the people who simply hear us out quietly, are also priests. They encourage us as we look around us in the border country, examine the unfamiliar terrain, and begin to give expression to our experience and our discoveries. Speech directed to a patient and attentive audience often brings to the surface revelatory qualities that we had not noticed in our lives.

Teachers and learners are priests to one another, encouraging and supporting each other in the border country. Growth in knowledge and understanding carries with it certain risks. We cannot learn without taking a risk that it will change our world, quite probably in ways we had not anticipated. We have to risk the possibility that what we have valued in the past may cease to seem valuable, that new light may call us to new ways of thinking and living, that we may see old landmarks from new perspectives and therefore, for a time, feel that we have lost our bearings altogether. The person who is formally the student is not the only one at risk, for the student brings a distinct perspective to the material that may compel the teacher to see it in new ways. They are poor teachers who do not learn from their students. Teacher and learner

---

31. Traherne, *Centuries* 3.1–5; Wordsworth, "Ode: Intimations of Immortality from Recollections of Early Childhood." The priesthood of children is often difficult for adults to accept. Robert Coles tells us of his own irritation when Anna Freud said to him, "Let the children help you with their ideas on the subject": "At the time, I was rather put off—I thought she was telling me that close attention to boys and girls as they talked about religious issues would bring me closer to the way my own thinking, some of it childish, made use of religious interests. But years later, as I looked back . . . , I realized that she meant precisely what she said; she had in mind no condescension or accusation of psychopathology." *The Spiritual Life of Children* (Boston: Houghton Mifflin, 1990) xvi.

encourage one another in the face of these risks, forming a priestly community that has agreed to venture together into the unknown.

Politicians are priests—I mean the true practitioners of statecraft who have a genuine care and regard for the body politic, not just people trying to impose an abstract ideal on it or to make a profit. They encounter that HOLY REALITY that animates our life as communities and seek to show us how to live in conformity with it. They seek to mold, out of the motley materials of our jumbled histories, a society that will be a blessing and not a curse. There have been too few of them in the tormented world of the last few decades. The same kind of priesthood belongs, at another social level, to faithful executives and managers of all sorts. They are priests to the communities that they lead and serve, seeking not just short-term profit for a corporation, but a community in which work is a human and not a degrading activity. Neither politicians nor managers can perform such a priesthood entirely on their own. They can do it only as they enter into priestly conversation with the communities they guide and serve and begin to understand what lies in the communities' depths. The community is priest to them, as they are to the community.

Our spiritual counselors are priests to us. Perhaps they speak to us most overtly and explicitly about our relation to the HOLY, to GOD, to TRUTH, though they have no monopoly on such matters. We expect them to hear us out and to speak to our particular experience, not with prefabricated answers, as mere mouthpieces of religion sometimes do, but with a deeply rooted wisdom that can interpret and respond to our most varied needs and uncertainties. It is a commonplace of spiritual direction that the attentive counselor will also learn from the person who is seeking counsel, that there are no one-way streets in this sort of human interaction.

Perhaps our most common experience of priesthood—and often our most powerful one—is found in friendship. In friendship, desire and opportunity combine to allow us the truest knowledge of another person we are ever likely to get. In old friends we can see the flaws as well as the good points, and yet we still delight in them, still recognize their uniquely human beauty, accept that they, like us, stand in GOD's presence at the border with the HOLY. Our knowledge of our friend and our friend's knowledge of us enables us to serve one another particularly well as priests, often in ways so casual that we barely notice that priestly ministry is going on.

Priesthood is part of the warp and woof of our existence. Even the most casual of human interactions may involve an element of priestly ministry, perhaps without our actual consciousness that it is so. If we identify certain people particularly as priests—artists, for example, or holy women and men, or people who have come close to death—we do not mean that they are the only priests. For most of us, most of the time, our priests are people like ourselves—and are all the more valuable to us for that.

Up to this point, I have been speaking of priesthood entirely in positive terms. This is appropriate because priesthood is an intrinsic necessity for human life—as necessary as air and water and food. Such necessities are, in their inmost essence, life-giving and good. Yet, in practice, priesthood is not always benign. The roots and connections and limits of human experience run deep beneath the surface. Priesthood provides our access to them. But the border country is dangerous country. Not everyone who enters it emerges as a priest of TRUTH. Some of us linger long without ever paying real attention. Our impressions are jumbled and half-submerged. Others may take into that country shortcomings of character that will make us try to bend our meeting with the HOLY to our own ends. In such cases, we will return to the everyday world having seen not so much REALITY as a magnified version of our own internal untruth.

To become a true priest of the LIFE-GIVING HOLY requires a certain loving detachment. We have to enter the border country and live among its secrets without having our eye fixed too much on how we can make use of them. We are there for love and communion and enjoyment, not for use. We must often learn to let the HOLY set the question as well as give the answer. We must accept the gift of insight as sufficient reward. If we enter the border country to control it or organize it, or to have our prejudices confirmed or to make some gain, we risk having our humanity warped or destroyed. And we shall usually harm others in the process.

If we enter the borderlands "knowing" too much in advance, if we only want answers to our prefabricated questions, or escape from an everyday reality that we are tired of grappling with, or proof of our own righteousness and wisdom, or a chance to satisfy our own grandiosity by taking possession of great mysteries, we cannot grow in truth—except by having our expectations shattered. If we are distracted by self-interested motives, we cannot be fully present to TRUTH; we cannot be attentive long enough to grow in it. TRUTH, after all, can be humiliating; it can deprive us of our most treasured lies and plunge us right back into the problem we were trying to escape. But TRUTH is also what grounds us and our everyday world. What is not true is not of GOD, is not, finally, HOLY or real. To live safely in the border country, we need to cultivate a quiet openness to the unexpected and to let go our hopes of ever controlling GOD. If we use the priestly arcana to gratify personal ambition or to protect us from whatever we fear, they will be distorted and become malignant. If we use them to satisfy the passions of a group, they will become demonic.

In the scriptures of Israel, one of the first stories about human life in this world is about priesthood and how it can become entangled with personal ambition. In the stories about Adam and Eve after their expulsion from Eden, the first characteristic human activities mentioned are sex, childbirth, and the naming of children (Genesis 4:1). After these activities, we hear of productive labor, specifically herding and farming (4:2). Third, the scriptures mention priesthood (4:3–4).

Abel and Cain each offered sacrifices to GOD, choosing good things from the fruits of their work. Sacrifice is one of the ancient sacraments of priesthood; it represents the entry into the border country, with its attendant loss of control and self-possession. But like any rite, it cannot guarantee a divine response. The HOLY always remains in its own power, not in ours. It shows itself to us as it wishes; it holds back when it chooses. The first sacrifices were like all the later ones in this regard. GOD, the story says, accepted one sacrifice and rejected the other. No reason is or can be given. It was an exercise of the sovereignty of the REAL. At one moment, the HOLY shows itself; at another, not.

Cain, however, refuses to accept the judgment of GOD, of the HOLY. He will not let go of his insistence on satisfying his own desires. The differing response to the two sacrifices creates jealousy in him, and from this spring hatred, falsehood, murder, judgment, exile, alienation, revenge, and a host of other ills. In this Hebrew story, one man competing with another over priesthood brings about all the troubles that the Greeks blamed on the curiosity of a woman who opened a forbidden box. Cain could not consent to let GOD be GOD, the HOLY be the HOLY, because to do so would confront him with his own limits. His only concern was to prove that he was as good as or better than his brother. To this end, he tried to use the DIVINE. When he failed, he grew angry, his priesthood became malignant, and he made himself a murderer.[32]

Priesthood becomes dangerous partly because we try to use it as one more opportunity for human competition. In every age, claims to possess unique (or at least superior) access to the HOLY are rife. Such claims are often entangled with struggles for power or financial gain, but they cannot simply be reduced to them. If anything, our desire to exceed one another in our "command" of ULTIMATE REALITY is even more decisive than the struggle for everyday goods. We are constantly frustrated by the impossibility of gaining any clear, decisive advantage over our competitors. The lust to be recognized as the unique priest can easily lead a person into falsehood, extravagance, vituperation, demagoguery, and pandering to popular bigotries.[33] At the same time, of course, this lust leads one away from true priesthood, which can flourish only in company with an unaffected regard for TRUTH.

The person who subordinates priesthood to the passions not just of an individual, but of a group, makes of it something even more destructive and evil—something we can legitimately call "demonic." As Simone Weil wrote, "The flesh impels us to say *me* and the devil impels us to say *us*, or else to say like the dictators *I* with a collective signification."[34] Hitler must have spent time in the border country. The very power with which he evoked and encouraged and fed the passions of his audience identifies him as a man with experience of the arcana. But his desire to sway an audience, to become their leader, and to satisfy

---

32. "If . . . the terror, the loss and the fear of the unknown abyss is too much, we will retreat from the edge. . . . Our fear and our terror will set like wet cement and we will become increasingly rigid. We then move from being quarrelsome, annoying, and irritating toward becoming theological and religious bullies. . . . [T]he rigidity is not primarily motivated by the desire to control other people; rather, it is primarily motivated by the desire to control God. . . . " Michael Dwinell, *Fire Bearer: Evoking a Priestly Humanity* (Liguori, Mo.: Triumph Books, 1993) 162–63.

33. This lust can infect communities and institutions as well as individuals. "It is only because we are so accustomed to this—taking churches for granted, even when we reject them—that we do not see how odd they really are: how curious it is that men do not set up exclusive and mutually hostile clubs full of rules and regulations to enjoy the light of the sun in particular times and fashions, but do persistently set up such exclusive clubs full of rules and regulations, so to enjoy the free Spirit of God." Underhill, *The Life of the Spirit and the Life of Today*, 116.

34. Simone Weil, *Waiting for God*, trans. Emma Craufurd (New York: Putnam, 1951) 54.

their demands led him to become demonic and to sanction the demonic in them. Hitler had indeed seen demons in the border country. But he mistook their nature. He mistook the demons for Jews and Gypsies and gay men and the others he hated, when in fact they were reflections of himself and his audience—of their own evil grasping after control and exaltation. When our internal evil comes, in this way, to be externalized and to take power over us, it is not too much to speak in terms of demons and demon possession.[35]

The results were powerful—but, as it turned out, only for death and destruction. Hitler satisfied the worst of his nation's passions and in doing so destroyed the lives of millions—many of them his own partisans, still more of them people who became his enemies only because he insisted on being theirs, few of them people who held any deep ill will for him before he attacked them. The results were not only appalling but bizarre, a great conflagration beyond rational comprehension, a *holocaust*, as it has come to be called. And what is a "holocaust"? It is a whole burnt offering. The language is sacrificial language. The language is about approaching the arcana—an approach turned in this case to evil and destructive use. The borderland is dangerous country.

Priesthood, then, has the capacity to do harm. In the case of Hitler's priesthood, as in that of Cain's, the harm continues to ricochet through history. As Genesis declares, one murder will beget others (4:13–15). How long will it be before the people of Germany and Austria will be free to think of themselves in terms that are not radically conditioned by the holocaust, whether through acknowledgment of it or through denial? (Denial, after all, is merely the postponement of acknowledgment; and when the debt is finally paid, it carries heavy interest.) How long will it be before the modern world can free itself from the self-replicating specter of genocide? How long will it be before the Jewish people can think of themselves in terms that are not overwhelmingly

---

35. ". . . all of the demonic claims against human life have a common denominator. Typically, each and every stratagem of the principalities seeks the death of the specific faculties of rational and moral comprehension which distinguish human beings from all other creatures. Whatever form or appearance it takes, demonic aggression always aims at the immobilization or surrender or destruction of the mind and at the neutralization or abandonment or demoralization of the conscience. In the Fall, the purpose and effort of every principality is the dehumanization of human life, *categorically*." William Stringfellow, "Resisting Babel: Preserving Sanity and Conscience" (excerpt from *An Ethic for Christians and Other Aliens in a Strange Land* [1973]), *The Witness* 78/9 (September 1995): 16.

dominated and driven by this one event? In one sense, the answer to all these questions is "never." The Hitlerian history is a permanent accretion to our identity as human beings, just as its own roots stretch back into the distant past. In even the most superficial sense, the answer is "not for a very long time."

Such priestly evils reverberate through the history of many nations, perhaps all. In the United States, they have to do particularly with the evils involved in two aspects of our history. One is the conquest of the continent by people of European descent, who often justified what they were doing in religious terms as the triumph of Christian light over pagan darkness or, in a thinly secularized form, as the fulfillment of Manifest Destiny. The other was slavery, for which a religious apologetic was also offered.[36] In each case, evil priesthood, claiming access to ultimate TRUTH, shaped the everyday world in ways that burden us still. When our national priests claimed that GOD *willed* the evils of conquest or slavery, they effectively justified both the deeds themselves and the passions of greed and racial hatred that informed them. Doctrines of Manifest Destiny, based on the history of Israel, and a professedly literal interpretation (actually a racist allegory) of the curse of Noah gave weight to a whole series of lies about white superiority that still permeate our culture. Americans go on living with the consequences of our demonic priesthoods. Perhaps it is much the same with other nations.

Priestly experience, then, is frightening and sometimes dangerous. To be a priest entails living on the everyday plane with an awareness of the DEEP under our feet. In reality, of course, all human existence is lived out on this boundary; and yet, we are not, as human beings, con-

---

36. Some advocates of slavery argued that it was GOD's providence for the conversion and gradual perfection of Africans. I have, for example, a rebuttal to such arguments by Cornelius H. Edgar, *The Curse of Canaan Rightly Interpreted, and Kindred Topics* (New York: Baker & Godwin, 1862) 33–40. For a good survey of Christian polemics about slavery and their use of scripture, see Willard M. Swartley, *Slavery, Sabbath, War, and Women: Case Issues in Biblical Interpretation* (Scottsdale, Pa., and Waterloo, Ont.: Herald Press, 1983) 31–64. Peter J. Gomes identifies the "culturist" element in the use of scripture texts to support slavery and other forms of racism in *The Good Book: Reading the Bible with Mind and Heart* (New York: William Morrow, 1996) 46–51, 85–101. The same basic points hold true for the use of scripture to justify the European-American conquest of the North American continent.

scious of it all the time. We can and do retreat into the shallows of the everyday; we prefer, most of the time, the lower stakes of day-to-day existence. But, as Genesis puts it, humanity was created from dust and the breath of GOD (2:7); we belong to both worlds. When we encounter the HOLY, we are encountering what is essential to us, even if it seems beyond us. We are drawn inescapably. From the beginning, in Cain and Abel, humanity has been approaching the border with gifts and with fear.

The fear is well-founded. TRUTH, as such, is beyond our grasp. We can at most grasp lesser truths of varying degrees of inclusiveness. The flaws in ourselves distort the lens through which we look. The person who wants to be important will look for a truth that is distinctively his or her "truth" and will make it out to be better than the next person's. The person who happens to despise others, whether Jews or people of color or homosexual persons or some other group, will find some plausible pretext for prejudice and hatred—and will not notice how these lies distort all areas of life. The person of intense partisanship will concoct some device to prove that his or her group alone possesses the truth and all others are contemptible. It is hard for us to turn our competitiveness, our schemes, and our preconceptions loose and simply to live in communion on the boundary.

TRUTH, as a whole, is beyond us and, at a certain obvious level, almost unaffected by our existence. TRUTH, in our grasping at it, however, falls prey to all the twists and turns that human evil can inflict. Going to the boundary, meeting the TRANSCENDENT, does not deliver us from our humanness. Sometimes it may even magnify our human potential for evil to an appalling degree. The egomania that brought suffering and death to the people of Jonestown is an extreme example of something endemic to humanity; but it gained its particular power, at that specific moment, from the perverted but powerful priesthood of one man. Xenophobia and violence were in central Europe long before Hitler; but Hitler's priesthood gave him the power to focus the passions of his audience in obedience to a chimerical god of racial purity. The power of Hitler or of Jim Jones came from their having been in the border country. But their own evil distorted what they found there, and the warping of their priesthood destroyed them and many others.

Priesthood is dangerous for us, both as priests and when we have recourse to another's priestly ministry. If it were possible to rid ourselves of the arcana and to live a human existence untroubled by such dangers, one would be more than a little tempted to do so. But it is not possible. We would have to extinguish our human drive to look around us and to seek meaning and value. We would have to lose our ability to commune with one another and with the universe. We would have to forswear our desire to understand, our delight in beauty, and every creative impulse. We would have to cease being human, which is not, finally, within our power.

Rather than seeking to escape from priesthood, we shall do better by learning to practice it with humility, honesty, disinterestedness, generosity, an appropriate degree of self-doubt, and an awareness of fundamental human equality. Given these qualities, we shall learn to be priests who also accept the priestly ministry of our neighbors. We shall aim at being priests who celebrate life rather than destroy it. If we cannot altogether avoid being the heirs of Cain and Abel at the boundaries of human existence, we can at least aim to contribute further to the wreckage that perverted priesthood inflicts.

One factor in determining how well we succeed is the question of how we name the arcana. I do not mean by this statement that there is one "correct" name that will somehow protect us from the effects of our own evil. Christians name the HOLY "GOD." It is a good name. But, however appropriate, it has not saved Christians from killing or degrading both outsiders and one another in order to "prove" our intimacy with the ULTIMATE. Still, our names for the HIDDEN REALITY do influence what we seek at the boundary and what we bring back with us into the world of the everyday. Probably we do best if we acknowledge that one name has never been and will never be sufficient.

If we understand the arcana as our border with POWER and not also with TRUTH, we shall feel no obligation to honesty in pursuit of our priestly goals. If we conceive the HOLY as objective and not also personal, we may find that we have little sense of one another's human potential for holiness. If we conceive of the TRANSCENDENT only as LAWGIVER, we shall understand our world, our lives, and ourselves very differently than if we conceive it also as LOVE. If we know it as KNOWLEDGE and not also as WISDOM, we shall abandon ourselves to the pursuit of something too narrowly intellectual, not rich nor human enough. No single name suffices to hint adequately at what lies beyond our grasp. Responsible priesthood therefore involves a conscientious attempt to learn those combinations of names that give us most adequate direction, that falsify our experience least, and that put us most surely in touch with our shared humanity as well as with the transcendence of REALITY.[37]

The search for the authentic names of GOD is a search for authentic priesthood. Happily, we do not have to begin the search from scratch. We inherit priestly traditions. We learn from other priests as well as from our own encounters on the boundary. Yet we have an ongoing responsibility to test and purify the tradition as well as to absorb and hand it on. The tradition of priesthood is no more secure from abuse than the individuals who belong to it. We must all be its purifiers and renewers as well as its preservers and practitioners. The priesthood we share is forever in process of formation.

All that I have written thus far has to do with the universal human priesthood. My argument is that all human beings are priests, by virtue simply of our humanity. To be sure, we share this priesthood with the whole of creation, giving and receiving these ministries in exchange with oceans and continents, angels, trees, stars, rivers, and everything that is.[38] (This is a subject deserving of fuller treatment, but not one I can pursue here.) At the center of our experience as *humans,* however, is our priesthood to and with one another. We can perform this priesthood badly, but we cannot escape it. Nothing really useful can be said about the subject of priesthood in the life of the church until this fact is firmly in place as the foundation and starting point.

The more specifically Christian dimensions of this priesthood derive from the work of Jesus, who took up this priesthood that belongs to all of us and lived it out in a particular way. He handed it back to his followers in a form not so much altered as *interpreted* by his life and teachings. Before we can understand how Jesus interpreted our shared priesthood, however, we need first to take a look at another sort of priesthood—one that is sometimes placed in opposition to the priesthood we all share. Not only do we human beings practice the shared

---

37. The "names," of course, are much more than words or titles. Each evokes not only an image of God, but a metaphor of how God is related to the everyday world. See Sallie McFague, *Models of God: Theology for an Ecological, Nuclear Age* (Philadelphia: Fortress Press, 1987).

38. Among contemporary authors, Annie Dillard has shown particular insight into this truth. The spiritual world of *Holy the Firm,* for example, includes far more than just humanity and GOD (New York: Harper & Row, 1977).

priesthood that belongs to all by right of our shared humanity, we also create models of this fundamental priestly ministry in the form of a sacramental priesthood, the priesthood of the ordained, the clergy. This is not an occasional aberration, but a strong, widespread human tendency. The next chapter will examine the purposes, benefits, and dangers of this sacrament of our common priesthood.

2

The Priesthood of Religion

The fundamental priesthood belongs to all of us by virtue of our human-ity. The only preparation or authorization for it is what comes from liv-ing our common human life honestly and attentively in the presence of the HOLY. There are, of course, some people who turn out to be excep-tional priests, in whom our shared priesthood becomes particularly clear and who help the rest of us become aware of who we are. But there is no formula for producing such priests. Our priesthood—like the rest of our human individuality—is the result of unpredictable encounters among temperament, social definitions, personal history, and the uncon-trollable will of GOD. For better or worse, we cannot make the neces-sary encounters with the HOLY happen at our own bidding. We can make ourselves available to them, but we cannot command GOD's presence.[39]

There is an element of surprise that is integral to our every expe-rience of the HIDDEN. We can treat this surprise as a gift and delight in it. But, often, its very unpredictability strikes us as a problem. Human beings are not content simply to wait on the unpredictable HOLY. If we cannot control it, we at least want some map of it. We want to cel-ebrate the HOLY, to hand on our knowledge of it. And so we com-memorate our encounters with GOD by composing songs and stories about them, by reenacting them in ritual, and by constructing models of them in the form of sanctuaries. This process is the creation of

---

39. "We resist living with the doubt, incompleteness, confusion, and ambiguity that are inescapable parts of the life we are called to live. Living by faith means living in unsureness. . . . We cannot bear having to take a risk that this is the way to go. We cannot bear our inability to know absolutely. So we hurry up and create some certainties that will relieve us of the anxiety. The temptation in the Garden of Eden is that 'you will be as gods,' knowing all things, and we succumb to that tempta-tion all the time." Verna Dozier with Celia A. Hahn, *The Authority of the Laity* (Washington: Alban Institute, 1982) 8.

33

religion, with all its traditions and sanctuaries and ritual observances—
and the priestly orders that serve them.[40]

Religion is not the same thing as the encounter with that HIDDEN
TRUTH that is within and under all our days, the encounter with
the HOLY, with GOD. "Map is not territory."[41] Religion belongs not
to the border country, but to the everyday world, the world of
surfaces, where it reproduces the pattern of our most profound spiritual experience in the concrete, everyday terms of rites and doctrines
and sacred times and places. What I have called by such names as
GOD, TRUTH, or the HOLY in the preceding chapter, religion represents
in terms of "the sacred" and "the pure." It contrasts these with "the
profane" and "the unclean," which function as images of what I
have been calling "the everyday world." "Sacred" applies to places,
rites, things, and people set apart as symbols of the HOLY.[42] "Profane"
(literally, "before/outside the shrine") signifies the opposite of the
sacred. "Clean" or "pure" refers to whatever is in accordance with the

---

40. The point of religion is always what it points toward, never itself. "We seldom
recall that being religious means that our whole life is so ordered that every moment
we are aware that we are not the final explanation for ourselves. It means that the
ethics that control our work are the ethics of a servant, because we are not our
own masters. It means that our relationships to our fellow human beings are under
the lordship of our Creator. . . . We do not have to stop and think about being
religious because that is the way our lives are lived." Dozier, *The Authority of the
Laity*, 7.

41. I would argue that the map is inevitably incomplete and imperfect because of
the uncontrollable quality of the HOLY. Hence I would echo, though for different
reasons, Jonathan Z. Smith's statement: "We need to reflect on and play with the
necessary incongruity of our maps before we set out on a voyage of discovery to
chart the worlds of other men. For the dictum of Alfred Korzybski is inescapable:
'Map is not territory'—but maps are all we possess." Jonathan Z. Smith, *Map
Is Not Territory: Studies in the History of Religions* (Leiden: E. J. Brill, 1978)
309.

42. "Ritual is not an expression of or a response to 'the Sacred'; rather, something
or someone is made sacred by ritual (the primary sense of *sacrificium*). . . . The
sacra are sacred solely because they are used in a sacred place; there is no inherent
difference between a sacred vessel and an ordinary one." Jonathan Z. Smith, *To
Take Place: Toward Theory in Ritual* (Chicago and London: University of Chicago
Press, 1987) 105–6.

sacred, what can safely enter the sanctuary; "unclean" and "impure" define the people and things that are to be excluded from shrine and rite.[43]

I am using this terminology in a quite particular way in order to give some clarity to these pages. The words are susceptible of many meanings, of course, and others will use them differently. I am not claiming to define them for good and all—only for purposes of the present discussion. My usage is not without foundation in ordinary language, particularly the distinction in ancient Latin between *sanctus* and *sacer*; but ordinary language tends to be muddled on these matters. Religion, it turns out, models our encounter with the HOLY so successfully that we often fail to distinguish the original from the copy. In what follows, I will use the arcane names, particularly GOD and the HOLY, to refer to what we encounter in the border country. I will use "sacred" to refer to the institutions of religion that serve as models, images, or maps of the arcana.

This does not mean that religion is completely divorced from the HOLY. Like everything else in the everyday world, religion may, at any moment, surprise us by opening onto the HOLY. GOD may— and often does—meet us through it. Religion prepares us to recognize and interpret the HOLY when we do encounter it. The young Samuel, for example, heard the voice of GOD in the Temple at Shiloh, but the old priest Eli had to tell him what he was hearing (1 Samuel 3:1–18). The rites of religion accustom us to certain patterns of encounter with the HOLY. Religion maintains the language and patterns and traditions of spirituality that help us interpret what we encounter in the border country. Still, we should avoid confusing the sacred with the REALITY

---

43. Religion is not confined to the purposes I have suggested here, though I believe it originates from them. It may also become a way of organizing all reality, including political and ideological as well as spiritual concerns. Speaking of the complex "maps" of Jerusalem and Israel found in the later chapters of Ezekiel, Jonathan Z. Smith writes, "Ezekiel, by employing complex and rigorous systems of power and status with their attendant idioms of sacred/profane and pure/impure, established structures of relationships that were capable of being both replicated and rectified within the temple complex. Being systemic, they could also be replicated without." J. Z. Smith, *To Take Place*, 73.

it stands for. Such confusion constitutes idolatry and can cause pro-found harm.[44]

Religion is almost as inevitable as our fundamental priesthood.[45] It is not hard to understand why. The HOLY that we keep bumping up against in our lives is both all-pervasive and also hard to find when we want it. Our experience of it, the experience that grounds our priest-hood, is elusive. Because we are creatures of time and space, we feel the need to settle this omnipresent but ungraspable REALITY into the concreteness of a sanctuary, a fast or feast, a rite—in short, in religion. GOD, TRUTH, ULTIMATE REALITY, the HOLY—these we cannot see or hold or visit at will; but we can make pilgrimage to a sacred shrine, per-form sacred gestures, recite sacred texts, sing hymns, and join together in celebrating sacred occasions.

If these rites are of more than the simplest sort, if (for example) they require the combined efforts of many people or take several days to perform or involve many different activities, they will probably require the services of religious specialists. The approach to GOD, remember, is dangerous. If our shrines and festivals and rites are to be good images of the HOLY (their very purpose in being), they, too, must be presented as foci of power and danger. Otherwise, they are of no value. We grant them power ourselves, through our reverence for them; and then we seek help to deal with their ascribed power without endan-gering ourselves. The power we grant them is real power, for it repre-sents the culture's or community's collective extension of authority to the designated signs and rites. The power of those appointed to help us in the presence of the sacred is equally real.

---

44. " . . . the institution, since it represents the element of stability in life, does not give, and must not be expected to give, direct spiritual experience; or any onward push towards novelty, freshness of discovery and interpretation in the spiritual sphere. Its dangers and limitations will abide in a certain dislike of such freshness of discovery. . . ." Underhill, *The Life of the Spirit and the Life of Today*, 121.

45. The oldest evidence for religious rites is usually said to be the burial practices of our Neanderthal cousins (E. O. James, *From Cave to Cathedral: Temples and Shrines of Prehistoric, Classical, and Early Christian Times* [London: Thames and Hudson, 1965] 38–39). It is possible, however, that some sort of mortuary rites go back beyond Neanderthal times; see Paul G. Bahn, "Treasure of the Sierra Ata-puerca," *Archaeology* 49/1 (January/February 1996): 45–48.

Hence the creation of priest-specialists, whom we might also call "priests of religion." Their office comes into being in order to replicate or reproduce, on the level of religion, the role of the fundamental priest in life itself.[46] As we live out our fundamental priesthood on the margin between everyday life and the HIDDEN REALITY, so the priest of religion (in serving that role) lives on the margin between the profane world, with its spaces, times, and people, and the separate and sacred sphere of religion. The worshiper lives, for the most part, in the profane sphere, all those aspects of life defined by religion as nonsacred. She or he approaches the boundary of the sacred as if a stranger, seeking guidance from someone more at home there in order to enter the sacred realm and depart unharmed. All this replicates the experience of the fundamental priesthood in the presence of the HOLY—an experience that is too diffuse, too scattered throughout our existence, and too unpredictable for us to maintain a clear grasp of it. Since we cannot afford to lose sight of such important things in our life, we create maps, icons, and images to point us toward them.

Religion and its priesthood have as many different forms as there are different conceptions of the HIDDEN HOLY and different methods of mapping it. We are concerned here, ultimately, with the life of the church and its priesthoods—the priesthood of the whole people and the priesthood of the ordained. But if we are to understand how Christian religion deals with priesthood, we have to pay attention to its roots in the ways the people of ancient Israel ordered their religion and its priesthood. Much has been written on this topic by historians of Israel and of religion in general, and no doubt much more remains to be said. We do not need a detailed account, however, or a complete history of how the institution developed and changed in response to changing times—only a broad sense of its basic outlines and its particularity.

---

46. The exact nature of institutional priesthood varies greatly from religion to religion, but the common features are involvement in rites and a special relation to the community's tradition. The community remains priestly in its own right. Joseph Kitagawa has pointed out that the notion of a priestly people is very widespread in the major religions and that it is the religious communities that "ultimately play the priestly role of mediating between concrete human experience and the sacral reality, no matter how it is called" ("Priesthood in the History of Religions," in *To Be a Priest: Perspectives on Vocation and Ordination,* ed. Robert E. Terwilliger and Urban T. Holmes, III [New York: Seabury Press, 1976] 52).

I do not want to overemphasize the uniqueness of the religion of ancient Israel. The sacrificial system at its heart was, in fact, broadly the same as that of other Mediterranean cultures.[47] Still, each religion is significantly unique, significantly different from all others. Each takes materials from a common stock of human religiousness and fashions them into its own unique essence in an effort to reflect a particular experience of the HOLY. In learning and living with our faith, Christians, like other people, have to learn and value the specificity of our own tradition. It gives us our ongoing character and provides the building materials with which, under the guidance of the SPIRIT, we create our future. Even elements in our tradition that no longer have living force are still part of our collective memory and therefore of who we are. They live on as powerful metaphors and symbols even now. And the roots of our identity, without doubt, are in ancient Israel.

The religious rites of ancient Israel were largely centered on sacrifice and the altar where it took place. Given what we have said about meeting the TRANSCENDENT at the boundaries of human life, it is not difficult to see why the ritual killing of an animal might effectively symbolize the encounter with GOD. We do not have to find these rites to our own liking in order to grasp their potential power. Probably they seemed quite natural to farmers and pastoralists like the early Hebrews. In their world, human life depended in part on the life and death of animals, a process with which they were directly involved.

The Israelite tradition was of two minds about the altar, the place of sacrifice. On the one hand, the nomadic element in the tradition militated against a fixed, localized sanctuary. This element continued to be evident in the rule that the altar must be built of unaltered stones, which were not reshaped for the purpose with human instruments (Deuteronomy 27:6). In other words, it was the sort of altar one could build anywhere in the stony pastures of Canaan. On the other hand, by the time the documents of the Old Testament were reduced to writing, most Israelites were settled farmers and strongly attached to their local "high place" and to the great pilgrimage shrines such as Shiloh, Dan, Bethel, Beersheba, and, above all, Jerusalem.

The more nomadic strand of Israel's traditions probably did not place much reliance on a separate order of sacred priests, since a small

---

47. Royden Keith Yerkes, *Sacrifice in Greek and Roman Religions and Early Judaism* (New York: Scribner, 1951).

traveling band could not afford to take them along as it moved from one pasture to another. Nomads might make use of the settled sanctuaries that lay along their path; but in the main, the elders of the nomadic group were their own religious experts. The settled farmers of Israel, however, could create settled sanctuaries with more elaborate religious rites. With that practice, an important niche for the priest of religion appeared. The high place of a small village, to be sure, might still make do with the wisdom of the village elders or the expertise of an occasional visitor—like Samuel when he came to Bethlehem in search of David (1 Samuel 16:1–5). If the village grew to be a town, however, it could support its own resident priest. A great pilgrimage center could do better yet, eventually supporting a whole corps of priests in its sanctuary. In due time, sacrificial worship was limited, at least in theory, to a single temple—the royal sanctuary in Jerusalem, with a very large body of religious officials.

While some of the older documents in the scriptures of Israel reveal the gradual development of this priestly efflorescence, documents that lay out the priestly role in detail, such as Leviticus, are relatively late. They reflect the highly developed religion of the Jerusalem Temple. For these texts, Jerusalem and its one Temple were GOD's residence on earth, the place where GOD's name dwelt. Here the HOLY comes dangerously close to being collapsed into the sacred place of religion. There was still an awareness that one could not control the HOLY through the rites of religion. Yet to worship at the Temple was at least the religious equivalent of approaching GOD. The worshiper had to purge the self of all uncleanness and to leave the profane world behind in order to draw near. The only thing to bring along was the sacrifice, and it had to be of the very best that the profane world could offer, an unblemished specimen of an animal considered clean for human consumption-along with lesser offerings of flour, oil, and wine.[48]

The priest met the worshiper at the Temple, not so much to kill the sacrifice—the usual rule seems to have been that the worshiper did the slaughtering—as to *offer* it or consecrate it by splashing some of its blood around the altar and burning the assigned portions of the flesh. These actions bridged the gap, as it were, between the worshiper's

---

48. For a good survey and interpretation of the Jerusalem sacrificial system, see Richard D. Nelson, *Raising up a Faithful Priest: Community and Priesthood in Biblical Theology* (Louisville: Westminster/John Knox Press, 1993) 55–82.

profane status and the sacredness of the sanctuary, and so brought the worshiper symbolically into contact with GOD.[49] One of the ways of bridging this gap was that the worshiper gave the priest certain parts of the sacrificial animal. In one sense, this was a fee for the priest's specialized service. In another sense, what went to the priest also served to consecrate the sacrifice, for the priest was a part of the sacred more than of the profane sphere.[50]

Israelite priests, accordingly, lived under various restrictions designed to separate them from the profane world that might defile them. They had to be male. (Women were particularly prone to impurity, in the Israelite view, because of menstruation.)[51] They had to be from a single tribe, that of Levi. Those of the first rank had to be from a single line of descent in that tribe, the house of Aaron. They had to be very certain to eat no unclean food. They had to maintain their purity in order to avoid eating the sacred gifts in an inappropriate state. They could marry only the purest of pure Israelite women and take no chances on the legitimacy of their offspring. They were not to mourn for any but their closest blood relatives, not even for their own wives, since contact with the dead rendered one impure. Even those who enjoyed correct descent could not serve at the altar if they had any physical imperfection.[52]

This stress on purity fits with what we have already said about the nature of the worship in which these priests served. They took part in a ritual focused at a particular place, a place whose sacredness imaged the transcendence of GOD. By the time Leviticus reached its final form, it was taken for granted by most Israelites that there must be only one sanctuary for sacrificial worship in the land of Israel and perhaps in the whole world. This reemphasized the singularity of the Temple and its remoteness from the profane sphere. Even a person who lived in the very shadow of the one Temple had a long way to go in traveling from

---

49. Nelson, *Raising up a Faithful Priest,* 59–62, 83–85.

50. Eli's sons, in 1 Samuel 2:12–17, violated the traditional way of collecting the priest's portion and treated it simply as a fee, and therefore as purely at their own disposal. Their innovation was greeted by the worshipers with great indignation.

51. For fuller treatments of the subject of purity and impurity in ancient Israel, see L. William Countryman, *Dirt, Greed, and Sex: Sexual Ethics in the New Testament and Their Implications for Today* (Philadelphia: Fortress Press, 1988) 11–44, and Nelson, *Raising up a Faithful Priest,* 17–38.

52. For restrictions on the priests, see especially Leviticus 21.

the everyday world at the foot of Mount Zion to the sacred sphere at its summit.[53]

The priests were indispensable to anyone who wished to make this journey. For one thing, they dared to enter into the innermost court of the Temple, where no layperson could safely go. One of them, on one day of the year, even entered the innermost chamber (Leviticus 16). That their identity and their daily life lay within the Temple and that they maintained a high level of purity authorized them to move through the sacred precincts with relative freedom. In addition, since they knew the parameters of safe behavior, they could instruct the outsider in matters that were beyond his or her profane knowledge. In the sacred world, the wisdom of the profane seemed of little use.

The work of priests, however, was not limited to the Temple and its rites. If the sacred drew people to itself, it also reached out to shape the life of the profane world. We are apt to think of the offering of sacrifice as the priest's principal job—and there is a great deal on this topic in the scriptures of Israel. But another major aspect of the priest's work was to give instruction in the right way to live. The Hebrew word for such instruction is *torah*, often (but perhaps misleadingly) translated "Law." It means direction for the kind of life that, even in the profane world, would accord with the sacredness of the Temple. Not that the same degree of sacredness would be required (or even possible) in the profane world, but that the ideal of daily life should stand in relation to what the sanctuary represented.

This extension of sacredness into the profane world took place primarily through the observance of purity. The network of purity connected Israelite people to their sanctuary through the very substance of the profane world. What they ate or avoided eating, what they wore, how they planted their fields, how they cleansed themselves after sexual intercourse, how they dealt with the dead or with lepers—all these served to connect them with the sacredness centered in the Temple. Purity also served to set Israel apart from the far more profane world

---

53. "Ritual is a relationship of difference between 'nows'—the now of everyday life and the now of ritual place; the simultaneity, but not the coexistence, of 'here' and 'there.' Here (in the world) blood is a major source of impurity, there (in ritual space) blood removes impurity. Here (in the world) water is the central agent by which impurity is transmitted; there (in ritual) washing with water carries away impurity. Neither the blood nor the water has changed; what has changed is their location." J. Z. Smith, *To Take Place*, 110.

of "the nations," the Gentiles, who lacked even the most basic connection with the sacred center of Israelite religion. It was the priest,
originally, who taught these things.

The sacramental priests of ancient Israel thus had a pivotal role in
the religious life of the people as a whole. This did not mean that their
priesthood simply replaced that of the people as a whole; the scriptures
continued to assert that the whole of Israel is a "kingdom of priests
and a holy nation" (Exodus 19:6). Nor did the priests of religion
monopolize all access to GOD, for it was accepted that GOD would also
speak with kings and prophets and had a special relationship with the
poor. Their priesthood had a critically important role, however, in that
it served as the religious model for interpreting the more fundamental
priesthood of the whole people.

As we have already observed, our understanding of the fundamental priesthood will always be closely connected with our understanding
of the HIDDEN. Both the one and the other belong to that category of
things to which it is hard to give definitive expression. We can know
them only tangentially and in fragments, never face-on or whole. Our
language has no direct, ordinary vocabulary for these two concepts. To
give enough specificity to them that we can at least begin to deal with
them, we make concrete models in the form of religion and its priesthood. Thus, for example, the Temple created an image of the borderlands. Its sacredness was an image of GOD's holiness, its purity an icon
of the distinction between the HIDDEN and the everyday world. Its rites
and traditions offered a concrete model of how one might approach
GOD, through offering something valuable and shaping one's life with
reference to the sanctuary. The Temple's priests were an image of the
fundamental priesthood by which we sustain one another in the border country.

Such models of things ungraspable and inexhaustible are called
"sacraments." One classic definition of sacraments is that they are "outward and visible signs of inward and spiritual grace."[54] They put us in
touch with that grace in a tangible way. They may even be said to con-

---

54. The Catechism of *The Book of Common Prayer.*

vey grace, for behind them stands the boundless generosity of GOD.[55]
Yet they hold no monopoly on grace, which is an uncontrolled and
uncontrollable gift of the HIDDEN REALITY itself. Rather, they point
toward grace; they map it for us; they remind us of its pervasive (and
therefore ungraspable) presence by creating images of it in concrete
rites, objects, and persons.[56]

Sacraments do not *exhaust* grace, as if one had no access to grace
except through these sacramental rites or objects or persons. Grace
always remains free of human control. GOD is always free to address us
by any means whatever. If an Israelite made a pilgrimage to the Temple and there made use of the sacramental priests to guide him or her
through the appropriate rites, and to carry the blood and choice portions of the sacrifice to the altar, that did not mean that that person
had no other avenue of access to the HOLY or that GOD could not deal
with that person directly. The lay Israelite, though not a priest of religion, continued to be a true priest and to participate in the priesthood
of the whole people. Such a person might be surprised by an encounter
with the HIDDEN ONE at any moment. For the priesthood of the people of Israel was and is the fundamental priesthood bestowed on all
humanity—in the particular form shaped and conditioned by Israel's
particular encounter with the HOLY. If the fundamental priesthood of
the people of Israel were to disappear, the sacramental priesthood would
lose its significance, having nothing to signify.

What the sacramental priesthood of the Temple did for the Israelite
was to set forth in visible and tangible form the shape of every Israelite's

---

55. "Remember the church exists to foster and hand on . . . the spiritual life in all
its mystery and splendour—the life of more than this-world perfection, the poetry
of goodness, the life that aims at God. And this, not only in elect souls, which
might conceivably make and keep direct contacts without her help, but in greater
or less degree in the mass of men, who *do* need help. How is this done? The answer
can only be, that it is mostly done through symbolic acts, and by means of suggestion and imitation." Underhill, *The Life of the Spirit and the Life of Today*, 129.
56. "Uncreated grace, the loving self-giving of God to all men and women, exists
long prior to any sacramental action. . . . But, as with the boy who does not recognize the girl's love for him, so neither do men and women always recognize the
presence of the God who is grace. To realize the possibility of grace, they need to
make grace, as he needs to make love, in some symbolic action." Michael G. Lawler,
Symbol and Sacrament: A Contemporary Sacramental Theology (New York: Paulist
Press, 1987) 56.

priesthood. The one Temple, with its rites and priesthood, figured GOD's oneness. The purity rules of the *torah* figured GOD's graciousness in choosing Israel and in instructing the people in clean behavior and so separating them from the nations. The worshiper's purification and the cautious and obedient ascent of Mount Zion alluded to Israel's acceptance of the covenant at Mount Sinai. The sacrifice shadowed forth the danger and cost of our approach to GOD—and also its bountifulness, for most sacrifices culminated in a sacred banquet.

The purpose was not to replace the ordinary Israelite's priesthood—that fundamental priesthood which he or she exercised in the way uniquely possible within the called people of Israel—but rather to illuminate it, to help the worshiper remember and interpret the truths that informed it, to guide each person living and ministering in the border country that is the very presence of the HOLY. The sacramental priesthood was a secondary priesthood, derived from the priesthood of the whole people (which, after all, went back, in the biblical story, to a time when there was no distinct priestly caste in Israel) and representing that priesthood to itself. The grace to which this sacrament points and which, in appropriate ways, it nourishes in the worshiper is the fundamental priesthood itself. Without such sacraments, there is a real danger that the people would lose sight of their shared priesthood amid the everyday preoccupations of life. What is everywhere is hard to see anywhere. The sacrament refocuses attention on the almost unnoticed pervasiveness of grace.

Of course, the religion of ancient Israel did not always work this way. There is nothing human, including most certainly the works of religion, that cannot be turned to evil purpose. Our hankering to compete, to make much of ourselves, to protect our sense of self-importance, to place TRUTH, if possible, in our debt, is always looking for an opportunity of self-aggrandizement. The sacramental priest finds such an opportunity by reversing the relationship between sacrament and grace, so that the sacrament appears to be primary and the HIDDEN HOLY merely a backdrop to it. In this way, the Temple came to be seen not simply as sacred (in the sense in which I have been using the word) but as HOLY in its own right, not just as the sacrament of GOD's presence, but as its guarantee.[57]

---

57. Biblical Hebrew does not seem to have had the vocabulary to distinguish "holy" and "sacred" in the way I am using the terms here. Instead, the prophets attacked these distortions by asserting that GOD does not care about sacrifices and other religious observances.

In the same way, the priesthood of the Temple came to be not just the sacrament of the priesthood of all Israel, but a superior religious caste.

There are protests against this state of affairs throughout the history of Israel. Prophets objected to an excessively high opinion of the Temple and its sacrifices. They found that some Israelites had so literalized the metaphor of GOD's presence there that they imagined the city could not possibly fall to an invading army.[58] Others had such confidence in religion that what they did in the profane sphere seemed to them irrelevant; they assumed that, as long as they maintained the prescribed religious rites, they were free, under GOD's protection, to grind down the poor.[59] They mistook sacrament for the ultimate REALITY behind it.

In the language of scripture, this error is called "idolatry." The first of the Ten Commandments is to have no gods but GOD; the second is to make no idols. We are apt to think of idols as being equivalent to "foreign gods" and to treat the second commandment as little more than a reiteration of the first. But one can make idols of the real GOD, too. And the most dangerous idols are those made from the best materials. Whatever can serve as a true icon of GOD can serve as an idol, too. Whatever can serve as a true sacrament of GOD's grace can also serve as a convincing idol to be worshiped as if it were the grace itself. Thus the Temple, the sacrifices, and the priesthood went, at times, from being sacraments to being idols and drew down on themselves prophetic condemnation.

All this leaves us in something of a quandary. There is no religion without sacraments. And there is no sacrament that cannot be perverted to the uses of idolatry. This statement applies to modern Christianity as much as to ancient Israel. The fundamental priesthood is the central thing; but, because it is so universal and inevitable in human life, it forgets itself if it is not represented in concrete and accessible fashion. Yet when it does create concrete sacraments of itself, it is apt to forget that they are images and to take them at face value. We may even so far forget ourselves as to suppose that the fundamental priesthood is derived from the sacramental one, that only the sacramental priests enjoy real

---

58. E.g., Jeremiah 7:1–15.
59. E.g., Hosea 6:5–10; Amos 5:18–27.

intimacy with the HIDDEN, that the priests of religion are the real priests, and that the rest can only be humble worshipers.

The ministry of Jesus resolved this problem in a striking way. Jesus did not, of course, manage to resolve it once for all; in every age, people must struggle through its difficulties once again. He did, however, resolve the problem in principle by reasserting the dignity of the fundamental priesthood in his own person and by setting a decisive question mark against the excessive claims of religion and its sacramental priesthoods.

3

The Priesthood of Christ

According to the Law of Moses, Jesus was not a priest at all in the sacramental sense. He belonged to the tribe of Judah, not Levi, and to the family of David, not Aaron. As such, he had no more access to the inner parts of the Temple or knowledge of its rites or authority to preside over them than any other male lay Israelite. He was not, in other words, one of those to be reckoned particularly close to the sacred. Our reports of Jesus' life and ministry say that he taught occasionally within the perimeters of the Temple, but only in those areas open to the Jewish lay public. On one occasion, he assumed a kind of revolutionary authority in the Temple by driving out the people who changed money and sold sacrificial animals there.[60] This act infringed on the prerogatives of the priests and no doubt had much to do with his eventual arrest and crucifixion. But he was no priest of religion—at least not of the sacrificial rites of ancient Israel.

There was another kind of "priest of religion," however, in the Israel of Jesus' time—the rabbi. I put the term "priest" in quotation marks because, although the rabbi was a priest in the sense in which I am using the word, Jews of Jesus' time would not have called rabbis "priests." For them, the term "priests" referred strictly to persons authorized to offer sacrifice at temples, whether Jewish or Gentile, and not to the other kinds of religious specialists who fall into this category as I am using it. The rabbinic "priesthood" was focused not on Temple and sacrifice but on the synagogue and on instruction (*torah*). They gave people insight as to how they should practice their religion in day-to-day life. Such instruction had been an important aspect of the work

---

60. "Jesus' disturbance in the Temple signaled the new social arrangements of God's reign. His statements and threats against the Temple, his attacks on the Temple priesthood, and the implicit authority in those claims threatened the control of Jerusalem and the people by the priests of the Temple." Robert Goss, *Jesus Acted Up: A Gay and Lesbian Manifesto* (San Francisco: Harper, 1993) 145.

of Temple priests in earlier Israel; but, in Jesus' time, it had become more the work of scribes and rabbis.[61]

A couple of brief (and admittedly loose) definitions will help: scribes (literally, "writers") were literate people expert in the text of the written Torah; rabbis were teachers who handed down interpretations of the written text and also a parallel "oral Torah." Like the priests of the Temple, they brought people into contact with the sacred, but they used the sacred text as their medium rather than the sacrificial cultus. Jesus came into some conflict with these religious authorities, yet he himself was perceived by many as a rabbi or teacher. He participated, then, in this other sort of priesthood, centered on the sacred text of scripture and the tradition of its interpretation. People came to him for explanations of religion, advice on how to frame their lives, and insight into GOD's will for them.

In this sense, then, Jesus did serve as a priest of religion. But he did not fit the role perfectly. He had no specific commissioning for it, and he framed his teaching in a way that raised questions. We are told that some doubted his qualifications. People noticed that his style of teaching was more direct than that of the scribes, introducing a note of personal authority that the scribes eschewed (Mark 1:22, 27). They asked, "Where did he get all this?" (Mark 6:2), and wanted to know the sources of his education (John 7:15). There was anxiety, in other words, about whether he was a legitimate teacher of religion—a credible priest of religion, in the sense in which I am using the term. Did he know what he was talking about? How did he know? Would his advice really help people in the presence of the sacred or perhaps lead them to commit some egregious error?

There was reason to ask these questions, for Jesus preached and practiced a kind of religion that, even though it was clearly at home in the first-century Jewish world, contrasted with both that of the Temple priests and that of the scribes and rabbis. Both groups distinguished themselves sharply from the profane world and the unclean majority of

61. The rabbis ultimately refocused Judaism so that it could survive the loss of the Temple. See Johanan ben Zakkai's oft-quoted dictum that the destruction of the Temple in 70 C.E. was not an absolute disaster, since acts of loving-kindness are also an atonement. See Jacob Neusner, *First-Century Judaism in Crisis: Yohanan ben Zakkai and the Renaissance of Torah* (Nashville and New York: Abingdon Press, 1975) 169.

people. This was as true for the scribes and rabbis as for the Temple priests, though their actions took somewhat different forms. For the Temple priests, separation from the profane meant a quasi-enclosed existence, at least while they were actively serving in the sanctuary. For their dissident cousins, the Essene priests who withdrew to Qumran, it meant an isolated life of rigorous purity in the desert. For the rabbis, theirs was a life lived among the general public but still focused on maintaining purity.[62] Jesus, by contrast, behaved in a way that cut across purity boundaries and called their usefulness into question.

Rather than pulling away from the crowds in order to guarantee the purity of his person and work, Jesus habitually welcomed them, taught them, conversed with them, healed them.[63] He chose his inner circle of disciples largely from among ordinary working people, who probably did not have a detailed knowledge of purity law or the commitment to be meticulous in observing it.[64] He welcomed women among his close followers, despite the fact that, according to the Torah, they were especially prone to impurity.[65] He associated with "tax collectors and sinners" and even ate with them, no doubt at great risk to his own purity.[66] He defended his followers when they transgressed normal purity customs. He touched a leper in cleansing him and a corpse in raising a dead girl.[67] When a woman who had a hemorrhage (and was therefore chronically and contagiously unclean) touched Jesus for healing, he turned around, caught her in the act, and, rather than rebuking her, told her to go in peace.[68]

In short, the Jesus of the Gospels shows a surprising indifference to the purity code. He moves among "the great unwashed," breathing the air of the profane world rather than the more rarefied atmosphere of sacred precincts and schools. Unlike the sectarians at Qumran, he

---

62. Countryman, *Dirt, Greed, and Sex*, 45–65.

63. Jesus does, to be sure, retreat from the crowds at times, either because they threatened his safety (sometimes by their sheer size, exuberance, and eagerness to touch him), or in order to pray, to continue his ministry in a new place, or to teach his immediate disciples privately. There is nothing to suggest that he avoided crowds in order to escape the risk of contamination from them.

64. E.g., Mark 1:16–20.

65. E.g., Luke 8:1–3; 10:38–42; 23:49

66. E.g., Matthew 9:9–13.

67. Mark 1:40–45; 5:35–43.

68. Mark 5:25–34. For a more detailed account of the treatment of purity in the gospels, see Countryman, *Dirt, Greed, and Sex*, 66–96.

does not redefine the details of purity and create around himself a new zone of sacredness, which only those who were pure according to the new definition could enter. He does not even concentrate on ensuring the purity of the food he eats. His disciples occasionally try to form a barrier around him and limit access to him. For example, they try to prevent people from bringing their children to him (Mark 10:13–16), and they distrust his openness to Samaritans (Luke 9:51–56; John 4:27). But Jesus will have none of these efforts to "protect" or separate him from the unwashed.[69]

At the same time, Jesus does not reject those who are pure. He includes at least one person in his inner circle who was probably very meticulous about purity—Simon, called "the zealot." And one of the highest compliments he gave anyone, according to the Gospel of Mark, he pays to a scribe (Mark 12:34). Jesus does not, then, scorn the pure or merely reverse the valences of sacred and profane, clean and unclean. He neither abolishes the distinction of pure and impure nor substitutes one polarity for the other by declaring what was formerly impure pure. Instead, he mixes the opposites together in a potentially explosive combination. This procedure threatened the status quo, alarmed the religious specialists of the day, and has continued to produce significant tensions in later Christianity.[70]

Jesus, then, even while conducting himself in such a way that he could be seen by the public as a rabbi, a kind of "priest of religion," also was at home in the profane, unclean world. He accomplished this in such a way as to suggest not that the profane world was somehow superior to the world of the sanctuary or that it could dispense with

---

69. I write here of the "Jesus of the Gospels" rather than the "historical Jesus," not to deny the usefulness of the quest for the historical figure, but in awareness of its methodological fragility and the uncertainty and lability of its results. What remains authoritative for Christian faith is always the Jesus of the Gospels rather than any of the possible figures that can be abstracted from them, and which often seem rather jejune in comparison with the richness of the figure in the Gospels themselves. The "historical Jesus" is a useful hermeneutical tool for modern people, but is no more identical with the actual first-century Nazarene than is the Jesus of the Gospels.

70. "Earnestly seeking to live out the implications of being God's people, the Pharisees democratized the purity rules for the priests so that all Israel should keep them. . . . In contrast, the Jesus of the Gospels crosses and thus obliterates the barriers between clean and unclean, Holy [or 'sacred,' in the sense in which I am using the terms here] and profane." Nelson, *Raising up a Faithful Priest*, 170.

the world of the sanctuary, but rather to show that the two must some-how be brought together in a greater priesthood. Everyday life is not the less holy or priestly when it takes place outside the sanctuary; nor is the sacred knowledge of the sacramental priest contaminated by being brought into the midst of unclean life. Jesus was pointing us toward the recognition that the goal of sacramental priesthood is to illuminate the priestliness of all human existence.

Jesus' priesthood, as it is reported in the Gospels, is perhaps most evident in his way of dealing with the people around him. He behaves with a simplicity and directness that many people have found profoundly puzzling. He is not always friendly and "supportive," as we would some-times wish.[71] He deals out praise and blame as he sees fit. He speaks to rich and poor, respectable and marginal, weak and powerful with the same freedom. He draws followers from a broad cross section of soci-ety. He eats with everybody, taking no particular care about purity. He takes no real steps to protect himself as he wades into the political quag-mire of his time and place. He does not speak primarily to political issues, yet his words are heard as having practical implications in all areas of life.

Above all, the Jesus of the Gospels rejects familiar *roles*. He rejects his family and replaces them with his followers (Mark 3:21–35). He is a sort of rabbi, but not quite. He is a miracle worker, but not always a willing one—and often attributes miracles to the faith of the person healed rather than to his own powers.[72] In Mark's Gospel, he often silences those who would identify him as "Messiah" or "Son of God."[73] He has a high notion of his mission and his message, but no great inter-est in controlling how people perceive him. He only wishes to avoid being identified with a formula. He refers to himself as "Son of Man"—a phrase whose full array of connotations is still unclear, but which basi-cally means simply "a human being."

Jesus has no religious institution such as the Temple or a rabbinic school behind him to legitimate him. He seldom appeals to scripture or tradition as authority for his teaching, though he cites them in

---

71. E.g., Mark 7:24–29; 8:14–21; 9:14–29; Luke 12:13–21. I have had more than one student complain that they thought they liked the Jesus of Mark's Gospel until they actually read the book with care.

72. E.g., Mark 5:34; 10:52.

73. E.g., Mark 3:11–12; 8:29–30.

argument with his opponents.[74] He teaches as if his authority were resident in himself and his message rather than by appealing, like the scribes, to the external authority of the text.[75] He demands attention to his message for its own sake—for its ability to transform the listener's perception of reality and to give rise to *metanoia*, conversion. His authenticity, that is, the coherence between his life and his message, was the greatest argument for the latter.

Jesus' priesthood is not limited to his death and resurrection. Such key shapers of Christian tradition as the Pauline school and the later creeds tend to focus almost exclusively on the end of Jesus' earthly life, but the Gospels assume that his meaning is equally to be known through his daily works and his dealings with all sorts of people.[76] It is a ministry that constantly transgresses boundaries. He teaches the crowds as well as the disciples. He engages in conversation with complete strangers. He heals indiscriminately, sometimes without being asked. His table fellowship includes the impure.[77] He crosses the line that separated Jew from Gentile. He even admits that a Gentile woman has taught him something.[78]

Jesus insists repeatedly on the necessity of integrity and the destructive potential of hypocrisy. He uses no high-pressure evangelistic methods to persuade people to conform to his teaching. He utters the word, lets it fall where it may, and respects the freedom to refuse as well as to consent.[79] He gives no creeds, no do's-and-don'ts of the usual reli-

---

74. E.g., Mark 12:18–27.

75. E.g., Matthew 5:21–48; Mark 7:1–15.

76. Leo Janáček, in his *Glagolitic Mass,* recognized this and sided with the Gospels by inserting an instrumental interlude in the Creed to represent Jesus' ministry of prayer and blessing (Robin Golding in liner notes to the EMI recording of the *Mass* by Simon Rattle with the City of Birmingham Symphony Orchestra, CBSO Chorus, and soloists).

77. The Gospel narratives "run true to life when they depict Jesus as a man who drew a strange mixture of individuals to himself. The collective presence of these companions, especially at meals, caused a number of good upstanding people to regard Jesus' ministry as something immoral. For Jesus himself, however, the gatherings of his diverse friends called for joy and feasting like that at a family reunion." John Koenig, *New Testament Hospitality: Partnership with Strangers as Promise and Mission* (Philadelphia: Fortress Press, 1985) 26.

78. In Mark's version of the story (7:24–30), it is the Syrophoenician's discourse (*logos*) that sways Jesus rather than her faith, as in Matthew.

79. Jesus' parable of the sower (Mark 4:1–20) acknowledges the unpredictability ⸢ results from his mission, as do his instructions to the disciples to shake the dust ⸢ir feet and leave if they are not welcomed on their mission (Mark 6:7–13).

gious sort. Much of what he says is riddling; it leaves the hearer to sort out its true import. His parables conceal his meaning but thereby open up in the listener an opportunity for surprise and new understanding. "Let the one who has ears to hear, hear!"[80]

Jesus the priest makes no effort to create a religion that might substitute for actual encounter with TRUTH. He aims less to structure his listeners' approach to the sacred than to spark their encounter with the HOLY. As a result, his teaching has about it a quality of incompleteness. It is not a closed, finished whole, but asks to be completed in the lives of the hearers. Even Jesus' choice of the medium by which his message would originally be preserved suggests this: he neither wrote it down nor had his disciples commit it to rote memory, but relied on their being transformed by it and then reproducing it in a manner that would enable the process of transformation to continue for others in new and changed contexts.

In his ministry, Jesus stood not above, but alongside those who came to him. In him, they found a person who was truly one of them, even though far more at home in the border country. He introduced them to the HOLY as to HEALTH, to HOPE, to GOOD NEWS, to LOVE. All this was as disturbing to his original listeners as it is still to us. To be in the presence of the ONE WHO IS, the POWER that created all things, and the LOVE that can never be driven away is both exhilarating, because it means we are in the presence of ultimate GOOD, and terrifying, because it seems to threaten our rather puny control over our own lives.

It is not surprising that Jesus' priestly ministrations evoked hostility as well as a large popular following. They awakened in all who heard him our deep human ambivalence about the HOLY. The authenticity of his priestly service is what gave his message its power and also what got him killed, in part because it reasserted the centrality of the fundamental human priesthood. Jesus did not so much attack the established priesthoods of his religion (though he did do that at times) as bypass them. He showed that one can encounter GOD in the midst of the profane life of the world and without benefit of clergy.

Early Christian thinking often summed up this refocusing of priesthood by describing Jesus' life as a *sacrifice*. Instead of the sacred sacri-

---

80. According to Mark, the use of parables (or riddles) to conceal was deliberate (4:11–12).

fices of the Temple, Jesus made his whole life, lived out in the profane sphere, a sacrifice of himself. This was an exercise of the fundamental human priesthood—the kind of personal self-giving for which the sacrifices of religion are sacraments at best and idolatrous substitutes at worst.

Unfortunately, we are almost certain to misread this language, given what "sacrifice" has come to mean in modern English. The problem is twofold. One aspect of it is the way we have moralized sacrificial language. For most of us, "self-sacrifice" has come to signify a kind of behavior in which certain persons set their own lives aside in order to care for others whom they believe to be in need of their ministrations. In the past, the religious often spoke well of such self-sacrifice and encouraged it. On the other hand, we did not always think very highly of the people who did it. In truth, this "sacrificial" behavior was often sociologically determined. The sacrificers tended to be female, younger, poorer, or more pious people, while the recipients of their ministrations tended to be male, older, richer, or less scrupulous. We were apt to see the sacrificers as rather empty, pallid people, and we distrusted the "martyr complex" that often accompanied such behavior. More recently, we have learned to call some of this behavior "codependent" and to see in it something destructive both to the caregiver and to the one cared for.

This is not to deny the reality or the value of genuinely self-giving love, generosity, and altruism. It exists, and when we find ourselves in its presence, we are moved with wonder that this splendor could be a part of human existence. This is the kind of self-sacrifice that flows from a sense of great fullness, of having riches to share—riches of energy, wisdom, property, even life itself. It is not pale, helpless, or self-pitying, but impresses us with its vitality and openhandedness. It is unfortunate that the moralistic interpretation of self-sacrifice and our tendency to impose it on the weak have given the terminology of sacrifice a bad name in our time.

Jesus, in any case, did not fit the pious notion of "self-sacrifice." He was not a "victim" in our modern sense of the word. He did not surrender his life because of undervaluing it. He was a demanding person who required as much of others as he gave them, and he did not accept every demand made on him. It was his generosity, vitality, and power and his provocative, even subversive, teaching that attracted people, not some sort of pallid, plaster-saint "goodness." He had a clear notion of his own mission and allowed neither fear nor favor to interfere with it. He baited the authorities and forced them into a position where they had either to accept his criticism of them or get rid of him. And this sort of life was the "cross" that he challenged his followers, too, to take up. He was no "martyr" in the whining modern sense. If we are to speak of Jesus in sacrificial terms, we have to distinguish what we mean by such language sharply from the pale imitations of later piety.

There is also a second source of difficulty with the language of sacrifice—one that comes from certain medieval and modern distortions of the ancient Christian doctrine of atonement. At their most extreme, they take the form of the "penal substitutionary" theory of atonement, which reduces the whole relationship between GOD and humanity to the single metaphor of indebtedness. It holds that the human debt to GOD was so great that only GOD could pay it. The Father, therefore, sacrificed the incarnate Son, thus paying the human debt with divine resources. One is left wondering why a GOD generous enough to die for humanity could not simply forgive the debt. There seems to be an element of needless bloodshed here; we are left with the picture of a bloodthirsty DEITY who calculates what is owed down to the last penny and who somehow reckons the debt satisfied by human suffering and death.[81]

It has long been known that the earliest Christian interpretations of the cross were quite different from these later developments. For one thing, they did not isolate the cross from the resurrection, as if the cross were the single saving moment and the resurrection something of an afterthought. For another, these early interpretations inclined to see the cross not as a payment to GOD, but as a victory over the powers of evil and death or, alternatively, a ransom paid to these powers in order to buy us back from captivity to them. None of this has much to do with later "sacrificial" doctrines of the atonement. In every case, GOD is seen as working in Jesus to give a gift, to bring freedom and new life, to turn back the ravages of sin and death.[82]

---

81. This picture is a misreading of the whole biblical treatment of sacrifice. "Certainly our most ingrained interpretation of sacrifice, mediated by centuries of Western culture, is that of a vicarious and substitutionary death. However, this concept was hardly part of the fundamental logic of Israelite sacrifice." Nelson, *Raising up a Faithful Priest*, 79.

82. Gustaf Aulén, *Christus Victor: An Historical Study of the Three Main Types of the Idea of the Atonement*, trans. A. G. Hebert (London: SPCK, 1953).

When early Christians used sacrificial language about Jesus' death, it had specific reference to the sacrificial system prescribed in the Torah—not to payment of debts. We have spoken about the human situation of living in the borderlands between the everyday world and the TRANSCENDENT REALITY that lies behind it and gives it existence and meaning. The sacrifices at the Temple were sacramental images of this boundary: images of death and life, of gain and loss, of risk, of approaching the unapproachable, of surrender. They were also images of the bridging of that boundary—of life in communion with the HIDDEN HOLY. The sacrificial element of Jesus' life does not pertain only to his death. He stayed unfailingly in the border country, without seeking to escape from it. He did this throughout his life. And when he died, he died in that border country. Even in the face of the worst terror, abandonment itself, he called on the GOD he felt had abandoned him (Mark 15:34). His faith continued to tell him where he was and with whom, even when he could no longer sense the place or the PRESENCE.

The most extensive early treatment of Jesus' work in priestly and sacrificial terms is in the Epistle to Hebrews, which draws its images from the priesthood of the Jerusalem Temple or, more exactly, of the tabernacle that prefigured it in the days of the wilderness wandering.[83] The theological argument of Hebrews is difficult for the modern reader to follow. The reasoning is dense, and the animal sacrifices on which the author bases his analogy have long been foreign to most Christians. Still, this is a powerful interpretation of Jesus' priesthood—powerful enough to gain Hebrews a place in the New Testament canon despite uncertainties about its authorship and long-standing doubts about some aspects of its theology.[84]

Hebrews argues that Jesus belongs to an order of priesthood older, more enduring, and more significant than the priesthood of the Temple—the order of Melchizedek. Because of this, Jesus' priesthood—above all, his sacrifice of himself—reconnects humanity with GOD in a way that the Temple priesthood never could. It is not simply a religious "shadow" of true priesthood, but actually succeeds in reconciling humanity with GOD, removing all the alienating effects of human sins.

83. The author draws his references to the sacrificial cultus from the Torah rather than from the practice of the first-century Temple.

84. Harold W. Attridge, *The Epistle to the Hebrews,* Hermeneia (Philadelphia: Fortress Press, 1989) 1–6; Robert M. Grant, *A Historical Introduction to the New Testament* (New York and Evanston, Ill.: Harper & Row, 1963) 31–32.

Because Jesus' sacrifice is so powerful and complete a priestly act, it never requires repetition. There will be no further sacrifices, according to this author, only the ongoing priestly ministry in which Jesus, now in GOD's very presence, presents this one perfect sacrifice eternally before GOD, bringing our humanity into GOD's presence once for all.[85]

In itself, this is, as I have said, rather alien language for the modern Western reader. Reading Hebrews can remain a powerful experience, even today, if only because of its author's skilled use of rhythm, balance, and imagery; but it is difficult for us to imagine the impact of its ideas on someone for whom the Temple sacrifices were still very much alive—in memory if not in actual practice.[86] If there is something here that can still speak to us directly, I think it is the author's discussion of the priestly meaning of Jesus' humanity.

The basic principle of priesthood in Hebrews is this: "The one who hallows [i.e., the priest] and the ones being hallowed [i.e., the worshipers] are all of the same origin" (2:11). Otherwise the priest is of no value. The purpose of the priest, after all, is to stand *alongside* others in the presence of the HOLY. The priest knows not just the HOLY itself but also the perplexities that we human beings experience in its presence. The priest knows *both* sides of the experience and can help form a bridge between them. Angels, too, dwell in the borderlands between their created reality and the transcendent reality of GOD. Since we share with them the status of creatures, they may, at times, serve as priests to us as well as to one another. But they will never be perfect priests for us because they cannot know from within what it is to be human. They do not share our particular experience of finitude or of connection with one another. True priestly service cannot be offered out of condescension, but only out of a shared identity. We can be priests to one another only insofar as we share a common life.

Since Jesus' priesthood is a priesthood for all humanity, we can understand it only by understanding what all human beings have in common. There are many possible ways of addressing that issue, but for the author of Hebrews, the principal answer is easy: Jesus shares

---

85. Hebrews 6:19–10:31.

86. The date of the writing of Hebrews is much disputed. The work was long regarded as late, but a number of scholars in the latter half of this century have assigned it an early date, even before the destruction of the Jerusalem Temple in 70 C.E. For a survey of issues and proposed solutions, see Attridge, *The Epistle to the Hebrews*, 6–9.

with us death, suffering, temptation—weakness of every sort.[87] I do not suppose that our author meant this as a complete description of what it is to be human; he was not writing a treatise on human life as such. But he did mean, I think, to underline, as the single most determinative aspect of our humanness, our *finitude*. In the presence of the HOLY, we know, above all, our limits, our weakness, our death. We also know life and joy and transcendence. But we know them as gifts from GOD, not as things of our own creating or possessing. This means that even life and transcendence are signs of our limitations. We can embrace them as pure joy only when we can embrace them with the humility of acknowledged creatureliness.

It was appropriate, then, for GOD "to perfect [Jesus] through sufferings once he had led many sons [and daughters] into glory—the one who was the pioneer of their salvation" (2:10). It was needful that "[Jesus] be assimilated in all respects to the brothers and sisters, so that he might be a merciful and faithful high priest with respect to GOD, for expiating the people's sins" (2:17). The faithful can dare to approach GOD boldly now because we have a high priest "capable of sympathizing with our weaknesses and tested likewise in all ways without sin" (4:15–16). Jesus' priesthood is not merely a priesthood of religion, isolated in the sanctuary from all things ordinary or impure. This priesthood is carried on in the very midst of ordinary life. Jesus is fully sensible of our uncertainties and fears and struggles, having experienced them to the full. Yet he stands by us, without fail, in the intimidating borderlands to minister to us. Jesus' priesthood is not Aaronic or Levitical, not a priesthood of religion, based on sacred shrines and rites. It is the priesthood of Melchizedek, named for a Gentile king (Genesis 14:17–24) and shared with all humanity.[88]

Weakness and limitation, then, are characteristics intrinsic to our humanity—characteristics of which we become particularly conscious when we approach the boundary with the HOLY. The SON, in assuming our humanity, also assumes this weakness. Yet this is not the weakness of the self-appointed "martyr," who sees himself or herself as less

---

87. Hebrews 2:5–18; 4:14–5:10.

88. It is ironic that the phrase "a priest after the order of Melchizedek" later became a part of Christian ordination rites and was applied to priests of religion, thus reversing the point made by the author of Hebrews, i.e., that Jesus was *not* a priest of his own religion.

than a full human being, and who seeks attachment to some person or cause that might be more "valuable." No, this is the weakness and limitation that characterizes all human life equally. It is our finitude. Finitude does not forbid us to lead a rich life, giving and receiving in abundance, loving, taking risks, creating, losing, grieving, hoping, and all the rest. If anything, it commands us to do all these things, because this is the way human beings live in the borderlands with GOD. We have, then, a little space in which to create something of significance in conversation with GOD. Indeed, we truly know our limitations only as we come to know our glory and our glory only as we come to know our limitations. Whether in our weakness or our strength, we find that we are still on the same border with the HIDDEN HOLY—powerless to move that border or to cross it and, yet, engaged across it in a rich and life-giving communion with GOD.[89]

The Jesus who ate with sinners, who walked all over Galilee and Judea and the surrounding territories, teaching and healing and outraging the religious and political authorities, who gathered a motley assortment of disciples and stopped to talk with nobodies, who died at last on the cross, with its attendant public humiliation, knew the boundary with the HOLY as well as a human being can know it. He knew both the fear and the love associated with it, and did not back away. He stayed on the border, there to live and die and to serve as priest for the rest of us. This is what it means to speak of Jesus as having offered a sacrifice of himself. As the author of Hebrews insists, Jesus was no priest of the Temple (7:14). For that matter, he was not even a proper rabbi. Yet our author took the image of the sacramental priesthood of Israel and showed how Jesus brought it back to its roots in humanity's fundamental priesthood. Jesus brought this common, fundamental priesthood to full expression by living it out, right through the completed sacrifice of his own life and death in the borderlands.[90]

---

89. Ignoring our finitude tends to produce disastrous results. "The *hero with power* . . . is able to reorder and temporarily fix. The *hero of no power* is able to transform. Every solution that the hero-with-power provides simply sets up the next set of issues, dilemmas, and conflicts; the hero of no power changes the whole 'gestalt.'" Dwinell, *Fire Bearer*, 45.

90. ". . . following Jesus the pioneer high priest eventually calls for a reversal of movement away from the sacred back to the secular. . . . [The followers] are to leave the security of holy [I would say 'sacred'] space for the cruciform 'disgrace' of profane space." Nelson, *Raising up a Faithful Priest*, 152.

As a result, Jesus has now been revealed for us not only as the supreme instance of our human priesthood, but as the place of our truest and most gracious meeting with the HOLY itself. It is difficult to understand, at first sight, why the earliest Christians, monotheists as they were, should have begun to speak of Jesus as being, in some sense, GOD. And yet in writings such as Hebrews or the Gospel of John, it seems that Jesus' divinity could be taken almost for granted. What required explanation rather was Jesus' humanity. Why did the WORD (in John's language) have to become flesh? Why did the SON (in the language of Hebrews) have to become, in all ways, like his human sisters and brothers?[91]

The truest priest is the one who truly knows both the HOLY that undergirds all human existence and also the human reality that is on our side of the boundary. These can be known in only one way: through experience. Religion is only a model or a map. Theology is only a *vade mecum*—a kind of ongoing conversation among priests that may serve as a guidebook during the journey. The ultimate knowledge is gained only by *being there*. The early Christians saw in Jesus the fullest and most profound instance of the human encounter with the HOLY, in all its terrifying and gracious power. It was a short step (albeit an astonishing one) for them to conclude that Jesus was actually the eternal embodiment of the perfect communion of humanity with GOD. Not only is Jesus the true high priest, Jesus is the very border country in which our human priesthood is lived out; Jesus is the HOLY made flesh.

The early Christians spoke of this in two ways—in terms of incarnation and in terms of resurrection. In the birth of Jesus, they said, GOD entered into true union with a human being so that what the man Jesus experienced, GOD the WORD, GOD the SON, experienced, too. Here, a perfect meeting bridged the boundary between us and the TRANSCENDENT, so that the UNCREATED and the created, the DIVINE and the everyday are held, in this person, permanently open to one another. "The WORD became flesh." Jesus was named in prophecy "Immanuel," "GOD among us." This language of incarnation, like all language about GOD, is riddling and unclear. Its purpose is not to confine or delimit the reality to which it refers, but rather to point toward it and to release it to work in our lives. The earliest Christian writers

---

91. John 1:1–18; Hebrews 1–2.

were minimally interested in metaphysics; they were seeking ways to express their *experience* of Jesus. In Jesus, they felt they were encountering not only our human priesthood, but GOD's act of reaching across the boundary to meet us.

This feeling was also expressed by saying that, after the death of Jesus on the cross, the HIDDEN took Jesus' humanity up into its own deathless and life-giving power. Jesus died a real human death, and GOD raised him from this death into a new and larger, but still human, life. I suggested earlier that death is, for us, one of the principal manifestations of the border with the ABSOLUTELY REAL. The resurrection is a sign that, even in death, the border is still, contrary to our expectations, open. The Jesus who is now in and with GOD is not any less human than before, but still carries his past experience of human weakness and loneliness, of fear and uncertainty, and brings them into the very heart and mind of GOD, who knows us now from within. Once our death is carried into the heart and mind of GOD, it is transformed into life by the FOUNTAIN OF LIFE. The border is now open, in a new way, from both sides, because it is located, for us, in Jesus' life, death, and resurrection.

Our own exercise of the fundamental priesthood does not cease to be frightening. The resurrection of Jesus has not abolished death, even though it has called us to look beyond it and to set it in a larger framework. We approach the border, then, with a mixture of faith and uncertainty. We do not know what, exactly, our encounter there will mean for our lives. We do not know how much the encounter with GOD will change us. We do not like coming to the edge of our sphere of control. We do not like the fact that death and new life are all mixed up together here. The news of Jesus' death and resurrection, however, creates at least a hope that his priestly experience will finally shape ours—a hope that has already proven strong and true in the experience of faithful people.

Jesus' priesthood belonged to the fundamental priesthood of humanity, not to the sacramental priesthood of ancient Israel or to the later Christian church. Jesus did not belong to any priesthood of religion, except in the ironic sense that he was seen as a maverick rabbi. Jesus was even willing to disrupt the workings of religion and its priesthoods, treating purity as a matter of indifference or interrupting the flow of sacrificial animals at the Temple. He disrupted the religious system precisely in order to reemphasize the fundamental priesthood, to draw attention away from the religious model and back to the true encounter with the HOLY in the context of ordinary human existence.

Jesus' life embodied our common human priesthood perfectly. By "perfectly," I do not mean *exhaustively*, for no one human life can do that. Human perfection does not lie in the realms of the abstract and universal. Human beings find their perfection in the realm of the concrete, where human life actually goes on. Jesus' priesthood was and is a particular human life lived out under earthly conditions specific to the first-century Palestinian Jewish world. Jesus' priesthood was deeply formed not only by his humanity in general but by his concrete social and cultural location as a male Israelite of his time and place. All our other expressions of the fundamental human priesthood will also be lived out in terms of a particular time and place. To say that Jesus embodied our priesthood "perfectly" is simply to say that there is always a profound, deeply rooted accord between his priesthood and that of every other human being—provided that our priesthoods are lived out with integrity and love, generosity and courage.

What made Jesus' priesthood perfect was its authenticity and clarity. Jesus' life was so filled with TRUTH and so open to the HOLY that it admitted no falsehood and no dimming of its transparency to GOD. It becomes a kind of touchstone by which our own authenticity and clarity may be gauged. It becomes the supreme example of priesthood. It becomes the priesthood that counsels us in our own deepest encounters with the HOLY. And, therefore, it becomes our best image of the maturity toward which our own priesthood is growing and moving. Yet with Jesus as with our every other encounter with the HOLY, we find it difficult to stay aware, to remain in the PRESENCE. And, therefore, with Jesus as with every other encounter with the HOLY, we find that we must (and do) construct religious models. The priesthood of Jesus is still being worked out in the lives of the people touched and illuminated by his priesthood. To give us language to speak of it and maps to help us find our way toward it, the followers of Jesus, like all other human beings, resort to the models of religion and of religious, sacramental priesthood. But the fundamental priesthood is still the key to human life in the world.

4

The Priesthood of the Christian People

The priesthood of the Christian people is the priesthood of all humanity, interpreted and formed by the priesthood of Jesus. To suppose that Jesus created a new priesthood from the ground up, as if no priesthood had existed before him, would be a radical break with our tradition.[92] The earliest Christians insisted, despite prolonged challenges from Gnosticism, that the GOD of Jesus was also the original CREATOR of humanity. The HOLY does not deny its former work in its later work. The CREATOR does not push aside the grace of creation in order to make room for the grace of resurrection, for the two are, at their deepest level, fully continuous. But Jesus interpreted the fundamental priesthood through his own service in it, as he taught and celebrated and lived out the good news. The priesthood of the Christian people, then, is the fundamental priesthood of humankind, understood afresh in terms of Jesus' message and experience.[93]

The GOD of Jesus remains, in many ways, as unpredictable and difficult of access as ever. This is always the nature of the HIDDEN HOLY. Jesus, on the cross, felt himself abandoned, which confirms that, even in drawing near to us through the incarnation, GOD cannot be *owned*, but continues to be beyond all human power to grasp, control, or

---

92. ". . . the distinction which is often drawn between 'natural' and 'revealed' faith is an artificial one, set up by theologizing minds. That awed conviction of the reality of the Eternal over against us, that awareness of the Absolute, that sense of God, which in one form or another is the beginning of all worship, whether it seems to break in from without, or to arise within the soul, does not and cannot originate in man. It comes to him where he is, as a message from another order. . . ." Evelyn Underhill, *Worship* (New York: Harper Torchbooks, 1957) 7.

93. "People have *Christian* experiences in and through *human* experiences with men and women in our world history, within the natural environment in which we live, but always in light of the faith-content of the Christian tradition of experience." Schillebeeckx, *Church*, 25.

confine. Even Jesus, as human, cannot control GOD. No excellence of ours, earned or ascribed, can force GOD's hand. Neither our own goodness nor the great gift of the incarnation, in which GOD has become one of us, makes us deserving of any specific blessing. We have no claim of particular individual merit to use as leverage on the HOLY. We cannot exert such a claim through repentance, either—by appealing to GOD's compassion for those who have come to their senses and turned around. Hebrews is quite explicit about this, observing that Esau's penitent tears gained him nothing (12:17). Neither does our sense of need or our most urgent prayer compel GOD. I do not mean that the BLESSED ONE is indifferent either to our good or to our evil, to our bounty or to our need. I mean only that GOD is transcendent—not a creature of our imagination nor subject to our will. The HOLY, finally, cannot be compelled.

At the same time, GOD has chosen to draw near in Jesus—and for the specific purpose of giving us gifts. For *gift* is the principle on which the CREATOR has based human existence; it is the most pervasive, even if little noticed, reality of our lives. We have life itself by others' gift of procreation, pregnancy, and childbirth. We are sustained in life by the good things of nature and by the labor, generosity, and society of other human beings. We are educated by the self-giving of our teachers. We are sustained constantly by gifts—love, forgiveness, reconciliation, pleasure. Our entire life is a fabric woven of gifts received, and we ourselves contribute our gifts to the lives of others. GOD is the first source, the prime mover and most lavish giver of all these gifts. So much so that, in Jesus, GOD drew near enough to give even GODSELF into a human life and to take up priesthood among us.

The GOD of Israel and of Jesus is a GOD afar off and also a GOD who is near.[94] As Christians, then, we know that we live in a border country filled with all the richness of GOD's inexhaustible gifts, a country where the PRESENCE has become palpable. And yet it remains also a country of ABSENCE, where we sense that the fullness of the HOLY is beyond us in any number of ways. It is beyond us in that we do not have an immediate sense of GOD's presence throughout our lives, in that our lives are unfinished and unpredictable, in that we cannot shape our lives exactly to the truth we perceive, in that we must, again and

---

94. See Jeremiah 23:23.

again, take risks without knowing exactly what GOD has in store for us. We do not even know what gifts the HOLY ONE has given us to share until we risk using them.[95]

One of the great conundrums of human existence that is not alleviated—it may even be intensified—by the good news of Christ is that, even when we have discovered the centrality and primacy of GOD, we still have to live our own lives. We cannot simply escape into the HOLY. Our human finitude pulls us back into this world of ordinary things, where we must be prepared to stand at the center of our own lives—now with a heightened understanding of our opportunities, our limitations, and what is at stake in the life of this world. I live a life that is still in a growing, maturing, provisional state. I am commissioned to shape it within the limits of my capacity, taking it both lightly and seriously, acknowledging both its smallness (in comparison with GOD) and its richness (in relation to myself and those who love me), standing with it, falling with it, rising again with it. GOD's ultimate and unbounded centrality does not abolish my subordinate and finite centrality. I really do live—and was created to live and am intended to live—in this world. I can live here in communion with GOD. GOD has even come here to live with me. I may experience moments of mystical union with the ONE WHO IS. But I cannot migrate out of this human world into GOD's own boundless freedom.[96]

We remain, then, residents of the borderlands that are in the midst of life, in the midst of the everyday world. We remain as priests, experiencing the borderlands' danger and also their riches. Jesus introduced us to the HOLY as GIFT, as LOVE. This GOD who gives and loves does not immediately cease to be alarming to us. GOD still limits us by the simple fact of being GOD. The border is therefore still a place of death for us, literal and metaphorical. Yet it is also a place of life, a surprise that pervades and shapes all our ministry.

---

95. Moses, at the burning bush, asks for a sign to assure him that his call from GOD was genuine. GOD responds by saying that *after* he has done what was asked he will serve GOD on this mountain (Exodus 3:12).

96. ". . . God's being is not a negation of the creature; he creates the creature in its finite but own autonomy and value. In God one experiences that in absolute freedom he is essentially creator, the lover of the finite, loving with the absoluteness of a divine love which is unfathomable to us. In this mystical view he then wills to be the beloved of all creation." Schillebeeckx, *Church*, 180–81.

The ministry of human priesthood, then, is not less important because we are Christians. The necessity of it is the same or perhaps even greater. The border country where we live and minister as priests allows us glimpses into the undergirding TRUTH, moments of brushing up against that deeper REALITY, even instants of immersion in it; and we dwell there in a repeatedly renewed state of communion with GOD in the incarnate WORD. But the border remains in place and will continue to remain, and we shall always be rooted on the human side of it. What we encounter in Jesus is not an abolition of the border, but an opening in it. GOD's gift crosses over to us in a tangible form with which we can readily identify—the form of a human life, of Jesus and the good news. GOD offers us gifts and takes our hand, not to draw us away from the border country into the wholly HIDDEN, as much as to provision, strengthen, and steady us for living authentically human lives where we are.

The priesthood of Jesus' people, then, is not, in the first instance, a sacramental priesthood serving a tangible sanctuary with religious rites. We cannot fulfill the priesthood of the Christian people by making ourselves pure, sacred, remote inhabitants of some sanctuary. If we cultivate a remoteness from daily existence, to create the impression that we have already, at least in principle, passed over into the HOLY, we are getting it all wrong. Just the opposite is true. The priesthood of the Christian people will be most itself when it is ministering where Jesus ministered—in the midst of profane existence and in the company of the unclean. There is indeed a place for a sacramental priesthood in Christian religion—a topic I shall explore more fully in the next chapter. But the Christian religion arises from the existence of the Christian people, the people who are being transformed by the good news, not the other way around. Even if the two—the Christian people and the Christian religion—now nourish one another, we should not confuse the order of their coming to be. The primary Christian priesthood, like the fundamental priesthood of all humanity, belongs to the sphere of everyday human activity. It is not divorced from the profane world; it stands in the center of it.[97]

---

97. "Those who choose to turn an open ear to the world should be able to hear more than mere noise, more than mere sound. They should be able to hear the song of life that resonates throughout the created universe and even in their own personal existence." Charles Cummings, *The Mystery of the Ordinary* (San Francisco: Harper & Row, 1982) 8–9.

This does not mean that all forms of Christian priesthood must be overtly activist or that retreat—even long-term, eremitical retreat—is intrinsically wrong. Jesus retreated for periods of rest and prayer, and Paul stressed that a religion fascinated and dominated by works will turn out to be a religion obsessed with what *we* do, rather than holding itself open to GOD. Priestly withdrawal, even that of the hermit, is still a way of living everyday human life. It may constitute simplification of human existence, reducing it to its barest essentials so that these essentials become more truly and honestly visible. The monastic, even when living in community, is rather like a minimalist artist. Just as such an artist's work can restore to us a sense of pure form or color or line, often submerged in more complex works of art, so the monastic's vowed commitment to a simplification of life—a household uncomplicated by sexual relationships, the surrender of all pretense at supremacy over the self, and stability of life—serves to bring the basic elements of human existence to the forefront of our awareness.

The primary question regarding our priesthood is not the traditional polarity of active versus contemplative forms of life. The question is rather one of *engagement*, of being genuinely present to one's life and world. The great danger of modern Western life is the way the rushing stream of events and persons and roles and tasks and identities and entertainments and distractions and luxuries and unmet needs threatens to overwhelm all sense of our humanity, individual or shared with others. Paradoxically, the most active person may turn out to be the most remote and isolated. We are in danger of never being truly present for anything, even our own lives. When we do achieve some engagement, it too often turns out to be defensive—an effort to stake out some sphere that is ours alone, from which we can exclude anyone or anything that is alien or displeasing to us. The important question, then, is to what degree we are prepared to live *with awareness* the true life of human beings, which is priesthood. To what degree are we prepared to understand ourselves in terms of our life in the border country, which means to understand ourselves both in terms of our link with the HOLY and in terms of our link with other human beings?

Failure to understand ourselves in priestly terms leads to a number of grave ills. It has led modern Western culture to ignore the HOLY altogether at times, to pretend that we can lead an existence that does not refer beyond ourselves. It encourages a supreme egotism that is contemptuous of the rights of others and of the larger creation of which we are a part. It authorizes an individualism that sees other people only as tools or, if they are uncooperative, as obstacles. Or it allows us to seek the good of our particular community—family or clan or tribe or nation or religious community—at the expense of other human beings. It permits us to favor our immediate good at the expense of the larger ecology to which we belong and at the expense of our own future generations. The neglect of the HOLY works an apparently disproportionate harm because of our immense human hunger for communion with the TRANSCENDENT. When we recognize no HOLY external to ourselves, we wind up trying to put ourselves, whether as individuals or as groups, in its place.[98]

Even in the current renewal of interest in spirituality, we sometimes misinterpret our connection with the TRANSCENDENT as a personal possession—a matter of self-cultivation that need not affect the way we conceive the world at large or the way we deal with others. Without a strong sense of the priestly communion that is life in the borderlands, we may lose the sense of our own humanness. It is a common disease of modern life to identify ourselves to such an extent with the certainty and power of the ABSOLUTE that we feel free to impose our peculiar conceptions of the HOLY on others. Or perhaps we may be content to luxuriate in a sense of special privilege, thinking of ourselves as somehow holier or purer or more pleasing to GOD than the "lesser breeds without the law."[99] But those others are the very people whom Jesus described as "the least of these my brothers and sisters" (Matthew 25:40). Jesus was not being romantic in using this turn of phrase, but practical. If the least person, the alien or the enemy, is not our kin, exactly where will you draw the line of kinship? And how can you be confident that the limits of kinship will always include you?

---

98. "The deep, deep need that each of us has to be called forth into the fullness of being by creative love, often makes itself felt in a hunger to be worthwhile, to be valued or appreciated, to have a purpose or goal in life. It has been observed in the contemporary world that those who most insistently complain as adults of finding that hunger unfulfilled, are also those who individually or collectively are amassing and hoarding and wasting so much of the material resources of the world, that others are kept on the verge of starvation in great numbers." Monika K. Hellwig, *The Eucharist and the Hunger of the World* (New York: Paulist Press, 1976) 18.

99. Rudyard Kipling, "Recessional." Kipling was using this phrase to signify a danger of arrogance he perceived in the West, but it has often been misused as if it were a straightforward reference to non-Western peoples.

Loss of our sense of priesthood, in other words, leads to a mass of problems. Once we drive the TRANSCENDENT as independent REALITY from our everyday world, we begin to identify our own quirks and desires and fears as the ULTIMATE. We no longer fear or respect TRUTH. We claim the HOLY as an adjunct of our own political aims. Then we distance ourselves from the rest of humanity, whom we feel free to treat with scorn. We imagine that we have escaped from the great, ongoing exchange of gifts that is human existence. Identifying ourselves with GOD, we may even try to seize control of other people's encounter with the HOLY. In all these ways, whether we abandon the HOLY altogether or claim it as a private possession or even identify ourselves with it, we cease to have any value as priests. The great priestly conversation dies into a succession of tedious and often brutal monologues.

If we imitate Jesus' priesthood, we shall find ourselves, instead, entering the company of "tax collectors and sinners," conversing on an equal footing with the unclean, gratefully accepting hospitality in the houses of "Samaritans" and "lepers," justifying lapses from the purity code, and saying, with the authority of our own experience, "Your sins are forgiven." We shall also find ourselves leaving others the freedom to say "no," to find their own way in the borderlands with or without our help. Jesus' priesthood is rooted in the ordinary world and expressed in the most familiar human moments of communion and love. It is founded on the assurance that GOD's great conversation with us is unending, that the HOLY will go so far as to forgive all and build the world anew on the rubble of our past wrongs. Jesus' antidote for our craziness—our arrogance and hypocrisy and lovelessness—is the unflagging love of GOD, so rash and excessive that it will even blithely leave the ninety-nine to seek out the one stray (Matthew 18:10–14).

What, then, are some of the characteristics of Jesus' priesthood that could be shaping the priesthood of the Christian people in our time? I say specifically "in our time," because one of the consequences of our finitude is that no two moments in human existence are precisely the same—not even in the life of an individual, much less that of a culture or of the whole human race. In Jesus, the WORD became incarnate in a particular person at a particular place and time. Jesus was a first-century Palestinian Jewish villager. Within a few years of his resurrection, his followers found themselves moving increasingly in the rather different orbit of first-century Mediterranean cities, with their sometimes volatile mix of Jew and Gentile. Even that early, they found themselves having to face problems and evolve solutions that had not been part of Jesus' own life experience.[100] In every age, then, the priesthood of the Christian people, though it remains the priesthood of Jesus' good news, will change along with and in response to the cues given by its historical and cultural context. We take our guidance from Jesus, but we have no complete blueprint handed to us in advance.

It is a process not unlike the creation of a garden. The plan of the garden arises in the interplay between the imagination of the gardener and the context of a particular place. The gardener will have to take into account soil, terrain, climate, water, exposure to the sun. There is a process of trial and error—if not in every individual garden, then at least in the life's work of the landscaper and, beyond that, in the tradition of gardening developed over the years in a particular region. In themselves, the conditions of soil and climate do not create a garden— nor does the imagination and work of the gardener. Only in conversation between them does the garden come into being.[101]

What, then, are the cues offered by our particular age? We live in a world of self-righteous destructiveness. It is characterized by hostility along the dividing lines of race, ethnicity, gender, sexuality, religion, and class; by complex economic and political justifications for arrogance, selfishness, and greed (I refer to the ideologies of the left as well as of the right); by new forms of homicidal absolutism in the world religions; by an intense desire to prove ourselves always in the right and our enemies always in the wrong; by an extraordinary ease in resorting to violence; by massive indifference to the fate of most children; by stunning ecological carelessness. Living in such a world, what priestly work falls to us as successors to Christ according to the order of Melchizedek? The traditions about Jesus enshrined in the Gospels are rich enough that one can read them many times over and still discover new insight. I will only emphasize, out of this rich storehouse, a central cluster of

---

100. For example the challenge of how to include Gentiles in a Jewish community, which forms a major issue in Acts and in many of the letters of Paul.

101. " . . . each site has it own special qualities of stone and earth and water, of leaf and blossom, of architectural context, of sun and shade, and of sounds and scents and breezes. Seek these out, and you will discover promises of formal order or of artful naturalism—the beginnings of your garden." Charles W. Moore, William J. Mitchell, and William Turnbull, Jr., *The Poetics of Gardens* (Cambridge, Mass.: MIT Press, 1993) 1.

themes in Jesus' teaching and behavior—central to the Gospels themselves—that will give us some direction: the themes of table fellowship, reconciliation, love, and integrity.

While Jesus' world was far from identical to ours, it was not altogether unlike it, either. Certainly, it was a world troubled by intergroup division, hostility, and spite. In this context, Jesus was distinguished by the extraordinary breadth of his table fellowship. He ate with the most religious. He ate with "tax collectors and sinners." Once, when he was at table in the home of a Pharisee, a woman of uncertain reputation came up to wash his feet with her tears, to dry them with her hair, and to kiss and anoint them. To the considerable distress of his host, Jesus made no move to rid himself of her (Luke 7:36–49). And this was in a world where religious leaders (all male) were not even supposed to speak with a woman in public.

This behavior is part of what made the contemporary religious leaders so suspicious of him. Committed as they were to a religion of purity, they objected to his casualness in eating with clean and unclean alike. It undermined the distinctions between "good" and "bad" that they took for granted. Jesus' followers were doing much the same thing when they decided, later on, to breach the wall of separation between clean Israel and the unclean Gentiles (Acts 10, 15). Jesus refused to let his behavior be governed by the deep-seated human opposition between "them" and "us," even when that opposition was undergirded by the institutions of religion.[102] Instead, he went out of his way to put all sorts of people at ease with him and so to place them alongside one another— alongside the very people whom they feared and despised.

If the priesthood of the Christian people in our own time is to follow the cues given by Jesus, it must concentrate on a similar transcending of human divisions and hostilities. This is particularly difficult in that the church is often deeply implicated in the very divisions that we are called on to overcome. This is not a new development. Already in late antiquity, for example, the remnants of the British church, driven by the barbarians into the western edges of the old Roman province of

---

102. That this behavior was not always easy at first for Jesus is evident in the story of the Syrophoenician woman (Mark 7:24–30), who has to overcome Jesus' own ethnic prejudices in seeking his help.

Britain, were reluctant to evangelize the Anglo-Saxon invaders. For them, "Christian" was no longer the name of a priesthood that would aim at overcoming the hostilities, but the name of one of the hostile parties.[103] That story has been repeated time and time again, sometimes with different sorts of Christians on either side of the dividing line, excluding and hating and even killing one another. Recognizing this, one becomes more aware of the astonishing grace in an event like Patrick's mission to Ireland, for he was returning to a people who had enslaved him in a raid on his homeland, and he was returning to bring them the good news of a common humanity in Christ.

How will the priesthood of the Christian people in our time renew its commission to overcome hatred between people who have defined themselves as opposite to one another? No single answer will suffice for the amazing variety of conflicts. A true priesthood, wherever it is at work, will be mindful of the familiar human realities that have emerged with particular brutality over recent years in Belfast or Sarajevo, will have to offer itself with humility and respect in the midst of suffering like that of Rwanda or Cambodia, Sri Lanka or El Salvador. Not that the context of priesthood is limited to such instances of political violence on the world stage. For the same ease in resorting to violence pervades our world and appears also within our cities, our families, our religious communities, and internally within ourselves, our spirits, souls, and bodies. The great challenge for us is to find our way back to the

---

103. I do not mean to sit in judgment on the life of the British churches of the time, which had, after all, been nearly shattered by the Anglo-Saxon invasions and continued to be terribly vulnerable. I am only pointing out that it is quite possible for Christians to lose the sense that the gospel was intended to bridge human religious divisions, not to create them. As Howard Thurman has written, "One of the central problems in human relations is applying the ethic of respect for personality in a way that is not governed by special categories." This is true in a particular way for oppressed groups: "When I was a boy growing up in Florida, it never occurred to me, nor was I taught either at home or in church, to regard white persons as falling within the scope of the magnetic field of my morality. . . . They were not read out of the human race—they simply did not belong to it in the first place. . . . What was true for me as a boy was true also of any little white boy in my town with an important and crucial difference! The structure of the society was such that I was always at his mercy." Thurman, *The Luminous Darkness*, 1–3.

fundamental ecology of gift, of grace, that alone can replace the violence of possessiveness and all its fear and anger.[104]

In the process, we will be rediscovering the giftedness of our own lives and the extraordinary freedom GOD grants to us as priests in the borderlands. That same freedom and giftedness is given to our neighbor, too, with the consequent implication that we must respect not only our neighbors' freedom to join the great priestly conversation but also their freedom to refuse. Priesthood has no power to compel. Its power is that it goes on being priesthood, goes on welcoming everyone who truly wishes to join with it in the presence of the HOLY, goes on seeking and hoping for the good of all in whatever setting we are called to minister.

I cannot tell anyone how to accomplish *your* particular priesthood in this regard. That is because it is yours and not mine. You are a priest. You learn your priesthood as you practice it in conversation with the HOLY ONE and with your world and with the other priests around you. I can say only what the Gospels say: that the priesthood of Jesus was a priesthood of generous reconciliation. It was rejected by some and accepted by others. And if that was the priestly ministry of Christ, then, in some form or other, it will be the priestly ministry of Christians as long as our world has any need of it. Both within the church and outside it, there is a great need for human beings to overcome our suspicion of one another, our isolation from one another, and the fear and hostility that arise from them. We need to "share food" with even the most impossible of our fellow humans.

This does not mean producing some single, homogenized humanity, which would probably imply absorbing the minority groups into the dominant group in any given place, to the disadvantage of both. Paul himself insisted that, in the context of the gospel, Jews will still

---

104. "Moreover, the fact that nuclear weapons were invented in the predominantly Christian West places a responsibility on people whose lives have been fundamentally shaped by Christianity to examine the tradition both for its destructive aspects and for its resources for the present. The nuclear world is at least partly the product of a tradition in which human bodies have not been sufficiently valued in spite of doctrines of creation, Incarnation, and resurrection of the body that would seem to affirm human body-selves." Margaret R. Miles, *Practicing Christianity: Critical Perspectives for an Embodied Spirituality* (New York: Crossroad, 1990) 12–13.

be Jews and Gentiles still Gentiles (1 Corinthians 7:17–19). It means rather that we form priestly bonds across the lines that have separated us, so that we understand that we share one humanity in the presence of GOD, even if it is diverse almost beyond our ability to tell. We share the love of GOD that created us and calls us into priesthood. We share our ability to give gifts. We share the ability to grow and mature. We share, alas, our ability to sin and to harm and to destroy. We share a common fear of death and a common hope of resurrection, which is our true life even in this world. Everyone was welcome to eat with Jesus. Will we dare extend the same welcome?

What would make this breadth of table fellowship possible? It is not possible as a response to moral demand, but only as an act of priesthood. Jesus' willingness to share food with all arose out of his intimacy with the HIDDEN REALITY, whom he met in the form of LOVE. It was one of his followers who summed it up most succinctly: "GOD is LOVE" (1 John 4:8, 16). But Jesus' priestly ministry is intelligible only as a living-out of this experience and understanding. All the beauty and achievement and power of his priesthood emerged from his encounter with the HOLY—as did all the demands and trouble and difficulty of it. For Jesus and the early Christians, LOVE took, particularly, the form of forgiveness, as I have suggested elsewhere.[105] But do not misunderstand. LOVE, even in the form of forgiveness, is not a sentimental and indifferent complicity in wrong, but a summons to the most profound generosity, seen as the basic motive force of all existence. If we are invited to participate in this generosity, it is not merely as passive recipients being offered a free ride, but as partners who receive gifts in order to share them with one another—that is, with all the other members of the human priesthood.

The practice of our priesthood calls for a certain transparency to this LOVE, so that the DIVINE shines through us to illuminate the opacity of everyday existence. Hence Jesus' insistence on integrity and his fierce attack on hypocrisy. We do not always notice that, in the Gospels, the most serious sin is not pride, as in the later Christian tradition, but hypocrisy (or "the lie," as John's Gospel calls it). Hypocrisy disables

---

105. L. William Countryman, *Forgiven and Forgiving* (Harrisburg, Pa.: Morehouse Publishing, 1998).

priesthood by putting a layer of pretense between us and the HOLY, by shrouding the self in a disguise so that we are no longer really involved as *ourselves* with GOD. Jesus leveled the charge of hypocrisy not primarily at the ordinary people of his world, but at the religious leadership, the priests of religion. He charged them with hypocrisy not because they were *worse* than anyone else, but because they saw themselves (and others saw them) as the *best* people of their day. Partly for this reason, they lost sight of their own imperfect humanity and grew accustomed to concealing their humanity from themselves and others.[106]

The grave temptation for every sort of priesthood is the temptation to think highly of ourselves because the HIDDEN TRUTH happens to have shown us something. In truth, the insight granted to us is a gift; it never redounds to our own credit. And if we elevate our fragmentary insight into a claim that we possess TRUTH—an error that is the very foundation stone of all fundamentalisms—the hypocrisy of this act will constitute a barrier between us and GOD that is almost impossible to overcome. The priesthood of the Christian people, then, must remain conscious of its contingent and dependent nature. However profound—even ultimately profound—the revelation of the HOLY in Jesus is, it does not give us a full command of GOD's own mind. We remain learners and seekers even while we serve one another and the world around us as priests.

Humility—this awareness of our own limits—is the best defense against hypocrisy. And it is intimately linked with Jesus' willingness to eat with sinners and the unclean. However much we as Christians may exalt Jesus in our efforts to explain his intimacy with GOD, Jesus himself did not place himself above even the least worthy of his contemporaries. The priesthood of the Christian people in our time will need the gift of such humility as it places itself at the service of a world riddled with alienation, suspicion, and hatred. The sources of this humility are integrity and love. Integrity is truthfulness, a true knowledge and acceptance of our limits. Love is the acknowledgment that our goal is not just some separate, individual perfection, but a renewed humanity marked by generosity and trust. Only with the help of integrity and love can we hope to lay down our own defenses of suspicion,

---

106. "Some of the Pharisees . . . said to him, 'We aren't blind, are we?' Jesus said to them, 'If you were blind, you would have no sin. But now you say, "We see." Your sin remains'" (John 9:40–41).

arrogance, and fear so that we can help welcome more of GOD's peace into our time.

The priesthood of the Christian people is not primarily a matter of religion—though religion plays its role in support of our common priesthood, as I shall say in the next chapter. Our priesthood is lived out primarily in the world of everyday existence. Here, too, Jesus offers us a sense of direction. Jesus did not reject religion, but he took it much less seriously than the religious authorities thought was right. He excused his disciples when they violated the sabbath—and overrode the sabbath himself to perform works of mercy. He sat loose to the laws of purity.[107] He assumed that women would understand him as well as men. As we have already noted, he was not a priest of religion himself. Instead, he allowed his nearness with GOD to be manifest in his living of everyday life—in the streets and marketplaces and houses of ancient Palestine as well as in the synagogues and Temple.

He reconnected the HOLY and the everyday, not in a pious way that might tend to submerge the everyday world under a cloak of religious ceremonies, but in a way that gave reverence to the PRESENCE that was already there. He was able to see faith in GOD in the sick, to hear TRUTH in the words of a Gentile woman (Mark 7:24–30), to see the bountifulness of the CREATOR in the fleeting glory of wild flowers (Matthew 6:28–30). He taught in the synagogue and the Temple, but it was not primarily there that he met GOD. He met GOD in the wilderness and in the streets. The priesthood of the Christian people will work itself out in the same sphere, standing alongside one another and the rest of humanity as we seek to understand our experience of the HIDDEN REALITY at the roots of our daily world.

Jesus gave a broad recipe for this sort of daily priesthood in the summary of the Law: You are to love GOD with your whole self and to love your neighbor as yourself. The specific actions and dispositions implied by these commandments will vary enormously depending on what the situation calls forth. But the broad, overall disposition is clear: a disposition to live in deep respect for the HIDDEN HOLY and to see one's neighbor as another self, who is also given the opportunity to live in GOD's presence and to participate in the common priesthood. It is worth noting that the Gospels do not present this teaching as belonging exclusively to Jesus. To begin with, Jesus here cites two quotations

---

107. E.g., Mark 2:1–12; 3:1–6; 7:1–15.

from the scriptures of Israel rather than beginning from scratch. But, in addition, one Gospel actually credits the summary of the Law not to Jesus at all, but to a legal expert with whom he was in conversation (Luke 10:25–28); and another places it in the context of a friendly exchange in which Jesus and the scribe with whom he converses come to full agreement on the matter (Mark 12:28–34). In other words, these two writers do not present the commandments of love as something unique to Christians but rather as a prescription for the priestly life of all humanity.

The commandments of love, then, are critical for our Christian priesthood, too. For ours is not some priesthood other than that of humanity as a whole, but the fundamental human priesthood as clarified, focused, and interpreted by the priesthood of Jesus. It is human priesthood following in the footsteps of Jesus' passionate life in the everyday world, expecting to find in the midst of it our most profound experience of GOD. It is a human priesthood that knows that we will begin to understand GOD only with the help of other human beings, including those who belong to groups from which we may long have divided ourselves. When Jesus was asked to explain what it means to love one's "neighbor" as oneself, he—a Jew speaking with Jews—told the story of a Jewish man who was assaulted, robbed, and left for dead beside the road to Jericho. After being ignored by two Temple officials, he was rescued by a Samaritan, whose nation had long been at sword's point with the Jewish people. "Who was neighbor here?" Jesus asked. "The one who helped," his interlocutor admitted.[108] The question is not, "Who is the neighbor to whom I owe priestly service?" The question is rather, "Who has become neighbor to me, and how can I, too, become a neighbor and so be part of the priestly interchange that constitutes and enables human existence?"

The priesthood of the Christian people is the principal product of Jesus' life of good news. Jesus' living out of the fundamental human priesthood serves to focus and guide our living of it in our own time and place. But it will never be enough if we try merely to copy what Jesus did. Instead, we pray that what we learn from Jesus will shape us so that we can live responsibly and generously, in our own day and place, as Jesus did in his. This life is lived in the shadow of death, but also in the confident hope of resurrection. It is lived by trusting the

---

108. Luke 10:29–37.

One who is. The person who takes on Christ's priesthood as the model of her own will find herself living in the dangerous borderlands by the power of Love.[109]

This will not be a timid existence. Jesus' life was anything but timid. Jesus embodied the ancient virtue of *parrhesia*—boldness, freedom of speech. He showed neither fear nor favor. He was not afraid of taking risks. His teaching has proved to be profoundly subversive, both in his own day and, repeatedly, in the subsequent history of Christian faith. Marginalized people—the outsiders, the nonreligious, the sinful, the disreputable, the oppressed—have read the teachings of Jesus or heard them preached and, again and again, have gotten the astonishing notion that they are loved of God, that they can afford to stand up straight and live lives filled with the secret and persistent power of our shared human priesthood. We gain this confidence not by being able to predict a successful outcome to our efforts—successful in this-worldly terms—but by trusting the One we have met in the borderlands, the One who created us and who raised Jesus from the dead.

By this gift of courage, however tentatively and weakly it works in us at first, we know ourselves as part of Jesus' priesthood, as priests of our common humanity guided toward the light of his resurrection and of our own. To live in this world as citizens of the age to come, as servants of the Holy and of one another, as bearers of good news, as subversive ministers of the resurrection that God is leading us toward— this is what it means to share the priesthood of the Christian people.

---

109. "The vocation of the baptized person is a simple thing: it is to live from day to day, whatever the day brings, in this extraordinary unity, in this reconciliation with all men and all things, in this knowledge that death has no more power, in this truth of the Resurrection. It does not really matter what exactly a Christian does from day to day. What matters is that in whatever he does it is done in honor of the triumph of Christ over death and, therefore, in honor of his own life, given to him by God and restored to him in Christ, and in honor of the life into which all men and all things are called. The only thing that really matters is to live in Christ instead of death." William Stringfellow, *Instead of Death* (New York: Seabury Press, 1963) 57.

Part II

Priesthood and the Church

5

The Two Priesthoods
in the Church

The Christian church belongs to the sphere of religion rather than to the more fundamental experience of our encounter with the HOLY. As such, it has both its values and its temptations. Despite the claims churches sometimes make for themselves, none of them enjoys immediate divine authorization. None of them has received directly from GOD a blueprint for its institutions, rites, hierarchies, theologies, moral instructions, or other traditions. None of them has control of the TRANSCENDENT, or even exclusive access to the ear of the DIVINE. To claim otherwise is to give the church an effective monopoly on the HOLY in this world and to render GOD's own self expendable and unnecessary. It is, in other words, idolatrous. The church is an institution of religion. It has a genuine value in relation to the good news proclaimed and embodied by Jesus, but it can fulfill its function effectively only if it does so with awareness of its limitations and with appropriate modesty.

It flows from this that a person can follow Jesus and participate in Jesus' priesthood without becoming a member of the earthly church. Such a person is a priest after the order of Melchizedek and a citizen of the age to come—and surely a member of the community of Christ. But that is not the same thing as belonging to the earthly church. There are occasions when the earthly church is even hostile to the priesthood of Melchizedek, when it is sufficiently self-idolatrous to be, in some ways and for the moment, a stumbling block to the faithful following of Christ. Yet, even then, the church continues to read the Gospels and to proclaim through them the message it no longer honors in practice. I do not, then, say that the church is ever entirely useless—only that its usefulness can, at times, be obscured.[110]

---

110. "That the treasure of God's grace reaches us surrounded by garbage will not seem surprising to anyone who is personally familiar with life in the church. . . . Grace comes to us, so Martin Luther argues, hidden *sub contrario*, 'beneath its opposite.' From this perspective, any idealized view of the church as only treasure is as faulty a vision of reality as any cynical view that the church is only garbage. Mangers, by definition, are found where there is manure." Morse, *Not Every Spirit*, 288.

The fundamental priesthood itself cannot be abolished by this state of affairs. It continues to exist both within and outside the church, not only in its universal human manifestation, but also in specifically Christian forms. Simone Weil, for example, has been a particularly powerful voice in twentieth-century Christian spirituality, yet she refused to be baptized because she could not accept membership in the church she knew.[111] Again, Emily Dickinson, who had a profound grasp of Christian faith, found little support for that faith in the contemporary church and wrote:

> Some keep the Sabbath going to Church—
> I keep it, staying at Home—[112]

Christians sometimes misinterpret our religion as a way of guaranteeing spiritual good standing: Do this (be baptized, attend church, be celibate, get married, be ordained, or whatever), and GOD will be pleased with you. But that, of course, is a betrayal of the gospel, which proclaims that GOD is already pleased to love us and humbly to request our love in return. Churchly conformity, then, is not essential in order for us to please GOD.[113]

Nor is churchliness necessary for a person to participate in the human priesthood in accordance with the pattern established by Christ. The claim that it is necessary goes back to the very beginnings of Christian faith—and so does Jesus' rejection of that desire. In the Gospel of

---

111. "She rejected all idea of the submission of the intelligence to a divine authority exercised by the Church. She feared and attacked, to the point of blasphemy, the 'patriotisms' of historical religions, whether of Judaism or of Christianity, equating these with 'social idolatry.' . . . A daring heterodoxy and the Church, as Simone Weil would insist, are manifestations of the Spirit. Her own heterodoxy is Christianity in its most concentrated form and intensity." George A. Panichas, in *The Simone Weil Reader*, ed. by George A. Panichas (Mt. Kisco, N.Y.: Moyer Bell, 1977) xxiii, xxvi.

112. Emily Dickinson, poem 324, in *The Complete Poems of Emily Dickinson,* ed. Thomas H. Johnson (Boston: Little, Brown & Co., n.d.). On Dickinson as a poet of good news, see Judith E. Bare, "A Gospel of Her Own: The Apostolic Secession of Emily Dickinson," Ph.D. diss., Stanford University, 1993.

113. "The paradox here is that it is almost impossible to hand down living belief in God without some alienation from the institution. A religion is not only the expression of a fundamental religious experience but also a 'domestication,' a taming of the overwhelming power of this experience." Schillebeeckx, *Church,* 59.

Luke (9:49–50), John says to Jesus, "Master, we saw someone casting out demons in your name and we told him to quit, since he isn't a follower along with us." Jesus responds, "Don't stop him. For whoever is not against you is with you." Later on, to be sure, Jesus says almost the reverse: "The person who isn't with me is against me, and the one who doesn't gather with me is scattering" (Luke 11:23). The context of each saying, however, makes a decisive difference. The first saying has to do with whether someone must belong to the company of Jesus' immediate disciples in order to participate in Jesus' priesthood. The answer is a resounding No. The second saying comes at the end of a story in which the religious authorities challenge Jesus' exorcisms by claiming that he is in league with Beelzebul. It is the rejection of Jesus' good news that disqualifies them in that case, not their being separate from the earthly church. "Whoever is not against *you* [the church] is with you." "The person who isn't with *me* [Jesus and the message of the good news] is against me."

The church, then, is not essential to the priesthood of those who would follow Christ. For most of us, however, it is, to some degree or other, inevitable, for the simple reason that priesthood, like all human existence, is intrinsically social. It takes place in our interactions with one another in the presence of the HIDDEN HOLY, and it therefore gives rise to some sort of community, whether we intend it to or not. Insofar as that community has a settled, continuing membership, it will give rise to institutions and be some sort of church, whether it calls itself by that name or some other. Ongoing communities of every sort require articulation of their lives in terms of their practices, their values, and their identity. We have to express what it is that holds us together and gives our common life meaning. We have to devise ways to communicate that vision to outsiders, to imbue newcomers with it, and to pass it on to children who are being raised within the community. The church is only a by-product of the gospel—but, given the needs of human beings, an inevitable by-product.

What is more, the church turns out to be the principal repository of the good news of Jesus' priesthood. However much it may, at times, try to distort that news to its own selfish ends, it keeps it in circulation and makes it available to new generations of priests. Without the living Christian community, the Bible would be, for most people, a dead letter. The writings of Christian spirituality might well have disappeared, and the tradition that gave rise to them would have withered. The social nature of our human priesthood means that no one possesses it purely as an individual. It is possessed only in the process of being exchanged. The same is true of the specifically Christian realization of this common human priesthood. We receive it from other people, we hand it on to other people. That, at bottom, is the reason for the church's existence.

Even those who choose not to be a part of the earthly church will have to remain in some kind of critical dialogue with it. Even if Simone Weil chose not to receive baptism, she developed her thinking in dialogue with Christian theology as well as philosophy, and her works find a principal audience today among people connected with the church. Emily Dickinson continued to be influenced by, to respond to, and to react against the religion of the contemporary church while keeping the sabbath at home. It is no accident that she wrote her poetry in hymn meters.[114]

Those who are consciously and deliberately fulfilling their human priesthood in the light of Christ's priesthood will find themselves engaged, in one way or another, with the church as the principal *religious* expression of our human priesthood as interpreted in Jesus. Even those who may feel themselves prohibited from joining with the church will find themselves significantly connected with it. Church members or not, we will find ourselves shaped by the institutions and sacraments of the church. This is particularly true if we are living in a culture that is or has been historically Christian, for we tend to assume the dominant sacramental models of priesthood in our own culture as the starting point for interpreting and understanding our fundamental human priesthood. There is no real alternative. Human meaning, as I have already said, is always built on the spot. But it is not built from scratch. We reuse what has come to us from the past, rejecting some pieces, moving others into more prominent locations, turning still others upside down to make them perform new functions. But we do not start from scratch. When our inherited sacramental model is clear and appropriate, it can give inspiration and clarity to the priesthood of all.[115]

---

114. Bare, "A Gospel of Her Own," 198–227.

115. " 'I do not believe that I am outside the Church,' [Simone Weil] wrote towards the end of her life, 'as far as it is the source of sacramental life; only insofar as it is a social body.' " Weil, *The Simone Weil Reader,* 9.

When it is distorted or clumsy, it is full of power for harm. I venture, then, to say that, in the Western world, no one who cares about the fundamental human priesthood can afford to ignore the religious model of that priesthood offered by the Christian churches.

The whole structure of the church and its teaching is relevant to our human priesthood, for the real purpose of all religious doctrine, ritual, and ethical guidance is to present a picture of what it means to be human and how we can fulfill the opportunities of our humanity in communion with GOD. Still, there are some aspects of the church's life that focus quite directly on this matter of our human priesthood— above all, the religious or sacramental priesthood that churches set apart in various ways, most commonly through ordination by laying on of hands with prayer. The key question before us in this chapter is how the sacramental priesthood in the church relates to the fundamental priesthood of the Christian people, which, as we have said, is simply our common human priesthood interpreted and clarified in Christ.

The fundamental priesthood of the whole Christian people is the basic priesthood. It can exist without benefit of clergy. Indeed, the ancient and classic model of the three orders of clergy (bishops, presbyters, deacons)[116] took more than a century to arise and be accepted. The earliest Christians depended on the relatively uncodified (and often chaotic) leadership of "apostles and prophets," people commissioned by GOD through Jesus or the SPIRIT, for leadership. In the New Testament, the term "priest" (*hiereus*) never applies to church leaders or officers. Apart from references to the sacramental priests of Jewish or Greek religion, the term is used only with reference to Christ[117] or to the Christian people.[118] Like all priesthoods of religion, the Christian clergy, then, is a model or icon of something richer and more profound, something that has priority over the clerical order both in importance

---

116. The term "priest" was subsequently applied to bishops and presbyters. In the sense in which I am using the term, deacons are also sacramental priests. Pseudo-Dionysius also seems to refer to them in that way in the fourth century (*Ecclesiastical Hierarchy* 5.2).

117. Hebrews throughout, especially chapter 7.

118. 1 Peter 2:5, 9; Revelation 1:6; 5:10; 20:6.

and in time, something that gives the sacramental ministry its vitality and purpose—namely, the priesthood of humanity.

Ordination itself, as I have written elsewhere, is a kind of language by which Christian communities speak of their identity and relationships. The ordained person is thus primarily a sign, a sacrament of the priesthood of all Christians, which is the priesthood of Christ. But, secondarily, the ordained also become signs by which the churches express their relationship to their own past, to the churches with which they are in communion, and to Christians of other traditions. The choices of who ordains, with what sort of prayer and ceremony, in what liturgical context—all these speak volumes about each church's self-understanding. But the universal reality is that the ordained person becomes a sacrament of the fundamental priestly ministry shared by all with Christ. The additional use of ordination as a way to identify specific church communities, while significant especially for ecumenical matters, is an epiphenomenon.[119]

The priesthood of humanity requires no ordination. This priesthood is the priesthood of the Christian laity—not in the sense of belonging exclusively to nonclerics, but in the sense of being the priesthood of the *laos*, that is, the whole people of GOD.[120] Ordination does not and cannot add anything to it, for it is the priesthood of Christ himself. It is our fundamental priesthood, lived out on the common human border with the TRANSCENDENT. It is the priesthood after the order of Melchizedek. It is not preparatory to some other, higher priesthood. It does not step back when some "better" priesthood arrives on the scene. There is no better priesthood. As I have already said, ordination simply creates a sacramental model, a religious icon that

---

119. L. William Countryman, *The Language of Ordination: Ministry in an Ecumenical Context* (Philadelphia: Trinity Press International, 1992).

120. The sharp contrast between "laity" and "clergy" arose at the beginning of the third century. At the time, the "laity" seems to have consisted of the adult male population of the church or even a more limited group of prestigious laymen, roughly the equivalent of the *plebs* in the older, republican Roman constitution, but considerably more powerful than the common people in contemporary political usage. Women were neither laity nor clergy, but a third, less public category. See Alexandre Faivre, *The Emergence of the Laity in the Early Church,* trans. David Smith (New York: Paulist Press, 1990) 43–132.

reminds us who we are and points us toward the living out of our priest-hood.[121]

Ordination does not subtract anything from the fundamental priest-hood, either. Christians who are ordained do not leave the fundamen-tal priesthood behind. Those who are ordained cannot afford to refocus their attention on their clerical distinctiveness as if that were the cen-tral definer of who and what they are. To do so is to lose touch with what is really central for all Christians alike, namely participation in the universal human priesthood as interpreted and illuminated in Jesus. Whatever ordination is about, it cannot bestow any priesthood higher than that bestowed in birth and interpreted in baptism; nor can it deprive a person of what birth has given and baptism shaped. In the fundamental and primary sense, laity and clergy are priests together. Any lesser claim for the priesthood of the *laos* calls the priesthood of Jesus himself, layman as he was, into question.

This way of understanding priesthood and ordination stands in sharp contrast with some other patterns of thought common among modern Christians—patterns so pervasive that we are barely aware of the way they control our thinking. It will be useful to try to raise some of these views to consciousness at this point so that we can discover how pervasive they are and, I hope, look at them clearly enough to rec-ognize them and perhaps reject them. These are not, primarily, official theological rationales for ordination (though they overlap with them in some cases), but practical images that govern ordinary perceptions of the clergy in the church today. They are so pervasive that they perme-ate the thinking not only of church members, but even of people who have little or no direct contact with the church. Some of the images are quite old, others of more recent origin.

- One very old pattern of thinking is the hierarchical pattern that treats the ordained priesthood as a conduit by which grace

---

121. "It is only to the extent that [priests] are ordained as *vicarii Ecclesiae* that they are also ordained as *vicarii Christi,* vicars of Christ, who is at once the source and the object of the Church's faith. Ordination establishes believers as ministers of the Church, that is, as believers who act in its name, and only as a function of that ministry as ministers also of Christ, as believers who act in his name." Lawler, *Symbol and Sacrament,* 239. Ironically, however, ordained priests already share in Christ's priesthood before ordination.

descends from GOD to the laity. This way of thinking is, of course, precisely opposite to what I am proposing, since it makes the ordained the "real" priests, while the priesthood of lay Christians is derivative and the priesthood of humanity as such probably nonexistent.[122] This perspective ultimately comes to grief on the reef of simple everyday observation.

Our common experience tells us that the ordained are not, as a class, holier or more intimately attuned to GOD than the laity. Indeed, over the centuries, the clerical orders have harbored at least their full share of arrogance, authoritarianism, indifference to the oppressed, sloth, gluttony, hatred, superficiality, and hypocrisy—not to mention the more conventional clerical sins touching on matters of sex and wealth. What is more, the simple fact of their being bound to the religious institution means that the world of the ordained is always in danger of shrinking to the confines of the church, where it focuses entirely on the maintenance and enhancement of the institution.[123] As a result, the grace of GOD, if it is thought to be ministered entirely by the ordained, will be defined more and more as a churchly phenomenon with minimal relation to the ordinary world. Thus it appears increasingly irrelevant to ordinary life. This is less a result of the increasing "secularization" of society, I believe, than of the inherent tendency of hierarchies to lose touch with common human reality.

---

122. A Roman Catholic author has written: "[In] the religious landscape in which the vast majority of Christians today have grown up, . . . one can disengage these principal articulations: *God*, through *Jesus Christ*, gives to the *clergy* a power over the *mass*. It is in the mass that the *church* truly realizes the fullness of its mystery. And it is from there that, nourished by the mass, it can go to the *world*. [These elements are arranged hierarchically with God at the top and the world at the bottom.] We thus find that the structure that predetermined clergy/laity relations now organizes the whole of our religious universe. . . . [O]ne can already presume that *each element will be considered as a passive object in its relations with the top and as an active subject of its relations with the bottom.*" Rémi Parent, *A Church of the Baptized: Overcoming Tension between the Clergy and the Laity*, trans. Stephen W. Arndt (New York: Paulist Press, 1987) 27–28.

123. "For me the problem is that Church has come to mean institution and not people—not the people of God. I do not think that most people, in response to the question 'What is the Church?' would answer 'the people of God.' They (accurately) view the Church as an institution with a professional hierarchy, concerned about maintaining itself. That is what institutions are always all about. They could not possibly be about anything else." Dozier, *The Authority of the Laity*, 3–4.

But the problem with the hierarchical model of priesthood is not just at the level of experience. The model also runs counter to the basic principles of Christian faith. The Bible, in particular, makes it difficult to justify such hierarchical claims. Priesthood, as we have already seen in Genesis, is one of the oldest human realities. The calling of Israel through Abraham and his immediate heirs long antedated the institution of the Aaronic priesthood, and the priesthood of Aaron was notoriously prone to implicate itself in idolatry from the very start.[124] In the New Testament, the texts giving detailed directions about the Christian clergy are late (reflecting developments in actual practice) and sufficiently unclear to provide models (and ammunition) for a whole array of post-Reformation polities. If Jesus thought grace would be available to his lay followers only through the ministry of males ordained in a specific way, as some have asserted, why is there not a word to that effect in scripture? Would this not be culpable carelessness on the part of the SPIRIT? Instead, the New Testament is quite vague on all such matters.

> • Another old pattern, rooted in the Reformation Era, is to think of the clergy as "graduate Christians," distinguished by a higher degree of religious or theological knowledge.[125] The churches spend a significant portion of their educational resources on candidates for ordination, which results in the clergy being theologically more educated, as a class, than the laity. For the most part, then, ordination is possible only for people who are willing to volunteer for theological education at the tertiary level—or, at least, willing to suffer through it. Thus, church policies sustain the notion of a clergy distinguished from "mere" laity by greater knowledge and

---

124. See the incident of the golden calf, Exodus 32.
125. ". . . the English village model [inherited by Episcopalians] . . . is centered and heavily dependent on the 'cleric,' who at one time was the most educated person in the village and thus also the primary teacher. This model tends to create vicarious religion, centered on the priest as the holy person, in whom is focused the religious power and knowledge. It also tends to create dependence, rather than interdependence. If the priest is 'father,' church members are children. . . . If the priest is pastor, members are always sheep intended to follow, not lead." Wesley Frensdorff, "The Captivity of Sacraments," *The Witness* 75/5 (April 1992): 5.

wisdom.[126] Yet the theory collapses when we note how many of the most influential theological or spiritual writers of our century, despite these policies, have not been among the ordained—people like Evelyn Underhill, Simone Weil, C. S. Lewis, or William Shoemaker.

Indeed, one of the worst mistakes churches can make (and have at times made) is to *restrict* theological education to the clergy, thus making informed reflection about faith and life a clerical monopoly and encouraging clericalism among laity and clergy alike.[127] This is a mistake because the clergy, as a class, tend to have a very limited view of what it means to be Christian. As noted above, they are more church-oriented than the laity, since they have careers that concentrate on service *within* the church. They become class-oriented, often without knowing it, seeking to perpetuate whatever prerogatives they have as a group. (That these prerogatives are increasingly few does not, of course, mean that they will be less vehemently defended.) Clergy members therefore tend to narrow the scope of Christian faith until it becomes meaningful only within a highly ecclesiastical culture, and loses its involvement in everyday life.

As a result, the laity, cut off from real theological dialogue with the clergy and suspicious of a dogma that claims to be beyond their questioning, often have to start theologizing from scratch, without benefit of the rich Christian tradition that the clergy have kept to themselves. Much of the mediocre and unreflective theology characteristic of popular American religion, alternating as it does between stony rigidity and spineless sentimentality, may be traced to just this origin: a clergy defined as belonging to a higher educational order (and therefore engaged in an increasingly abstract and irrelevant theological discourse) and a laity cut off from the tradition, except as bits and pieces of it

---

126. This is a general expectation in the church, not just a clerical claim to power. "What gives clergy the feeling that they ought to know everything? All too often lay people give them that feeling, and clergy feel guilty if they don't meet those unreal expectations." Dozier, *The Authority of the Laity,* 9.

127. "Symptoms of clericalism include intimidation, hoarding educational resources, controlling so-called 'real' theological language, congregational passivity, and renunciation of authority." Fredrica Harris Thompsett, *We Are Theologians: Strengthening the People of the Episcopal Church* (Cambridge, Mass.: Cowley Publications, 1989) 99.

might be doled out by the clergy for their own purposes. Repeatedly, the laity have turned to the sources that were readily available—primarily translations of the Bible and the platitudes of popular piety. The result has been the construction of new, makeshift, and often clumsy theologies in place of the classical Christian traditions. The "new" theology, in such a situation, then sometimes becomes a tradition in its own right, albeit an impoverished one, and the preserve of a new clerical order, as in American Fundamentalism.

If we are to break this particular vicious circle, it must be through joint participation of clergy and laity in renewing the richer and more ancient traditions of theological reflection. Our priestly work needs serious contemplation of both the world and the Christian message. To do this, we need a critical mass of Christians with a theological awareness strong enough that we can reflect together on our priestly experience. This does not imply making everybody go to seminary. The experience of Latin American base communities shows that when the world and the Christian tradition are brought into direct contact with each other, everyone is genuinely a theologian. Whether or not one agrees in all respects with the theologizing of these communities, they do clearly sustain serious reflection on the Christian message in the context of their world, and they do it without the presence of many advanced degrees.

All this is not, however, to diminish the value of higher education. There has been some tendency of late, even in churches traditionally serious about education, to argue that the only way to overcome clericalism is to keep the clergy closer to the laity in their formation. This has sometimes been interpreted to imply the circumventing of advanced theological education altogether. But the cure for an ignorant laity is not to set an ignorant clergy alongside them. The cure is a good supply of teachers. Seminary graduates, whether clergy or laity, need to see the sharing of the tradition as a principal purpose of their ministries. The tradition is of irreplaceable value, not because it predetermines all aspects of our priesthood, but because it enriches our priestly reflections by placing us in the ongoing priestly conversation of ages past and to come. "Higher" learning becomes genuinely valuable as it is shared in an ever widening circle of conversation.

  • Another common, powerful, and inappropriate image of the
    clergy is to take them as "the serious Christians" or "the real

Christians," in contrast to "the mere laity." This is a deeply traditional way of thinking about the clergy and has strongly shaped public attitudes, both inside and outside the church, for centuries. We assume that the clergy are purer, more moral, more disciplined than the laity—or, if not, that they ought to be. ("Clergy" in this particular sense includes not only the ordained but also such unordained icons of religion as monks and nuns and lay church professionals.) Because we think of clergy in these terms, we may simply refuse to see their faults; or, then again, we may apply extreme standards to them. Minor faults that we might overlook in a layperson become serious lapses in the official Christians. Areas that we would regard as private issues for a layperson we feel free to criticize in the clergy.

Here is a classic expression of this attitude from Thomas Comber, a seventeenth-century Dean of Durham:

[T]he Laity have but a single point to manage, *viz.*, to take care they do not offend God themselves, whereas a Minister must not only avoid that which is evil in itself, but also fly from the appearance of it and everything which may occasion his People to offend. So that there are several innocent Words and Actions which yet may be apt to be misconstrued that a Clergyman must abstain from lest others, taking the same liberty and wanting the like discretion, may stumble at the Stone which the other stepped over without hurt. . . . he must be Virtuous for his own sake, and unsuspected of Vice for the sake of others. Some company he may not keep, some places he must shun, some exercises he ought to forbear lest he give offense to weak but well-meaning People, or offer occasion to the wicked to speak evil of his sacred Profession.[128]

There is an element in this statement I would like to commend, namely its emphasis on the public responsibilities of the cleric. But we should

128. Thomas Comber, *A Companion to the Temple,* quoted in J. Robert Wright, ed., *Prayer Book Spirituality: A Devotional Companion to the Book of Common Prayer Compiled from Classical Anglican Sources* (New York: Church Hymnal Corporation, 1989) 436.

be wary of Comber's insistence on the moral superiority of the clergy, however pious, high-minded, and reasonable it may sound at first.

There are several reasons for skepticism. One is that Jesus himself would have been unordainable by Comber's standards. Jesus kept company with people and visited places and indulged in "exercises" for which he could be and was criticized severely—and not just by "weak but well-meaning People" or "the wicked," but by people as religious in their day as Comber in his. Few, if any, of Jesus' disciples could have met the Dean's standard. Comber's standard was not, it seems, Jesus' standard for his followers. It is analogous rather to the standard espoused by the religious sectarians of Jesus' time, people like the Essenes who were concerned to protect their own purity from being stained by contact with the ordinary Israelite laity. Jesus chose most of his disciples precisely from such ordinary layfolk. From the more religious he attracted mainly animosity.[129]

A second reason for skepticism has to do with the good news Jesus preached. Jesus insisted that the fundamental given in our relationship with GOD is not our goodness, but GOD's forgiving love. If we define the ordained in terms of exceptional holiness or purity, we are defining them in opposition to the basic good news of Jesus. We imply that, even though GOD's love may be sufficient for the layperson, the ordained person must be better—more deserving, more moral, more pure. This reduces (if it does not obliterate) the sacramental value of the ordained as images of the fundamental Christian priesthood. The good news of Jesus is about forgiveness, not purity. It was not Jesus who was committed to a superior standard of purity, but his opponents.

This is not to deny that Jesus demands a great deal of his followers. Ultimately, he calls for the full dedication of our lives in faith, hope, and love. Even from the beginning, he insists that we progress toward honesty and openness and away from hypocrisy and deceit. But these demands are quite different from a requirement specifying that only models of propriety can be ordained. Jesus did not object to observance of the traditional forms of piety and religion, but he was very

---

129. The rise of monasticism in the fourth century joined with other tendencies to create a notion of the clergy as an ascetic elite. Clergy who transgressed were punished not by excommunication, but by "demotion" to lay status, which identified the laity as a religiously inferior group. Faivre, *The Emergence of the Laity in the Early Church*, 162–64, 189–205.

clear that they were not conditions of GOD's favor. GOD's favor is given to us because GOD wills to give it to all, however sinful we may be, and not because we have deserved it. In the church's earliest decades, baptism seems to have been open to anyone who wished it. It had no complicated catechumenate leading up to it. GOD's gifts are free.[130]

If the church's sacramental priesthood mirrors and interprets the priesthood we all share with Christ, how can we justify reserving it to a pious elite? To draw sharp distinctions between worthy and unworthy gives the lie to the basic Christian message. In addition, it defeats its own aim. It creates a misleading public image of the clergy as quasi-angelic beings, free of human weakness. This, in turn, gives rise to a set of impossible expectations that the clergy cannot fulfill without denying their humanity. When their humanity rebels against such denial, it often does so in ways that prove destructive to others as well as themselves. The public is then outraged, and church officials hide behind walls of hypocrisy in an effort to evade the resulting unpleasantness.

This is not to suggest that clerical behavior is a matter of indifference. In many respects, it is of very great importance. (I will say more on this topic in chapter 7.) But the qualities to be sought are not the qualities indicated by Dean Comber. They are not the puritan qualities of precision in piety and avoidance of the unclean, the virtues that distinguish those who are holier than the common herd. They are qualities of responsibility and openness, which arise from the traditional "theological" virtues of faith, hope, and love. The clergy of the Christian church are not an elite—not a group of Gnostic *perfecti* who have passed beyond the weaknesses of the ordinary believer.

To be sure, the *numbers* of the ordained are and ought to be relatively small in comparison to the total number of the faithful, but not because the ordained constitute an elite. It is because sacraments are always more bounded, defined, and concrete than the mysteries to which they witness. It is of the nature of a sacrament that it should afford a relatively localized and tangible sign of a relatively diffused and pervasive grace. The water of baptism is a concrete, tangible expression of GOD's choice of the person being baptized—a choice that antedates the baptism, pervades one's life, and cannot be fixed to a single time

---

130. Baptism, to be sure, was originally limited to Jews. The baptism of the first Samaritans and Gentiles took place only with initial reluctance and was ultimately justified only on the basis of manifestations of the SPIRIT (Acts 8:5–25; 10:44–48).

or place. The bread of the Eucharist is a concrete presentation of GOD's nurturing care for us—a care that sustains us all our lives and cannot be limited to the brief moments of receiving the sacrament. Similarly, the relatively small numbers of ordained ministers within the church serve as icons of a priesthood diffused throughout the people of GOD. The ordained are sacramental images of the more fundamental priesthood all share with Christ.

The interpretation of the clergy as a religious elite rather than as a sacrament has a host of ill effects. For one, it means that ordination will often serve, de facto, to sanction differences of class or other cultural gradations by which some people are considered more worthy than others. The assumption will be that only the best (usually defined as the most respectable) people may be ordained. To prevent this, the clerical order should not be significantly different in composition from the church (or, better yet, the society) as a whole. Even conservative Christian theologies will acknowledge that it is not only permissible, but desirable, that the clergy include people of every racial or ethnic community. Indeed, one cannot say that the gospel has taken root anywhere until the community has begun to produce its own sacramental priests. If the Christians of the first century had admitted Gentiles to baptism but refused them any role in sacramental leadership, we should not now have a Gentile church.

For the same, equally orthodox reasons, it is important that women be ordained. The fact that, for a very long time, this was not done does not count against its orthodoxy. Orthodoxy is determined not merely by the hoariness of precedent, but by the overall coherence of any belief or usage with the central theological assertions of the Christian faith. The only conclusive argument is that a practice is in harmony with the good news, without which nothing, however venerable, can be orthodox. If women are not competent to be sacramental priests, why are they competent to be something much more important and to share the priesthood of Christ himself? It is an indefensible error to bar any person from ordination solely because that person belongs to a group defined by ordinary human characteristics such as race, language, culture, or sex.

The ordained priests are a sacrament of the fundamental priesthood. And therefore the inclusiveness of the clerical order is a sacrament of the inclusiveness of the fundamental priesthood in the church. Accordingly, the church should include openly gay and lesbian people in its

clergy. The argument that the Bible condemns such people as sinful is
unacceptable. At best, it is impossible of proof and, at worst, it is merely
a sanctification of bigotry, comparable to the way the curse of Canaan
(Genesis 9:20–27) was once used by Christians of European origin to
justify the oppression and exclusion of people of color. I have shown
elsewhere that the New Testament does not regard homosexual persons or acts as intrinsically sinful. Leviticus bans sexual intercourse
between males as impurity, but the gospel rejects the idea that such
physical impurity forms a barrier to relationship with GOD.[131] And,
since GOD has called many lesbians and gay men into membership in
the Christian people, they, too, are to be included in the ranks of the
sacramental priesthood. In the same way, Levitical purity laws that
excluded those with physical disabilities from serving as priests of the
Temple can have no legitimate analogue in Christian religion.

- There is another long-standing tradition that sees the clergy
  in parental roles and casts the laity in the role of permanent
  children. This is consecrated by the language of the more
  catholic traditions that traditionally address the clergy as
  "Father" (or, sometimes now, "Mother"); but it is by no means
  restricted to those traditions. The view is pervasive, for example, in modern American Protestantism, where it appears in two
  contrasting versions. One is the image of the ordained minister as the disapproving, judgmental parent, with a correspond-
  ing vision of the laity as bad children. The main task of the
  clergy is to tell the children what they have done wrong and
  to summon them back to the approved way. Such parents are
  expected to be rigid and authoritarian. They will be angry about
  offenses, but they can be appeased by a show of repentance. At
  best, the laity will prove to be good children by doing as they
  are told. More likely, they will be wayward and have to be
  rebuked. In any case, the clergy will need to remind them constantly of the correct standards of behavior, often by means of
  rebukes administered to absent third parties—those truly wicked
  folk who live somewhere else and are very different from the
  (comparatively) good sheep of the home fold. This disapproving-
  parent model is quite old in the churches and matches up with

131. L. William Countryman, *Dirt, Greed, and Sex*, 11–143, 237–67.

the use of parental models in other social contexts in which the assumption is that the common folk must be controlled by their betters, who are somehow endowed with greater insight and wisdom.

By contrast, the people of more "liberal" Protestant traditions often cast the ordained person in the role of the encouraging, liberal sort of parent who will treat children as good even when they are bad. Such a parent is expected to put up with any sort of behavior at all on the part of the child, while the child is not required to act responsibly, or constructively, or even civilly. The laity are thus permanently relieved of any necessity to grow up and take responsibility for their own faith. They can continue indefinitely to be dependent on the clergy, who are required always to be gentle and encouraging and consoling and never to demand too much. If the "parents" turn out to be less than perfect, the "children" are free to be as judgmental as the more disapproving type of clerical parent over what they define as the betrayal of their own relative weakness and dependency. The style of parental figure is different, but the basic opposition remains. Laity and clergy continue to be distinguished from one another as simple opposites. What the clergy are, the laity are not; and vice versa. The clergy are strong and mature, the laity weak and dependent. If the laity are to become mature Christians themselves, they can show this only by being ordained.

- A more modern way of distinguishing the clergy has been to describe them as "professionals," with the laity as their "clients." What constitutes a "professional"? It is a combination of specialized knowledge, a certain standard of skill in the use of that knowledge (usually determined by formal examination), an assumption that the person is entitled to be paid for the practice of the profession, and a supply of clients willing to pay for the services thus provided. Professionals belong to a "profession"—a community of related professionals whose evaluation of them largely determines their standing and their advancement. They have a career that they pursue, and this career gives shape to their working life. Implicit in this description is the assumption that the connection between the professional and the client is abstracted from other relationships and relatively distanced. To say that someone has acted "professionally" is to

say that they have acted in a way dictated entirely by their specialized knowledge and not distracted or distorted by personal
predilections or by personal knowledge of the client.

To see the clergy in these terms represents a sharp break from older
ways of viewing the clergy. At one time, clergy were forbidden to move
from one church to another.[132] They were conceived not as mobile,
independent professionals who might make their expertise available anywhere, but as leaders and officers of a local community, as attached to
their particular city as a municipal official. If they had a "career" (the
ancient *cursus honorum*), it was determined by the politics of the whole
community, not just that of the clerical order. And this is precisely the
point of difficulty in seeing the modern clergy as "professionals." While
there is much to be said for expecting certain standards of ability and
responsible behavior from the ordained, the clergy are not ultimately
reducible to isolated experts. Even if they are no longer entirely "home-
grown," their whole significance derives from their relationship to the
Christian community of which they are a part.[133] Once again, we find
clergy and laity defined here as opposites—and in ways that fit awk-
wardly with the actual life of the church.

> • Another modern image might, at first, seem better in this
> regard: the image of clergy as executives (or managers) of the
> church corporate. This does at least capture the importance of
> their link with the larger community. Unfortunately, the image
> also dissolves the sacramental quality of ordained priesthood,
> reducing the clergy to mere functionaries. It is a very ancient
> habit in the church to expect the ordained priests to take some
> responsibility for the leadership of the community, but that is

---

132. So the *Canons* of the Council of Nicaea, though they have often been flouted,
as in the case of St. John Chrysostom. The Council of Chalcedon forbade the ordination of clergy who were not tied to a particular church. On the tie between clergy
and community in early Christianity, see Lawler, *Symbol and Sacrament,* 229–31,
and Faivre, *The Emergence of the Laity in the Early Church,* 196.

133. "Yet what one senses in the shift to the professional model for ministry is
an insufficient attention to our sources, to the foundational texts and experiences
out of which the church emerged. What is missing is sufficient attention to Scripture. . . . [W]hat permeates the New Testament is the concern, indeed the passion,
that the gospel be proclaimed, served, and preserved." David L. Bartlett, *Ministry
in the New Testament* (Minneapolis: Fortress Press, 1993) 15.

not the same thing as simply defining them in those terms. Is the Pope the Chairman of the Board of the Roman Catholic Church? Yes, in a sense; but that statement captures little of the real authority or power of the office.

In any case, if the clergy are the executives or managers of the church, what does that imply with regard to the laity? A few may sit on the board, I suppose, and some will belong to middle management, but most are implicitly relegated to the status of workers. To be sure, these are "volunteer" workers and must be handled with the appropriate skills. But the relationship of clergy to laity becomes the job of managing volunteer personnel. The clergy remain other than the laity. The two groups may retain some common purpose, but their functions are opposite. In place of professionals and clients, we now have managers and workers.

This vision of the clergy is sometimes confused with the imagery of "servanthood." The image of the servant, in itself, is a venerable one for Christian ministry. It arises from Jesus' own identification of himself as one who came to serve, not to be served (Mark 10:45). It gives rise to the order of the diaconate (*diakonos* being Greek for "servant"). And, in itself, the image strikes a valid note: the sacramental priesthood exists only to serve the fundamental priesthood.[134] In practice, however, the image of "servant" must be viewed with a certain suspicion in our times. For one thing, it has come to prominence precisely at a time when servants have practically ceased to exist in the Western world. Since the metaphor of clergy as servants has no real foundation in our lived experience, it becomes a kind of blank check, capable of holding any content at all, while concealing the content under the apparent humility of "service."

Those who speak of the ordained as servants of the church seldom seem to mean by it that the ordained are at the beck and call of the laity, that they might be people who take orders or do as they are told. Often, the term cloaks an assumption that the "servant" knows what is best for the one being served and will dish it out whatever the one

---

134. Much of the modern theological discussion of servanthood, however, may be based on erroneous notions. See John N. Collins, *Diakonia: Re-interpreting the Ancient Sources* (New York and Oxford: Oxford University Press, 1990), which suggests that the Greek term *diakonos* can denote one acting as an agent, does not necessarily indicate low status, and was often used in specifically sacral contexts.

being served may think of the matter. It is hard to resist thinking that the image is less "cleric as servant" and more "cleric as nanny." One remembers that one of the ancient and treasured titles of the Bishop of Rome is "Servant of the Servants of GOD." Yet this self-designation does not seem to have impeded the papacy during its periodic displays of autocratic and dictatorial authoritarianism.

I do not mean to dismiss the image of servant altogether—or to reduce the servant to a merely instrumental role. The good and trusted servant combines a willingness to obey commands with an attentiveness to the true good of the person served. A good waiter (to take a type of servant still found in our culture) is not simply limited to bringing what is ordered, though that is fundamental, but can sometimes tactfully save patrons from ordering a meal they will regret! I have, in fact, seen clergy working from principles of servanthood perform analogous feats of humble and tactful charity. I do not, then, mean to dismiss all servanthood language—only to suggest that it requires careful inspection in our world, as the language is less clear or obvious than may at first appear and may sometimes serve as a cloak for clerical high-handedness.

> • The clergy may also be pictured as salespersons or, perhaps better, as managers of retail outlets. In this case, the laity are consumers to be lured into church and parted from their resources in return for the commodities (spiritual and social) that the church will convey to them. Many megachurches seem to operate in this mode. While they believe (or claim to believe) that they are simply making the gospel available to larger numbers of people, they are caught up in the same dynamics that affect any retail operation. They have discovered what sells, and they will have to continue to sell more and more of it in order to make ends meet. The clergy are the people principally responsible for the sales charts. Their task is to manipulate the customers (the laity) into buying the product (which they are, of course, convinced will be good for them).

Marketing, however, is chiefly concerned with the *moving* of goods, not with their quality. Having found the right key to unlock the sale, the marketer is satisfied. This is the reason why revivalist theology is so inexcusably thin and repetitive. It is only designed to make the sale, to gain the convert. Eventually it proves self-defeating, since it has no commitment to the long-run priestly conversations by which we grow in GOD's grace, conversations that need the depth of Christian tradition to sustain and enrich them so that, in their turn, they will bring the tradition to life in new ways.[135]

If the layperson is merely a commercial client, the economic task for the marketer is to work for a maximum of sales with a minimum of investment. The labor-intensive realities of the human priesthood cannot, of course, compete in this respect with the mass-marketing techniques of evangelistic "crusades" or televangelism. The more recent method of the megachurch may offer somewhat more hope, but that depends entirely on the spirit in which it is lived out. If done "cheaply," the megachurch will be a combination of social club (demanding a clientele drawn from essentially the same educational and social levels) with religious regimentation—a kind of mass production, in other words, that aims to satisfy social and spiritual needs together. Megachurches that are willing to encourage the kind of personal questioning that will help the fundamental priesthood come to maturity seem to be the exception rather than the rule.[136] It will be a challenge, at best, to make true priesthood "commercial."

> • In all these cases, the basic problem is this: we keep identifying the clergy as the opposite of the laity. They may be characterized, in the older images, has having greater knowledge or holiness or purity than the laity. The cleric may be characterized, in the newer images, as the professional in contrast to the lay client or as a manager in contrast to the lay volunteer worker or as a salesperson in contrast to the lay consumer. Each of these options, in its own way, deprives the clerical priesthood of its value as a sacrament of our common, fundamental priesthood, the priesthood of humanity and of Christ. By accepting the images above, we effectively undermine the real usefulness

---

135. I do not impose the marketing image on revivalism. I still remember hearing the most famous evangelist of our time, in my teenage years in Oklahoma City, urging us to get our tickets to the marriage supper of the Lamb as if it were a media event.

136. That it is at least possible I have learned from the example of All Saints Episcopal Church, Pasadena, California.

of ordained priesthood to Christian people. Conversely, if we can detach ourselves from such images of the ordained ministry, we may begin to see what the real value of a sacramental priesthood is.

The true power of a sacramental priesthood centers in its handling of religious rites. Through its approach to the sacred, it offers models of our common human and Christian priesthood. As I have been arguing throughout this book, we have few ways to speak of our encounter with the HOLY in the borderlands. The religious models that we human beings have constructed and inherited and endlessly revised and renovated are our principal language for speaking about GOD. They are not GOD; but by providing the sacred as a religious image for the HOLY, they enable us to reenact both the dangerous approach to and the transforming, life-giving encounter with the TRANSCENDENT.[137] This is the sphere in which the sacramental priesthood does its particular work.

In Christian tradition, the sacred takes two principal forms, traditionally called "word and sacrament." "Word" refers to the process by which the good news of Jesus is preserved and renewed from age to age; it is the whole verbal element in Christian worship that creates a spoken language for our experience of GOD's presence with us. "Sacrament" refers above all to the two most basic rites of Christian faith: baptism and the Eucharist (or communion). In a broader sense, "sacrament" can refer to any religious rite that mirrors and interprets our experience of the TRANSCENDENT, including such rites as penance, marriage, burials, or ordination. There are also many lesser sacraments, particularly in the form of sacred places and times—for example, churches, shrines, and the feasts and fasts of the Christian year. These provide a sacred environment for word and sacrament and therefore also figure

---

137. "Remember the Church exists to foster and hand on, not merely the moral life, the life of this-world perfection; but the spiritual life in all its mystery and splendour—the life of more than this-world perfection, the poetry of goodness, the life that aims at God. And this, not only in elect souls, which might conceivably make and keep direct contacts without her help, but in greater or less degree in the mass of men, who *do* need help. How is this done? The answer can only be, that it is mostly done through symbolic acts, and by means of suggestion and imitation. . . . [C]ultus has done a mighty thing for humanity, in evolving and conserving the system of symbols through which the Infinite and Eternal can be in some measure expressed." Underhill, *The Life of the Spirit and the Life of Today*, 129, 138.

in the work of the ordained. All these are matters in which the ordained have traditionally been given prominent roles.

In approaching and celebrating sacred rites, the ordained minister becomes an image of our common priestly experience in the borderlands. The sacramental priest draws near to the sacred places or objects as an image of our approach to the HOLY, performs the sacred rites as an image of our life in the presence of GOD, shares the sacred elements with the congregation as we share the HIDDEN with one another through our priesthood. In all of this activity, the ordained person is operating not by some magical power to "confect" sacraments, a power denied to the "ordinary" layperson. Rather, the ordained priest is manifesting in religious, sacramental fashion a more fundamental reality that pervades all our experience. The ordained presider is not introducing a new, hitherto absent element of GOD's presence into the community, but bringing to discernible focus the PRESENCE that is already there by virtue of our common priesthood.

Consider the role of the ordained in the sacrament of baptism. The rite is a sacramental act, witnessing to the priesthood of the whole people. In baptism, the candidate submits to the water, which is both threatening and life-giving. It becomes a sign of the borderlands themselves, the threatening "place" in our experience that turns out to be the womb of new life. The ancient imagery of baptism tells us that, through the water, we escape from the Egyptian bondage of our past, crossing the Red Sea with dry feet; in the water we pass through the flood with Noah and begin a new life in a new world (1 Peter 3:20–22); in it, we are reborn of water and SPIRIT (John 3:3–5); in it, we are washed clean, never to be filthy again in GOD's sight (Ephesians 5:26); in it, we pass through death itself and find ourselves alive with new life (Romans 6:3–4). As a sacrament of the borderlands, baptism brings us face to face with the uncertainty and dependency of our lives and helps us to understand that this place of apparent danger and death is really an encounter with the LOVE that sustains us in life.

The role of the ordained person in baptizing mirrors the priestly role that each of us experiences, whether as giver or as receiver, in the presence of the HOLY. Baptism is not about the power of the clergy to bestow grace. The ordained do not have power over GOD's grace. We can meet the HIDDEN HOLY without these rites. The rite is rather a showing forth of this experience, a concrete, sacramental re-presentation of it, reminding us and reaffirming for us how GOD meets us in the border country. The ordained minister is a sacrament of the priesthood that flourishes among us there and, ever afterwards, helps us plumb the meaning of our own priesthood as it grows from our meeting with the HIDDEN.[138]

We experience GOD's meeting with us not once but time and again, in ever new ways, in our daily life. Baptism manifests this experience sacramentally, but the meeting itself is not confined to baptism nor exhausted by baptism. Baptism confirms for us that we are living in the company of the HOLY, in the borderlands where deepest REALITY undergirds everyday existence. Baptism assures us that, even while we are absorbed in the world of the everyday, we are also living in the presence of the hidden POWER and BEAUTY. Baptism affirms that we have been claimed by LOVE and sacramentally sets the seal of that claim on us. Because of all this, we can live at the boundary with increasing confidence in GOD's goodness. We can risk staying on the border to assist one another. The ordained minister, in approaching the water of baptism with the person to be baptized, is not a priest over against the person being baptized, but a priest alongside the person—and so offers a sacramental image of the priesthood each of us lives out every day.[139]

Something similar is true of the Eucharist. The table or altar is traditionally at the focal point of the space where the church gathers. The bread and wine are the stuff of ordinary, physical life. Through their offering up in thanksgiving, they become a sacrament of the BEYOND that is in the midst of life. Like baptism, the Eucharist represents the border country as a place of both danger (the cross) and life (the resurrection). In this place, death becomes life, risk becomes nourishment, fear gives way to hope. When the community gathers and the designated person stands at the table to give thanks over the shared meal, the sacred ritual mirrors our actual experience of the HOLY as one in whose presence death opens onto life. In the communion service, we surrender our life liturgically before GOD along with Christ and receive it back as Christ's larger life, shared by all.

---

138. Juan C. Oliver has pointed out to me that the baptismal sponsors are also sacraments of the fundamental priesthood, most obviously in the recent revival of the catechumenate, where the sponsors help the adult catechumens in and out of the font.

139. This is particularly clear in the case of baptism, since, even in quite conservative traditions, laypersons have authority to baptize in case of emergency. The ordained person is simply the normal minister when baptism is performed in the presence of the whole church.

Even before or apart from its connection with Jesus' death and resurrection, the sharing of food is an aspect of our lives where we often find the HOLY meeting us. As we eat together, we find ourselves, at least in graced moments, nourished not only with the physical food but with the priestly presence of one another and an awareness of GOD's graciousness. The sharing of food often proves to be the occasion for the deeper priestly sharing of life. This sharing is possible only as we die to our own preoccupations and presuppositions in order to be present to the experience of another person. There is always risk in it, always at least a small element of death that proves life-giving only by the gift of the SPIRIT. In the rite of communion, this revelatory, grace-filled quality of eating together is taken up into a sacramental image of our priestly life in the Christian community and illuminated by Jesus' sharing of himself. The ordained minister at the table is, once again, not acting as a priest over against the other worshipers, but is shining a sacramental spotlight on the priesthood in which we all participate.

By GOD's grace, we find ourselves living in the border country. While it may seem, at first sight, to be a wasteland, it turns out to be for us, as for the people of Israel in the desert or for the crowds in Jesus' ministry, a place of feeding. We share food with others and find ourselves filled. This sharing is a repeated aspect of our experience of the fundamental priesthood. We receive this power to share life from the HIDDEN itself, not from the work of the sacramental priest. But the sacramental action sets before us and so reinvigorates in us the power we have received from the HOLY. It gives us a reminder of our priesthood and new courage to continue in it. Jesus directed his followers to perform this rite "for the remembrance" of him. The point is not that we should remember Jesus as someone from the distant past, but that the rite reminds us who we are in Christ here and now.

The ordained also minister the word, the whole verbal aspect of Christian religion: scripture, tradition, preaching, teaching, interpretation, most modes of prayer, and everything that can be put into words of any sort.[140] Words figure prominently in Christian religion as icons of GOD. In the Gospels, they convey Jesus' good news about GOD.

---

140. "The sacramental office belongs to the ordained person. . . . And I believe it is also the calling of the ordained to know the story, to hold that story in our remembrance, to recall it in the educational program, to act out that drama in the sacrament, to hold that community together so that the word can always be preached, and the sacraments offered." Dozier, *The Authority of the Laity*, 40.

Jesus' parables entice us or even trick us into encountering TRUTH. Jesus is himself acclaimed as WORD in the Gospel of John. It is above all the power of words to surprise, to subvert our sense of knowing the world and of being in command of it, to give new texture and nuance to what we thought we already knew, that gives them the power to mediate the divine WISDOM. Religious rites or sacraments may serve best to confirm us and reestablish us in what we have already learned; the word can, at times, lead us further, producing *metanoia*—repentance, conversion, the new vision of the world that brings us a step closer to TRUTH.[141]

This property of the word, of course, is not limited to the rites of Christian religion. It is not even primarily resident there. Jesus spoke it in fields and houses and streets and marketplaces more than in the synagogue or the Temple. The word of comfort spoken in a time of distress, the word of challenge spoken when needed, the unexpected comment that opens up new and unforeseen vistas in the world—all these are truly expressions of the word. Indeed, they are its truest expressions because they reveal its power to transform. All this, of course, can happen in church. But most of the time it happens just where it happened in Jesus' ministry—in the locations of our casual daily interactions with one another. The religious ceremonies at which the ordained preside are sacraments of this daily grace, not monopolies on it.

Liturgical usage, then, is not the only or even the primary home of the word. The word in liturgy is a sacrament of its pervasive presence in all reality. The deacon brings the Gospel book into the worshiping assembly and reads from it. Someone reads from other scriptures. There are psalms and hymns and prayers. Someone preaches. There are words of instruction, perhaps. There are words for celebrating sacraments. All these vary according to the traditions of particular churches, but they all stem from age-old Christian usage. Our worship is full of words, words mirroring that great word that breaks through our dullness of hearing, renews for us the great promise of grace, shows us the new possibilities for our own lives implicit in GOD's love for us.

The word of GOD, in Christian religion, remains subversive. If the sacramental words of worship cannot guarantee the presence of GOD's word, neither can they guarantee to keep us safe from it. The word

---

141. I do not mean to limit either sacrament or word to a single function, only to suggest where their primary strength lies.

keeps breaking through the boundaries of the sacred. This is related to the fact that the word, in Christianity, was originally oral, not written. The earliest Christians had no scriptures but those of Israel, and these did not speak plainly or unambiguously about Jesus. The central form of word, for them, was not scripture, but the oral tradition of Jesus' life and good news, communicated through teaching and preaching. This oral tradition was not primarily the repetition of memorized formulas, but rather a vivid and relatively free style of bringing the faith tradition to bear on the life of the hearer, surprising us with the presence of the divine WISDOM in the life of every day. In other words, the speaking of the word in earliest Christianity partook in the fundamental priesthood, placing us directly in the presence of the HOLY, as much as it did in the sacramental priesthood.

In teaching and preaching alike, the point was not merely to repeat a formula, but to bring the revelatory word that had transformed the speaker's life to bear on the lives of others. As one early writer put it, the speaker handing on the good news "used to adapt the teaching to the needs."[142] The audience wanted more than just a recognizable account of Jesus' teaching and ministry. They wanted spoken words that could bring them once again a word so unexpectedly powerful that it could produce *metanoia*: a new and life-giving perspective that would yield joy, repentance, conversion, radical change.

Christian teaching and preaching still aim to do more than just hand on the religious tradition. They must at least do that, of course. The word is part of the sacred rites. But it is also more—because of its inherent tendency, implanted in it by Jesus' own priesthood, to break the limits of the sacred, to step out from the familiar formulae and engage with the deeper and broader realities of human experience. The word is truly itself only when it can be heard as good news. Taken at face value, the words of Christian religion give access to the sacred, not the HOLY. Yet, at any moment, they may become the medium not just of the sacramental, but of the fundamental priesthood.[143]

Teaching and preaching are both sacramental of the word and share its power. They differ mainly in the social expectations attached to each.

---

142. Papias of Hierapolis, quoted by Eusebius, *Church History* 3.39.15.

143. It was such a moment, for example, that sent the anonymous Russian Christian off on the journeys he narrated in *The Way of a Pilgrim*. The words of scripture, read in the service, came off the page and posed themselves as a challenge to his particular life and priesthood.

We expect a teacher to tell us something new or to remind us of things known but half-forgotten. The teacher who is faithful to the fundamental priesthood uses this expectation of the new as an opening to impart not just new information, but new perspective, the first step in *metanoia*. We expect the preacher, on the other hand, to restate the familiar verities of our religion, but to do so in a way that renews our sense of their relevance and enlarges our understanding of them. The preacher who is faithful to the fundamental priesthood will use this expectation as an opportunity to evoke the HOLY behind the sacred, allowing us to sense that the apparently familiar is, in fact, strange— larger, more mysterious, more diverse, and more powerful and full of hope than we had supposed.

In just these ways, preaching and teaching, though they are formulated liturgically as tasks particularly of the sacramental priesthood, can at times become expressions of the fundamental priesthood as well. Here the line becomes blurred—an appropriate development, since the sacramental priesthood exists not over against the fundamental priesthood, but in and for it. The best preaching and teaching is rooted in our experience of the borderlands and may come as easily from laypersons as from clergy. So it is precisely in the ministry of the word that the lines between ordained and unordained become least meaningful.

The word emerges with true power only from a profound, humbling, and life-giving encounter with the good news of love and forgiveness— in other words, with GOD's own self. It is possible to counterfeit the power of true preaching through skill in rhetoric and a willingness to manipulate an audience and play on its prejudices. In fact, such manipulation has been common since the earliest times. As Paul says, however, the truest preaching can forswear all trickery because the message of GOD's grace has its own sufficient power, best heard when the style is the word's servant, not its master (1 Corinthians 1:17–25).

At times, true teaching and preaching are rare in the public worship of the churches, and the word may seem almost dead. Even then, however, it is still enshrined in the rites of Christian religion, witnessing *sotto voce* in the books and readings and prayers and other objects and formulae of the rites. Even the worst and most perfunctory of sermons still witnesses to the possibility of a life-giving word. Even overly familiar phrases, repeated by rote, go on witnessing to the principles of the gospel. They are merely waiting for "the one who has ears to hear"— one person here and another there. Eventually, a living voice again makes the gospel audible. That voice may as easily belong to a layper-

son as to one ordained. Indeed, by the sheer necessity of numbers, it
will more often be so. Some Antony of Egypt or Dame Julian of Nor-
wich begins to speak good news again, and the clergy may start to
awake from their sleep, too. The ambiguous quality of the word, sacred
and HOLY both at once, means that there will always be an ambiguity
of speakers, too.

It is a mistake, then, to try to limit the ministry of the word entirely
to the ordained. The ordained must have a liturgical share in this ministry or they will be sadly incomplete icons of Christian priesthood. But
the way the word overflows the realm of the sacred means that it should
also be ministered sacramentally by others—by people whose qualification is that they have lived on the border with the HOLY and have
something to tell of it. In the worship of the church, the word is most
compelling when spoken by many voices, having many tales of discovery to tell.

Outside the church's worship, the laity are usually better ministers
of the word than the clergy. After all, the clergy's close association with
the institutional life of the church can tempt them to be advocates of
the institution rather than of GOD. And since they are culturally defined
(however wrongly) as "wiser" and "better" than others, their message
will often be unconsciously dismissed as bearing no relation to ordinary human lives. The layperson, on the other hand, is free to be a
priest of the HOLY without this kind of distraction and to do so from
within an everyday world more easily recognized by others as their own.
In this way, the word presented as sacrament in the church becomes
once again the living word of good news, able to transform lives.

I cannot say too often that the priesthood of the whole people is
the fundamental priesthood. Even for the ordained minister, Christian
priesthood still means primarily one's exercise of the priesthood shared
with the whole people. The ordained priesthood is a sacramental service offered not so much *to* the whole people (which would imply a
stance over against the laity) as *in* and *for* that prior and more universal ministry. If there is a "higher" priesthood, it is the fundamental
priesthood, the priesthood of the whole people of GOD, the priesthood
of Jesus, the priesthood after the order of Melchizedek. It is not the
ordained ministry.

Yet, all this being said, what the ordained do in church, moving in
the realm of the sacred, is powerful for good or ill in shaping the priesthood of all. If the ordained ministry proffers a bad icon—incomplete,

blurred, distorted—there will be uncertainty and confusion in the priestly people. One might suggest that this is often true of Christian churches today. The meaning and role of the ordained is too often a puzzle both to the ordained themselves and to the larger Christian community. In the next chapter, I will explore some of our present uncertainties and ask how the explanation of priesthood that I am offering can help us understand these problems and seek solutions.

6

Problems about Priesthood

Fifty years ago, the role and purpose of ordained ministry seemed fairly clear in the Western world. Since then the task has become steadily more problematic, both for the public at large and for the churches—and, indeed, for the clergy in particular. While many clergy and congregations are still working together well, the signs of tension and uncertainty are everywhere. Some denominations have too few clergy for their needs, others a surplus. Many denominations are at war with themselves over the ordination of women and of gay men and lesbians. Ethnic and racial minority groups in mainline denominations sometimes find themselves at odds with the majority's cultural expectations for clergy. Some laypersons feel that the clergy are an impediment to the realization of the ministry of the whole people. Some clergy see emphasis on lay ministries as undermining their own roles. Some clergy confront a sense of burnout and acknowledge their failure to care for their own health and welfare. Others turn out to have been preying on their flocks with offenses ranging from abusive behavior toward individuals to embezzlement of funds. Seminaries find themselves caught in cross fire as different groups demand conflicting solutions to what they see as the deficiencies in clergy education. These problems give a more concrete countenance to the general malaise that afflicts ordained ministry in the churches at present, and they deserve closer examination.

These are not simply problems for or about clergy. These are problems for and about both priesthoods, since they are interrelated. The problem is impossible to resolve in terms of our long-standing tendency to define the laity and the ordained as opposites. As long as we proceed in that way, every statement about the clergy tends to imply the opposite about the laity. As we have already seen, a definition of the clergy as theologically educated has often implied a definition of the laity as ignorant, and so forth. In its most drastically simplified form, the opposition becomes, for some people, one of good and bad. If the clergy are seen as basically "good," all problems raised by laypersons must represent a simple failure of respect or a grab for power. If the laity are identified as the "good" people, the clergy are under constant suspicion, and one begins to think about how to circumvent them or even to do away with sacramental priesthood altogether.

One might be tempted to try to resolve the conflict by abolishing the clergy altogether. But the attempt is probably doomed to failure. Sacramental priesthood is deeply embedded in the institutions of religion; and religion, despite its dismissal by some modern thinkers, is apparently indispensable to human beings as a way of understanding and communicating our most profound and inarticulate experience. When we lose one sort of religious priesthood, we tend to replace it with another. When the moral authority of the Temple priesthood waned in antiquity and the ritual system that it administered largely disappeared with the destruction of the Temple itself, Judaism found a new "priesthood" in its rabbis. Most Protestants who rejected the medieval priesthood at the Reformation put comparable forms of ordained ministry in its place. As Milton wrote,

New Presbyter is but old Priest writ large.

The urge toward sacramental priesthood is virtually irresistible. Among Christian traditions, perhaps only the Society of Friends can claim to have resisted it with any success. Some kind of sacramental priesthood normally returns to haunt churches that have tried to dispense with it.

While I am endeavoring to move us away from definitions of laity and clergy that treat them as simple opposites, it will always be true that the definitions of the two will be interrelated. In order to know what either group is, we need to know what both groups are—and how they interpenetrate and support one another. The alternative to the opposition between laity and clergy is not abolition of one group or the other or radical subordination of the one to the other, but a redefinition of both that acknowledges their interconnectedness. We need to move away from seeing the sacramental priesthood as standing "over against the laity" and understand it as existing "in and for the fundamental priesthood." It is not only the prepositions that are different in the second formula; it is the definition of the group in relation to which the clergy are defined. "Laity" implies "clergy" as its opposite. "Fundamental priesthood" implies "sacramental priesthood" as a sacred representation of itself, projected into the sphere of religion.

Christian communities, laity and clergy together, have to make decisions about how to articulate their social reality. Failure to make these decisions leaves everyone without a practical sense of what they are responsible for or how to perform these tasks. Today, most churches seem to be in a state of considerable uncertainty about such problems. The clergy often seem uncertain about what their own tasks are—and may feel that they lack the skills and talents to fulfill them all. They ask whether they are to "do" ministry themselves or rather to "enable" the laity to do it. They wonder whether they should be generalists or specialists—and, if specialists, specialists in what. They ask where the limits of their responsibilities lie. They wonder how to balance the demands of the church and the needs of their families and personal lives.[144]

The laity seem often to be equally unsure of their role. They ask, What is the layperson's ministry? Is it necessarily done in church on Sunday or in relation to church organizations? Does it need the church's "label" on it? Or is it something that happens primarily in the midst of the everyday world? Why, for that matter, are there limits on what the layperson does ritually? Why should not the layperson be free to do anything an ordained person does? Why does the church separate certain people through ordination when priesthood is the work of all?

The complex dimensions of such questions emerge more clearly in the context of concrete problems like the ones I mentioned briefly at the beginning of this chapter, which therefore claim our further attention now. In considering them, we shall also be asking how the various models or images of ministry discussed in the preceding chapter may contribute to the creation of these problems.

- The larger public is perhaps most aware of the churches' difficulties through newspaper reports of dramatic cases of *clerical malfeasance*, particularly in the form of sexual abuse and misappropriation of church funds. It is difficult to say whether such problems have become worse or whether they have only

---

144. "It would be lovely if the minister felt responsible only to God, but that is a hope for heaven, not for this earth. Every minister feels and should feel responsible to and for the gospel, but also to and for the congregation, the denomination and its authorities, the community, and . . . the future of humankind. . . . To say that ministers are professionals means in part that no one else will have quite the stake we do in the day by day running of the institution we serve." Bartlett, *Ministry in the New Testament*, 17–18. For a survey of clergy confusions and distress in the Episcopal Church, see Loren B. Mead et al., *Excellence in Ministry: Study Document: Personal and Professional Needs of the Clergy of the Episcopal Church* (New York: Episcopal Church Foundation, 1988).

become more public; but, given the anecdotal evidence I encounter, I suspect that what has changed is not so much clerical behavior as our cultural response to it. The churches have never been able, even at their most vigilant, to guarantee absolutely the good behavior of the clergy. In past eras, however, clerical misdeeds tended to be dealt with quietly, even in secret, in order to "spare" the larger church community embarrassment. Police and journalists often cooperated in this concealment. In the process, those who had been abused were often silenced by community pressure, while the clergyperson in question might merely be transferred to a new position, without people in the new place being told why.

This process of concealment had its counterpart in other areas of public life. American journalists used to treat the sexual behavior of politicians, for example, as news that was "not fit to print," whereas it now appears routinely on the front page of newspapers. American culture, in its constant swaying between sexual permissiveness and restriction, is now at the restrictive end of the spectrum, and is inclined to treat sexual offenses with great rigor—and therefore with great curiosity, too. New recognition of the ways in which patriarchal domination of society has used sexual politics to silence women, and new awareness of the serious damage that sexual abuse can cause to the emotional maturation of children, have also encouraged the public to take such matters more seriously. All this has served to bring individual offenses that would previously have been concealed into the light.

Recognition of these offenses is particularly troubling (and fascinating) to the general public because they are violations of two of our most strongly held, if often unconscious, presuppositions about clergy: first, that they are morally superior to other people or even belong to a different moral level altogether (what we might call "clerical angelism"); second, that they are professionals who betray their very reason for existence if they cross the boundary of personal detachment between themselves and their clients. In this latter respect, the public's fascination with wayward clergy is closely related to its fascination with wayward psychotherapists who form sexual liaisons with their clients, or who use their position to gain power over the client's property. Where, in the past, the church community often chose to preserve the illusion of clerical angelism by concealing the faults of individual clerics, the professional image of the clergy has now added the necessary impetus to prompt exposure and a more open treatment of the issues. This, in turn, exposes the sometimes conflicting interests that our varying definitions of the ordained impose on us.

> • Within the churches, a constant though less dramatic difficulty centers on *problems of supply and distribution of clergy*. In the United States, the Roman Catholic Church has been experiencing a radical decline in the number of ordained priests, one that has now reached crisis proportions and effectively compelled the substitution of lay pastoral workers in most of the tasks formerly performed by clergy. The Episcopal Church, by way of contrast, has had far more clergy available than there are paid positions to be filled, but still finds itself suffering from a shortage of clergy in some areas, either because salaries are not attractive or because the professionally educated person does not always want to live in a small town or rural area. (The same problem has dogged the medical profession in nonurban areas.) Churches that have more centralized modes of clergy appointment (for example, the Methodists) are more able to assign clergy to such posts, which they can use as lower rungs on a career ladder, but they, too, have to confront the reality of shrunken rural populations and the inability of many smaller churches to pay for the services of a full-time professional. Problems of this sort are not restricted to the United States. Throughout the world, there are difficulties in sustaining old, established expectations about the "normal" ratio of clergy to congregations.

The uncertainty of clergy availability tends to undermine long-held customs and presuppositions regarding clerical and lay roles. If Roman Catholic nuns or other nonordained pastoral workers are increasingly the de facto "clergy" of their congregations, even performing most of the liturgical roles (apart from saying the prayer of consecration in the Eucharist or giving absolution), that raises questions about who these "lay" people are and about what difference ordination really makes. For this reason and others, it is not surprising that one now hears many Roman Catholics questioning (for the most part *sotto voce*) the need for an ordained ministry at all. It turns out to be a rather short step from having Christianity's highest, most differentiated definition of the sacramental priesthood to thinking of its abolition.

In other denominations, the tendency has been to meet clergy shortages through limited forms of authorization in which a lay leader of a local community that cannot find or afford a "professional" cleric is ordained or licensed without extensive educational preparation. Or, at least, authorization is given without the full process that would be normal for clergy whose ordination or licensing would be considered universally valid within the denomination. Such persons wind up doing much the same pastoral work they were already doing through their fundamental human and Christian priesthood. They are usually non-stipendiary, and there is little change in their responsibilities. But now they are sacramental priests as well. What difference, exactly, is their ordination or licensing understood to have made in their ongoing ministry? And how is their ministry to be related to popular notions of the ordained priest as the person of special knowledge or as the professional? Far from being the detached professional, whose primary identification is with the professional corps to which she belongs, the "local priest" has been chosen precisely because she is immersed in the community which she will now serve as ordained person. Her level of specialized knowledge may not be much different from before.

In a variety of ways, then, difficulties about the supply and distribution of ordained persons push the communities involved to rethink the roles of lay and ordained priesthood. Any time familiar patterns are disrupted, questions arise about what was formerly taken for granted. In the present case, the disruption of the old patterns has been long-lasting, and churches have not yet found acceptable new patterns with which to establish a "normality" for the future. We have yet to determine whether a congregation without "professional" clergy is really handicapped, and, if so, how or to what degree? Is more always better? May less, at times, be more?

On the other hand, what is the significance for the church of clergy without congregations—"surplus" clergy not in the church's employ? What does ordination mean in their case? How do such clergy fulfill their ordained ministry when they have no ecclesiastical appointment? Is there really, in some churches, an "oversupply" of clergy? From what perspective? From that of congregations? From that of clergy not employed by the church? From that of parish clergy who may be uncomfortable with having other ordained (and theologically trained) persons in the congregation who are not directly subject to their control? Are the clergy a corps of detached professionals, like psychotherapists and doctors and attorneys? Or are they defined entirely by their relation to a community? The difficulty in resolving such questions suggests the need for new and more satisfactory images of priesthood, both fundamental and sacramental.

 • Most churches have also found themselves embroiled, over the past few decades, in serious internal *conflicts about who is a suitable candidate for ordination*. More denominations have begun to ordain women, but ordination has not automatically meant full acceptance for them once ordained. The career advancement of ordained women still lags significantly behind the rate at which they have entered the corps of the ordained. And in some churches that do ordain women, there are still minorities that explicitly refuse to recognize their validity or authenticity as sacramental priests. This is true in the Church of Sweden, for example, which has ordained women to the priesthood for decades but has only very recently—and not without protest—selected its first woman bishop.

Other denominations have steadfastly refused to consider the possibility of ordaining women—even to the extent of prohibiting discussion of the topic. The question does not, however, go away. In the Roman Catholic Church, the increasing prominence of nuns and lay women in pastoral roles and in academic theology makes the tension between theory and practice a more and more difficult one. This is one of the factors, I should imagine, leading some Roman Catholics toward a radical suspicion of ordination as such. At some point, the Roman Church may be forced to ordain women if it wants to save the ordained priesthood at all.[145]

Opposition to women clergy has many sources and is connected with larger Western cultural patterns that have long demanded subor-

---

145. The inclusion of women will not leave the priesthood unchanged any more than it has left other institutions unchanged. "As in other well-established professions, women have been allowed or even invited into academic and professional theology with the understanding that the proper and respectable way to do it has already been established and that the newcomers will do it the way that it is done. . . . This is to some extent an inevitable process. But eventually the apprentices become not only journeymen but masters." Monika Hellwig, *Whose Experience Counts in Theological Reflection?* (Milwaukee: Marquette University Press, 1982) 30.

dination of women to men.[146] It is difficult to disentangle all the concerns behind the opposition. In part, it may arise simply from a reluctance to countenance any kind of change in religious institutions for fear that the institutions will seem less adequate to their task if they are not shrouded in a certain venerable antiquity. In part, however, opposition arises from age-old beliefs that women are less rational than men, that they are more emotional and therefore less stable, that they are more subject to impurity, that they are "weaker" and more prone to violations of sexual morality (which, oddly enough, coexists with the same belief about men), that they are more "natural" and more tied to the physical body and therefore less spiritual than men (which coexists, oddly enough, with a belief that women are *more* spiritual than men). All these beliefs have been or still are traditional within Western culture. They conflict with images of the ordained priesthood as knowledgeable, angelic, and detached.

A similar conflict over the ordination of gay men and of lesbians, particularly those who are not vowed to celibacy, is presently in a very heated state in many churches. A few churches have now approved the ordination of openly gay or lesbian persons, but, like ordained women, such clergy often find deployment difficult. For many Protestant congregations, the ideal cleric is a married heterosexual male, despite the fact that, as a group, they are most likely to find themselves involved in sexual transgressions that will embarrass the church. Other candidates will be accepted only reluctantly. This preference for heterosexual males is partly a reluctance to break with the past, but also an unconscious expression of the notion of priest as "father."

In most denominations, the issue of ordaining gay men and lesbians is far from settled, even in theory. Most still officially discourage or reject it, but without being able to suppress the ongoing call for change. Since the Roman Church requires celibacy of all those ordained priest, sexual orientation is theoretically irrelevant. It is impossible to say what percentage of that church's ordained clergy are in fact homosexual men living celibate lives. In practice, however, many of the church's gay clergy are sexually active, but the problem of low clergy

---

146. "Do not regard the ordination of women as deacons, priests and bishops as an end in itself, but as a symbol of the way in which the church regards all women in the community of faith and the community at large." Janet Scarfe, "A Pastoral Charge to the Episcopate in the New Order Which Has Already Begun," in *Episcopacy: Views from the Antipodes,* ed. Alan H. Cadwallader (North Adelaide, Australia: Anglican Board of Christian Education, 1994) 204.

numbers encourages bishops to wink at this violation as long as no issue
is made of it and it does not lead to open scandal.

In the case of gay and lesbian people, even more than in the case
of women perceived as heterosexual, a big part of the problem is the
way in which their ordination challenges notions of clerical angelism.
When people are described as homosexual, they are being explicitly
identified in terms of their sexuality in ways that heterosexuals are not.
(Who thinks of himself as heterosexual except when distinguishing himself from homosexual people? Heterosexual people are simply "standard issue" in our culture.) A large part of the anxiety about ordination
of lesbians and gay men, then, is that they will bring sexuality too close
to the sacred. Widespread confusion between the quite different categories of homosexuality and pederasty also plays a role here, as do a
few biblical texts that some read (rather loosely) as condemning all
homosexual relationships.

Here, as with the resistance to the ordination of women, the simple desire to see religious institutions as unchanging is undoubtedly a
factor. I doubt, however, that loyalty to scripture is a primary concern;
if it were, those who cite the Bible against the ordination of homosexual persons would show themselves more interested in the analysis of
what the texts in question actually mean as distinct from merely using
them as weapons. The real issue, I think, is that such ordinations
threaten the notion that sacramental priests are less fleshly and more
spiritual than the mere laity.

Interestingly, for many people the crucial issue is simply whether
an ordained priest *acknowledges* being homosexual. It is a fairly open
secret that the churches have long ordained gay men to the clergy. Many
churches would have a hard time staffing inner-city congregations without them, since married professionals with children are usually reluctant to live in such areas. Gay urban clergy have long been expected,
however, to remain very circumspect about their sexuality and never to
acknowledge it openly, which has led to a good deal of hypocrisy in the
matter. There was an English bishop of a major city, now retired, who
routinely opposed ordination of gays and lambasted gay liberation in
the press and then reassured his gay clergy privately of his personal support. This enabled him to keep his inner-city churches staffed while also
keeping his gay clergy on a short leash.

There have also been occasions when ordaining authorities have
been willing to ordain openly gay or lesbian candidates, but only on
the condition that they abandon their life partners. This enabled the

ordaining authorities to maintain their own fiction that the newly ordained were not really sexual beings. In still other cases, gay or lesbian persons have been knowingly ordained or accepted into an ecclesiastical jurisdiction and then abandoned as soon as anyone made an issue of their presence.[147] It thus appears that, for many ordaining authorities, the difficulty with having homosexual people in the sacramental priesthood is not any practical shortcoming on their part, but the danger that they will be seen as making a connection between the sexual and the sacred.

Women and homosexual persons are not the only people whose suitability for ordination is problematic. In theory, the major Christian denominations would all affirm that race and ethnicity are irrelevant to ordination and that ordination is as available to minority groups in the churches as to those who belong to the majority. In practice, members of minority groups may find that they confront significant cultural barriers, with reference to such issues as educational expectations, deployment opportunities, and the definition of the clergy as professionals. For example, most Western denominations expect that candidates for the ordained clergy will put themselves forward for consideration as in other professions. In some ethnic groups, to do so would be virtually a disqualification for the role, since it would imply setting one's own will above that of the community.[148] The only proper thing is for the community to say to someone that they see in her the gifts for this kind of priesthood and to inaugurate a process leading to ordination. Where clergy are perceived as a professional corps, however, the ordaining

---

147. E.g., James Ferry, who gives a moving account of his treatment—or, more accurately, mistreatment—by the church in *In the Courts of the Lord: A Gay Priest's Story* (New York: Crossroad, 1993).

148. "The western democratic bias toward self-nominating leadership and the rule of the majority excludes participation by people who look toward peer recognition and nomination and who value time-consuming decision-making processes by consensus that nurture long-term relationships and the well-being of the community over time-saving votes by voice or show-of-hand or secret ballot. As presently constituted and organized, the 'normal' vestry or Standing Committee or Diocesan Council or Commission on Ministry makes no concession to these different values and operational styles. Until it does, the church's organizational structure, and therefore its power base, will be dominated by those who know the rules of the game and are comfortable with them, and affiliation-oriented people of color will continue to be voiceless and faceless." Alberta Pualani Hopkins, "The Challenge of the Future: Creating a Place Called Home," in *The Challenges of the Past, The Challenges of the Future*, ed. John L. Kater, Jr. (Berkeley, Calif.: Church Divinity School of the Pacific, 1994) 78.

authorities might well perceive such a procedure as expressing too little personal commitment and drive and as suggesting that the candidate is too dependent on the wishes of others. At an extreme, the
candidate might even be defined as "codependent."

Similar problems can arise with regard to education. How is someone from a small ethnic minority to be educated for sacramental priesthood in his own community context, when the available forms of higher
education inevitably cater to those groups large enough to supply a predictable flow of students? In the United States at present, that means
that seminary education is usually shaped for only three groups, at most:
European Americans, African Americans, and Hispanics. It is much
more difficult to supply a context in which a Native American or Hawai-
ian candidate can receive a thorough grounding in Christian tradition
without being distanced, in the process, from his or her own culture.[149]
For that matter, even European American candidates from rural or from
blue-collar backgrounds may find themselves alienated to a degree from
their communities of origin as the candidates become translated, by the
educational process, into members of an urban professional class.

If candidates from an ethnic minority do make it through the
process of selection and education, they may then find that their sacramental priesthood is understood, de facto, to be limited to their own
ethnic group. Whereas European American clergy are often assumed to
be competent to officiate in all ethnic settings, clergy from ethnic
minorities may be shunted away from congregations that are made up
predominantly of members of the majority ethnic community. I suspect
that this practice is tied up with our image of priest as parent. Whites
have often claimed this parental role in the past, vis-à-vis people of color,
and we do not readily surrender it.

> • For those who have passed the hurdles and gained admis-
> sion to the "professional corps," the reward often seems to be
> a decade or so of productive labor followed by a serious dan-
> ger of *emotional and spiritual burnout*. When this affects

---

149. Similar problems arise elsewhere. Philip Culbertson notes positive indications
of grappling with these issues in New Zealand while also underlining the problems.
For example, he notes, "The traditional Clinical Pastoral Experience methodology
of direct feedback, constructive criticism, and confrontation is offensive to Poly-
nesians and Maori, particularly when delivered by a supervisor from a white culture." "Pastoral Theology and Multiculturalism," *Anglican Theological Review* 79
(1997): 179.

midcareer clergy, some become angry and abusive and eventually harm the congregations they serve because of their own disorientation and spiritual collapse; others simply disappear from the church, taking with them the resources of their education and experience. Older clergy often respond to burnout by continuing to "go through the motions" without any real personal engagement, which also proves harmful, since it leaves a vacuum at the heart of their ministry.

The causes of burnout are numerous. One element, at least in the United States, may simply be the cultural presupposition that being a professional means being constantly driven and overcommitted. This is certainly the image we have of physicians and attorneys, and, when we think of the clergy in professional terms, we tend to transfer those expectations to them. Indeed, the clergy may impose such demands on themselves as part of the proof that they really are professionals. A Protestant preacher of the nineteenth century, who was expected to spend many hours in preparing sermons, might be quite astonished to find how little time many of his twentieth-century successors spend in their studies. Instead, modern preachers are caught up in managerial and marketing roles, which may be less easy to relate to the common priesthood of which the clergy are sacraments than is the study of the shared religious heritage.

Other elements creating burnout may be more specific to the life of the church itself. One is that the structures of most denominations do not normally encourage collegiality among clergy (though some efforts are now being made to correct this problem). Each cleric is pretty much on his own in the task of shaping and nourishing a congregation. True team ministries have been too expensive for all but rather large churches, though they also appear increasingly now in rural or other areas where economics makes the yoking of several congregations necessary.

Many clergy feel they cannot trust their clerical colleagues. This distrust may arise in part from a sense of professional competition for advancement in their careers—something that encourages a degree of political astuteness and mutual suspicion. Long and faithful service in an impoverished context may be poorly rewarded while someone who seems less deserving finds a more effective route to influence and affluence. In such cases, other clergy are seen as rivals and as a source of danger rather than of companionship. This sense of danger is exacer-

bated by the ongoing conflicts within denominations over issues of doctrine and discipline, which sometimes leave the clergy with little sense
of common identity and purpose. The increasingly strict response to
clergy "malpractice" adds another danger. The ordained wonder
whether they really belong to a community of faith or whether they are
distanced and objectified—effectively excluded from the community—
by being routinely expected to be perfect. Professional "distance"
threatens to destroy the professional.

The prevalence of burnout raises questions about how appropriate
the community's expectations of its clergy are. By "community" here,
I mean both the laity and the clergy, who both contribute to shaping
the community's presuppositions in the matter. Do the laity want the
clergy to be superhuman—and thereby destroy them? Do the clergy
want to be gods instead of priests—and thereby destroy themselves?
The answer is probably "yes" to both questions. Both groups contribute
to the high expectations imposed on the clergy, and these are much
harder to meet now than they were fifty years ago because of the break-
down of cultural consensus and the increasing fluidity of religious com-
mitments. Whereas, fifty years ago, there was a fair amount of
denominational loyalty among the laity, and it was enough for the clergy
to be authorities on Methodist or Lutheran or Roman Catholic theology, now laity move pretty freely from one denomination to another
and do not assume the burden of being committed to any "pure" tradition. The denominations are themselves in disarray, internally, over a
number of issues. As a result, the parish clergy find themselves having
to be theologically creative in an entirely new way.

As theological consensus has disintegrated within the denominations,
the field of theology itself has become an ecumenical endeavor, and it
is therefore increasingly difficult to gain an authoritative command of
it—or even to know when one might have succeeded in doing so. It
is increasingly a collection of questions and methods rather than a body
of fixed answers. If the clergy are to be "graduate Christians," serving
as final authorities on Christian teaching, they find it difficult to validate their position and they may encounter objections from laity with
strongly held convictions of their own—convictions that may rest on
foundations quite different from those the ordained priest is assuming.

Something similar is true with regard to codes of clerical conduct.
In the 1950s there was a fair degree of consensus, even across denominational lines, about what constituted the measure of clerical morality
in our world. It was a fairly restricted definition, focused on personal

probity, sexual reticence, and a conservative manner of life. The cleric knew where the boundaries were and how to stay on the peaceable side of them. The experience of the churches during the struggles over civil rights and the Vietnam War called this earlier definition into question. Was the appropriate thing for the cleric simply to be an unexceptionable middle-class citizen? Or were there weightier matters of the law, such as justice and peace, that took precedence?

How does one describe the righteous person at present? There is no single agreed definition, though we may, each of us, think that we will know her when we see her. If the clergy, then, are trying to be examples of the old perfections—or even models of ordinary propriety—they may well find that they fall afoul of the standards of some even as they endeavor to fulfill those of others. Add to this mix our shifting definitions of sexual harassment and an increasing tendency to deal rather intransigently with clergy who are accused of committing any sexual offense, and one can explain a fairly high level of anxiety among many ordained priests.

Has the clergy job description become so all-encompassing that the job is now beyond human doing? Is the church as a whole so unclear about the nature and use of the ordained ministry that it cannot produce a humane job description? The aggregate impact of the developments over the last half-century is that we expect the clergy to be the official guardians of a consensus that has, in fact, lost its old coherence and is still looking for its new shape. We expect them to be paragons of a virtue that we cannot define in advance and which becomes an eternally shifting target in the cultural tug-of-war between liberal and conservative elements in society and the church. They are to be perfect parents in a world where many of the landmarks of adulthood have disappeared, executives of a fractious corporation, sales representatives in a world where brand labels seldom mean much anymore. On the whole, burnout seems a fairly moderate response to the burden. We should probably be grateful that the clergy have so little tendency to turn homicidal.

In the meantime, what does all this imply for the laity? It implies, on the whole, a laity that sees the clergy as "the others" who are responsible for the life of the church. While there are many who do not yield to this temptation, it has become all too easy for the laity simply to measure the clergy against shifting and ill-defined (and sometimes purely private) standards and to find them wanting. This choice costs the laity little. They can avoid having to take larger responsibility for their own religion or their own faith. Rather than recognize that we are in an era when our fundamental human priesthood is the only possible context for building a new consensus, both groups prefer to tinker with the broken consensus and to judge one another by it.[150]

- For me as a seminary professor, all these questions sooner or later take the form of how I am to prepare students to serve as sacramental priests or as educated laypersons in the present circumstances. What is the *appropriate education* that might help move us beyond our present quandaries? This is, of course, a subject of controversy within the larger church, too. Bishops worry about the alienating effect of seminary education or ask why they would wish to send candidates away for seminary education, at substantial expense, instead of having them read for orders with nearby parish clergy. The folk at home worry that the seminarian may lose her faith. Academic accrediting associations are afraid the students will not learn enough or not be held to high-enough standards. Different groups complain that the seminary does not prepare students well enough for ministry in the inner city—or in rural regions—or with young people—or with ethnic minorities.

Church authorities sometimes attempt to control the curriculum directly by mandating the addition of specific items that have come to seem particularly pressing (often because of bad experiences within the church): study of alcoholism, for example, or the particular ethics of peace and war, or evangelism, or the problems of eradicating racism, or the need to build bridges with a growing population that does not speak English . . . all worthy issues, but difficult to shoehorn into an already crowded curriculum. The various pressures on seminary education from the church, from the accrediting agencies, from the financial exigencies imposed on students, many of whom must uproot

---

150. "[William Stringfellow] complained about the professionalization of the clergy, about confusion in their roles (were they social workers? therapists? scholars?), but most of all the exclusion of the laity from the ministry of the Church in the world. Clergy had become mercenaries, 'a substitute laity.'" Gary Commins, "Death and the Circus: The Theology of William Stringfellow," *Anglican Theological Review* 79 (1997): 143.

themselves (and often their families) in their thirties or forties—all these will tend to shape the educational process piecemeal unless there is a clear vision of where the center of that educational process lies. But the seminaries cannot hope to enunciate such a center unilaterally or to be exempt from the conflicts that disturb the rest of the church. Clarification of seminary education depends on clarification of our common understanding of priesthood and vice versa.

A theological education will take one form if it is seen as equipping the ordinand to be the knowledgeable person in the church and a rather different form if it is viewed primarily as preparation for a profession. In the former case, it will be more like a graduate school; in the latter case, more like a school of law or medicine. It is probably fair to say that the history of seminary education over the past fifty years largely consists of a shift between precisely these two models, from graduate school to professional school. If the moral superiority of the clergy is the primary desideratum, then it must take yet another form, that of an enclosed community where close watch can be kept on the moral rigor of the seminarian and accurate evaluations given. Again, if the image of ordained priesthood is that of manager or of sales representative, the appropriate schooling will be still different, perhaps following the pattern of business programs and the short seminars so common in the business world.

Seminaries cannot dictate to the churches a resolution to the current problems about priesthood, but neither can the churches resolve the problems without involving the educational institutions in which they have invested so much. In both cases, what is called for is rethinking from the ground up. We need to decide what basic images of the ordained ministry we really regard as central. We need to reclaim the fundamental priesthood of humanity as performed by the whole Christian people. The sacramental priesthood must become genuinely an icon in and for the fundamental priesthood instead of grinding on in opposition to it.

> • For that is the ultimate question we have to raise here regarding priesthood in the church today—the question about *the relationship of the two priesthoods in the church*. "Lay ministry" and "ministry of the laity" are terms heard with increasing frequency, but with uncertain meaning. Some advocates of the

laity are quite articulate about the royal priesthood of the whole people and then have difficulty articulating why we have clergy at all. They ask whether the sacramental priesthood today is more help or hindrance to the priestly work of the Christian people. Some feel that the existence of an ordained clergy diminishes the priesthood of the whole people or may even usurp it altogether. They accuse it of fostering passivity on the part of the average church person and creating a climate in which the laity become mere consumers of religious goods supplied by the clergy. Some suggest abolishing ordination—or at least making some radical change in its administration or in the roles of the ordained.

The clergy, on the other hand, often prefer to see themselves as the real fountainhead of all priesthood. Just as physicians are increasingly expected to share information and gain informed consent from their patients, the modern clergy are prepared to share their ministry with the laity by "equipping" the laity for ministry or "enabling" the ministry of the laity. But they remain clear that the ministry is primarily theirs as a consequence of their education and of the special authority that derives from ordination.[151]

In either case, priesthood is being thought of as a possession, whether of the laity or of the clergy. It is thought of as something to be defended or shared at the will of its owners. I can see no way of moderating a dispute set up in those terms or even of achieving real conversation. Its basic mistake is one that we have already identified:

---

151. Behind this clericalist stance lies the long history of explaining the clergy as standing closer to Jesus and therefore functioning as a kind of channel conveying both the gospel message and the authority of GOD to the people. Such thinking is no longer very popular among theologians, but its implications linger in the churches. The profound contradiction in the clericalist stance is revealed in some remarks of Edward Schillebeeckx: "By [the] non-powerful rule of God's eternal love over all men and women through his special love for the poor and oppressed, his church, 'the community of God,' is called to life and we also come to build up the church in this world. The power of the church hierarchy or 'holy rule' does not transcend the *exousia* or authority of Jesus Christ" (*Church*, 222). The problem, of course, is that the hierarchy has often claimed an authority transcending that of Christ by accepting the very temptations to direct power over others that Jesus is said to have rejected at the beginning of his ministry.

the tendency to view clergy and laity as each other's opposites. If they are opposites, then the priesthood cannot belong to both of them at once in any meaningful sense.

This tendency pervades other aspects of the discussion, too. Is the whole lay-clerical polarity to be located primarily in the church itself, so that the issue is who does what on Sunday morning or in church government? Or is the polarity one between church and world, with the priesthood of the laity belonging to the world and the priesthood of the clergy to the church? To put it another way, is secular life the ministry of the laity or does ministry always relate to the church? In any case, how is the church to honor both priesthoods with the respect due to them? And how do they interact with one another? A definition that treats clergy and laity as polar opposites will never be capable of revealing their mutual interdependence. To get past this point of difficulty, we need to acknowledge that the priesthood of all is prior to and contains the priesthood of the ordained, while the ministry of the ordained provides sacramental focus in the context of the ministry of all. Without some recognition of our interdependence, laity and clergy will continue to find one another mutually threatening.[152]

Uncertainty and conflict about priesthood have pervaded the churches for decades—and at times been in danger of paralyzing them. The tension affects not only the areas of church life that we explicitly label "ministry." It affects every major area of our common life, including our understanding of the gospel message and our willingness to proclaim it. This situation, for reasons both spiritual and practical, demands movement toward resolution. We cannot be clear about the fundamental priesthood without becoming clear about the sacramental priesthood—or vice versa. We cannot become clear about the gospel without becoming clear about the character of the HOLY that both priesthoods serve, directly or indirectly. This is a critical and confusing time for us. To try to remain indefinitely in this present confused state is dangerous. On the other hand, such a state of indeterminacy offers particular opportunities for people to hear the call of the SPIRIT. The collapse of idols—or at least a weakening of their grip on our credulity—

---

152. Ultimately, the phrase "ministry of the laity" appears to describe a ministry confined to those who are not ordained or otherwise set apart within the church. But that is a negative definition that provides no real guidance. See Harlan Stelmach, "The Post-Laity Movement," *Laity Exchange* (Winter/Spring 1992): 8–9.

may create confusion, but it also gives us a chance to rebuild our religious institutions in less idolatrous ways.

Given the history of the Christian churches and the requirements of religious institutions, it seems wiser to try to rethink and refashion the ordained ministry in terms more clearly related to the priesthood of the whole people than to discard it. If we try to discard it, the likelihood is that we will merely be blindsided at a later date by some unintended and unplanned replacement for it. The goal of our efforts should be an ordained ministry that can readily be seen and understood as a sacrament of the ministry of the whole church and, ultimately, of all humanity. We need an ordained ministry that mirrors all of our priestly selves, that invites us to look beyond itself to what it signifies, to the more fundamental priesthood, the priesthood that resides in the midst of people's lives.

If this seems a daunting challenge, it may be of some comfort to recognize that this is not the first moment in church history when we have faced such difficulties. From the very beginning, it has been difficult to achieve a fully satisfactory resolution of the issues of church leadership and sacramental priesthood. The sacramental priesthood is constantly being reinvented. For one thing, it is always a hybrid office, with its nonsacramental aspects changing radically from one time and place to another.[153] In the first few decades, the church seems to have had little in the way of formally authorized leadership; various persons in the congregation might assume leadership at different moments. To identify leadership in the church, Christians relied not on official titles, but on evidence that a person was trustworthy and had received gifts of the SPIRIT appropriate to the purpose at hand—gifts ranging from prophecy to the hospitality (and fortune) that enabled a member to be host to the church assembled. Christians soon found, however, that such informal leadership could be divisive. There was a tendency for each spirit-filled teacher to have a somewhat different message and for

---

153. Scholarly discussions of ministry in earliest Christianity are as varied as the ministry itself. There is broad agreement on the summary that follows here, but not necessarily on its interpretation. See, for example, C. K. Barrett, *Church, Ministry, and Sacraments in the New Testament* (Grand Rapids, Mich.: William B. Eerdmans, 1985); Kevin Giles, *Patterns of Ministry among the First Christians* (Melbourne: Collins Dove, 1989); and Bartlett, *Ministry in the New Testament.*

each spirit-filled leader to compete for an exclusive, or at least a dominant, leadership role.

Already, by the end of the New Testament era, the authors of the Pastoral Epistles,[154] the *First Letter of Clement,* and the *Didache*[155] were insisting on a more stable, predictable, and unifying kind of leadership. They called for regularly appointed officers, given titles such as "elder/presbyter," "overseer/bishop," and "servant/deacon."[156] The author of the Pastorals laid down fairly detailed qualifications for these ministers, but we can sum them up in a very few words: they were to be adult males, stable, honest, effective in household management, and eminently respectable, especially in the eyes of neighboring non-Christians (1 Timothy 3:1–13; Titus 1:5–9).

This particular choice of qualifications was clearly related to problems in the life of existing churches. For one thing, the Christians were suspected of being socially revolutionary. They undermined family solidarity by converting women, children, and slaves without permission of the head of household. They allowed women to participate in their assemblies. Who knew what worse things they might be up to? The author of the Pastorals wanted Christians to look eminently respectable by the rules of the day. Another source of trouble was the churches' tradition of traveling teachers, fraught with opportunities for the disruption of settled communities. Some of these teachers promoted new and different versions of Christianity and fragmented existing congregations. The author wanted to keep such "creative" people away from positions of leadership. Then again, there were problems, within existing local leadership, regarding embezzlement of funds, and the author wanted to guard against that by entrusting the treasury only to people proven not to be "lovers of money" (1 Timothy 3:3; 6:9–10).

In the *First Letter of Clement,* written in the 90s of the first century, we find the church at Rome exhorting the church at Corinth not

---

154. 1 and 2 Timothy and Titus. The author presents himself as Paul, but is generally agreed by students of the subject to have been a second-century Christian.

155. Or *Teaching of the Twelve Apostles.* After some early debate, it was finally excluded from the New Testament and can now be found, with *First Clement,* in the collection of early Christian writings called "The Apostolic Fathers." Much of it may be older than the Pastoral Epistles.

156. The titles themselves are older than these texts, but their organization into the classic threefold ministry dates to the second century.

to replace its existing leadership with new people, but to honor the existing officers, whom the author claims were instituted by the apostles themselves. We do not know the exact reasons why the Corinthian church may have wished to appoint new leaders, but it may have reflected the wealth or social standing of some new converts.[157] At about the same time or a little later, the *Didache* writes of the leadership of the churches as consisting primarily of charismatic, spirit-filled persons who are called "apostles" and "prophets" and of other (?) persons called "teachers." These leaders were primarily wanderers, but might settle in with an existing congregation under certain circumstances. At the end of the *Didache*, in materials perhaps added after the rest was written, the author counsels the churches to "appoint, then, for yourselves bishops and deacons worthy of the Lord, gentle men and not devoted to money and truthful and tested, for they too minister to you the ministry of the prophets and teachers."[158] Unpredictable, charismatic leadership is being replaced by duly elected institutional officers.

We do not know exactly what role these early church officers played in the worship of the church. Were they sacramental priests in the sense of which I have been writing?[159] They became so at an early time, if they were not from the beginning. Ignatius of Antioch, writing about 117 C.E. (perhaps a little before the Pastoral Epistles), insisted that the bishop preside at the assembly for worship. Not all agreed at the time, but by the end of the second century that expectation seems to have been nearly universal. When the Christians in a particular city grew too numerous to meet in one place on Sunday, presbyters might

---

157. L. William Countryman, *The Rich Christian in the Church of the Early Empire: Contradictions and Accommodations* (New York and Toronto: Edwin Mellen Press, 1980) 154–56.

158. *Didache* 15.1.

159. ". . . there was no ministry which had this as its main function; no one was ordained or appointed to an office which consisted primarily of saying the eucharistic prayer, but whoever said it did so as the natural expression of what they already were within the community. . . . Thus because of their status within the community we should naturally expect the leaders to have assumed this function. Moreover, since the eucharistic prayer had to be improvised and essentially involved the recounting of the mighty acts of God, it is again natural to suppose that it would have fallen to someone with the gift of proclamation." Paul Bradshaw, *Liturgical Presidency in the Early Church* (Bramcote, England: Grove Books, 1983) 7–8.

be designated to act in the bishop's stead. Deacons read the gospel, led the prayers of the assembled people, presented the offerings and oblations, and cleaned up afterward. At a fairly early time, the local bishop came to be called "priest" (*hiereus* in Greek; *sacerdos* in Latin) and the term soon extended to include presbyters, too. Deacons were often called "Levites," a term that associated them with the priestly tribe of ancient Israel.[160]

From a very early time, then, Christians have been combining sacramental priesthood with the political, executive, and managerial ministries that articulate the life of the community, internally and externally, in practical ways. Probably no community can survive and propagate itself without some degree of internal articulation. Even in the most egalitarian of societies, there tend to be traditional patterns for making decisions and certain spokespersons around whom public opinion crystallizes. The early Christians, struggling to survive in a complex and sometimes hostile urban world, needed clear articulation of their public life as well. Christians and non-Christians alike wanted to know who spoke for the community, and outsiders probably judged the community itself largely by its public representatives. Early developments in the ordained ministry responded to the specific needs of the time and place.[161]

This is the legitimate side of the point Dean Comber made in the quotation in the preceding chapter. Ordained ministry exists, in part, as a way of articulating the life of the community. The ordained minister is no longer purely a private person, but a public figure as well, all of whose actions are taken to be characteristic of and decisive for a larger group. Of course, no human being can be totally public in terms of identity. Everyone remains to some degree a private person, with

---

160. Bradshaw, *Liturgical Presidency*, 13–14. There is evidence of laymen and deacons having presided, too, though this practice did not receive approval in the mainstream church (27).

161. "I am inclined to argue . . . that the priesthood . . . has from its earliest days represented a fusion of functions, and a curious fusion at that. . . . [According to the fathers of the fourth and fifth centuries,] the priest was shepherd or ruler. His rule was exercised, moreover, in three basic ways. He supervised the community's worldly affairs. He presided over its liturgy and in doing so imaged the great High Priest. Finally he was the teacher of the community, the servant and interpreter of the tradition which was its wisdom and which defined its beliefs, its values, and its way of life." Richard A. Norris, Jr., "The Beginnings of Christian Priesthood," *Anglican Theological Review* Supplementary Series No. 9 (1984):31.

one's own idiosyncrasies. Exactly how much of a private life an ordained person has left may vary from culture to culture or age to age. The anonymity of a large modern city, for example, creates quite different circumstances from the intimacy of a seventeenth-century village, where one could scarcely hope to have any secrets. But, in principle, the point holds: the ordained person has special, public responsibilities, like those of any political leader who represents a particular social grouping.

At this point, we may seem to be on a line of reasoning that could effectively reverse everything said up to the beginning of the present chapter. I have argued that the fundamental priesthood is shared by all Christians alike and that the sacramental priesthood exists to model it, for the benefit of all. The sacramental priest is not particularly different from other Christians; she or he should not be seen as distinguished primarily by magical power or greater knowledge or holiness or by the imagery of parent or executive or sales representative, but by her or his sacramental roles. But do not the functional leadership roles that I am now writing about require precisely the sort of superiority in education and purity that I had previously rejected as the primary defining qualities of the clergy?

Yes and no. The clerical office has always been and will always be a hybrid. The real question is not how many distinct images will go into our understanding of the clerics' work, but which image or images will be primary. Which one will hold the others together by offering a central point of contact? Which one will create a hierarchy among the demands made on the clergy so that we can discern how to establish priorities among them? Which one will enable the rise of a new consensus of clergy and laity about their interrelationship?

In any case, the Christian tradition is not bound eternally to the proposition that only the ordained can articulate the life of the community. Indeed, one can readily think of at least four periods in the history of Christianity when the church has assigned significant leadership to laypersons, and these are among the more creative, if also more turbulent periods of that history. One such period was the fourth century, when the Roman emperor, at one social extreme, and the common people of Egypt, at the other, played decisive roles in the formulation of Christian doctrine and polity and the development of Christian piety. A second was the rise of the Franciscans and other primarily lay orders committed to active Christian living in the thirteenth century. A third was the Reformation Era, when "godly princes" and other governmental bodies such as city councils had a decisive voice in the reshaping of Western Christendom. A fourth was the early period of American Christianity, when churches made the choice to balance the authority of laity and clergy in church government.

Functional patterns of church governance can be and have been ordered in a great variety of ways. Protestants have been fairly free in creating new modes of organization. But even in the Roman Catholic Church, often assumed to be relatively unchanging, centralized, bureaucratic control of worldwide church life by the Vatican is a relatively recent innovation. There is no reason intrinsic to Roman Catholic history why more power could not be shared with local bishops or with laypersons. In fact, the Second Vatican Council tried to increase the authority of the episcopal college. In denominations with less centralized regimes, such changes are easier because the whole worldwide community does not have to change all at once. The Episcopal Church, for example, when the first bishops were consecrated for the United States after the Revolution, made substantial alterations in the model of church life it inherited from the Church of England. One result was that bishops now shared their authority with church conventions that included lay representation.

No divine ordinance specifies that the ordained ministry is to be the only representative of the church community, either to itself or to the surrounding world. The church, from time to time and place to place, is free to arrange such matters in the way it deems best. The one necessary thing is that it seek to express through its life the good news on which it is founded. The only wrong forms of church governance are such as might intimate that GOD is better pleased with the particularly learned and pious or with the specially pure, or that the priesthood of the Christian people is of secondary importance. These forms would implicitly replace the good news of GOD's forgiveness with the bad news of human competition and triumphalism—and the fundamental priesthood of humanity with the derivative priesthood of religion.

The functional leadership roles in the church, then, can theoretically be carried by anyone. But, in practice, many of them are being carried by persons who are also sacramental icons of our common priesthood. The church has a long history of making the same people both sacramental priests and community leaders. This reflects a desire to have priestly icons in visible roles, since the sacramental role of the clergy influences the self-understanding of every Christian in a variety of ways.[162] Those interested in how a Christian community is encouraging and living out the fundamental priesthood have to be interested in how its clergy are modeling that priesthood.

If we are to reform our basic understanding of the ordained priesthood, it cannot be done by the clergy alone or even by the church's official deliberative bodies alone. The whole church will have to be involved. If the laity keep the same set of expectations they presently have, they will continue to get the same sort of clergy—or they will frustrate the efforts of those who are trying to bring about new possibilities. Only by making major changes in our expectations can the church as a whole move toward an ordained ministry shaped by the good news of Jesus, sustaining and not contradicting our common fundamental priesthood, and ministering out of the assurance of grace, not simply of their own learning, skill, or purity.

The sacramental priests need their functional tasks clearly and appropriately defined—and located in the context of the priesthood of the whole people. As a group, the sacramental priesthood needs to be as inclusive as the church itself—or even more so, so that they can serve as bridge to groups who do not yet feel welcome in the church. Clergy will need to develop ways of working with one another in a spirit of cooperation and trust rather than competition and with the whole people in a spirit of partnership rather than domination. It is a tall order, but a necessary one. And it will release new life for all members of the church by giving us clergy once again more clearly tied to the good news, in their functional as well as their sacramental roles.[163]

---

162. For purposes of thinking through the present-day problems with regard to the clergy, however, it is important to distinguish the two aspects. "In my mind there are two basic systemic problems, which are interrelated. One of these deals with our ministry delivery system, and the other with our system of leadership and governance. These are, in practice, too intermixed and intertwined to distinguish easily." Wesley Frensdorff, "Ministry and Orders: A Tangled Skein," in *Reshaping Ministry: Essays in Memory of Wesley Frensdorff*, ed. Josephine Borgeson and Lynne Wilson (Arvada, Colo.: Jethro Publications, 1990) 19.

163. "There are two distinct images I have of a re-invented congregation. One is of the laity, now come of age, fully integrated into the ministry and mission of the church, fully expected to act on their faith in their public responsibilities, and with the help of clergy and lay professionals acquiring the biblical and theological acumen necessary for that. The other image is of the clergy now finding freedom in the traditional role of preaching, teaching, liturgy, pastoral care, and with the help of laity, developing a mission strategy centered on enabling laity to connect their faith with their everyday life." Jean Haldane, "Private Faith and Public Responsibility," in Borgeson and Wilson, *Reshaping Ministry*, 193.

Even if the functional roles of the clergy are secondary, they none-theless interact with the sacramental roles and draw power from them. Even though the roles are revised from time to time, they are gener-ally stable enough, once set in place, that we begin to take them for granted—which gives them yet more power. It is important, then, for the whole church to unite in rethinking the ordained ministry now, when necessity prompts exactly such a reevaluation. We can use this moment as an opportunity to reunderstand the ordained priesthood in ways that will be supportive, for the future, of authentic Christian exis-tence and the priesthood of the whole people. As our understanding of our common, fundamental priesthood becomes clearer, it demands such changes in the sacramental priesthood. And if the sacramental priesthood becomes a better vehicle of the good news of Jesus, it will foster new maturity in our fundamental priesthood. The following chap-ter will offer some suggestions for exploring this conception of the sacramental priesthood.

7

An Ordained Ministry in and for the Fundamental Priesthood

The fundamental priesthood of Christians is no more and no less than the true life of humanity in the presence of GOD, illuminated by the priesthood of Christ. Whenever someone is living attentively in the borderlands where we meet the HOLY and is ministering and being ministered to there, that person is a priest. Since Christians believe that GOD is as fully manifest in Jesus as is possible for human beings, we also believe that the TRUTH anyone encounters on that boundary is fundamentally at one with the WORD incarnate in Jesus. If our Christian priesthood is unique, it is so only in that we have been graced, for no merit of our own, with the integrating clarity of that vision. Just as the Christian priesthood is, ultimately, simply the fundamental priesthood of all humanity, created from the beginning as an integral element of our being, so the fundamental priesthood is, ultimately, the Christian priesthood, informed by the TRUTH that we have come to know in Christ.

This priesthood, fundamental and Christian, can exist without benefit of clergy or even, when necessary, without benefit of membership in the community of the church. Still, as human beings, we have an ongoing need for religion with its sacramental priests, and these priests have a significant effect on the priesthood of the whole people. By the way they articulate the life of the community and the priesthood of the whole people, the ordained can contribute to a setting in which the fundamental priesthood can more readily do its work—or they can inhibit and distort the same. Their proper function is to model sacramentally—and so to foster and facilitate—the life of the whole priestly community.

They can do this only if they find their place *in and for* the larger priestly community; they cannot do it by casting themselves in a role over against the rest of humanity. The whole point of sacraments is not that they are anything at all in themselves, but that they concentrate and represent, in the form of the religious sacred, the otherwise diffuse and intangible HOLY. The point of the church's sacramental priesthood is not its own power or authority or even its sacredness, but the way in which it emerges within and points toward the priesthood that is dispersed throughout the Christian people and the whole human race.

Ordination (or its equivalents in the form of licensing or religious vows or acceptance by a congregation of a charismatic figure) makes a particular person a sacrament.[164] What does that mean? That the person ordained is henceforth a perfect priest? Hardly. Mere reference to the newspapers can disprove that proposition. The basic meaning of the sacramental priesthood is simply that the ordained person is an icon. Even if there is a certain tendency, in our world, to dismiss sacred rites as mere formalities, they actually have substantial power in shaping our world, and they form the foundation of the contribution sacramental priesthood makes. The ordained person is a sacrament who performs sacramental acts and thereby creates and maintains the larger religious model that helps us deal with our experiences on the boundary with the HOLY.

There is a sense in which all this is quite external to the personal spirituality of the sacramental priest, to that person's performance of her or his fundamental priesthood. A sacrament is a sacrament even if the materials are less than perfect. One may prefer the best bread for the Eucharist, but the worst will still serve the purpose. One might prefer, with the ancient directives of the *Didache*, to have cold, running water for baptism, but standing water will do.[165] One would be glad to have the best possible priest in every sense of the word standing at altar or font to preside at these sacraments, but we can participate fully in the sacred rites even with a sacramental priest who is far less than perfect.

This is the point made in antiquity by the doctrine of "indelibility of orders." Even the sacramental priest who has sinned in some quite serious way can still preside at the Eucharist and perform a genuine

---

164. "The person ordained is a baptized member of the Body of Christ in whom Christ dwells and whom the community has called and anointed for the express purpose of 'outward and visible' manifestation of that shared 'inward and spiritual' reality. Sacramental Orders function as effective symbols both of God's participation in the community's ministry and of the ministering community's participation in God." Joe Morris Doss, "The Unified Symbol of Ministry: Sacramental Orders," *Anglican Theological Review* (hereafter *ATR*) 63 (1980):31.

165. *Didache* 7.1–3.

sacrament of the body and blood of Christ. The alternative was to suppose that only the sacramental priest who had attained a certain level of perfection could legitimately perform the rites of religion. The consequences of that idea are too depressing to be seriously entertained. No one will ever be perfect enough to be beyond question. Perfection for human beings, in any case, is not a static state that can be reached and possessed; perfection for human beings means full and unresisting openness to growth in the SPIRIT. There is, then, no adequate or even conceivable way to quantify degrees of perfection so that we could be entirely confident of the sufficient merit of any sacramental priest. Must the usefulness of religion be held hostage to such uncertainty? What would be gained by doing so?[166]

What is more, the uncertainty of one's own worthiness would be extremely destructive to the spirituality of the sacramental priest. It would encourage all the diseases of conscience that produce anguished, paralyzed, defeated people: scrupulosity, fastidiousness, doubt of GOD's goodness, despair, hypocrisy, aridity, sloth, withdrawal from human emotion. We must presume that only imperfect human beings are available to serve among us as sacramental priests. If there are, perhaps, some few perfect ones among their ranks, they are probably the ones least likely to call attention to themselves. And rightly so, for their sacramental ministry is no more dependent on their perfection than is that of their least perfect colleague.

Sacraments function on their own level. They are not identical to everyday realities, nor are they purely spiritual, as if they belonged to the altogether transcendent side of the borderlands. They belong to the specifically religious sphere, which has its own reality and power (powerful for good or evil), which provides a language of word and gesture and form and image to grant us the ability to think and speak about the deeper realities we encounter in the borderlands, the realities of our priestly life in the presence of the HOLY. In their own way, sacraments are of great power, but this power consists precisely in their ability to refer us to the deeper TRUTH that underlies them, with all its life-giving and dangerous secrets. Whether the sacramental priest, then, is

---

166. The use of the idea of indelibility to identify the ordained as belonging to a categorically different level of being from the layperson, of course, must be resisted; but the doctrine does not have to be understood in that way. See Frensdorff, "Ministry and Orders," 29–34.

fulfilling his or her fundamental priesthood well does not necessarily affect the nature of the sacramental rites performed.

At the same time, no responsible person would intentionally choose for the role of sacramental priest a person who is indifferent or hostile toward the priestly life that we all share by virtue of our humanity. The dissonance involved in having a person who has perverted her or his fundamental priesthood presiding in the role of sacramental priest is, at best, difficult to justify. At worst, for the person who has perhaps suffered directly from the ordained person's misconduct, the sacramental rites may come to seem a mockery rather than an icon of the universal priesthood, a barrier rather than a point of entry. While, in principle, the sacramental rites function independently of the minister's worth, in practice they can become opaque under such circumstances.

The central desideratum, then, in the selection, training, and work of sacramental priests is that they should be people who are faithful to their roles as priests in the fundamental sense and are growing in the practice of that priesthood.[167] In choosing those who will be ordained, church authorities should rank no consideration more highly than this; they should look above all for evidence that the ordinand is already functioning as a priest in the fundamental sense in ways appropriate to the person's age and experience. Education should then encourage the understanding and development of each person's priesthood as well as give the students the information necessary to make them good sacramental priests. And the whole church, as it identifies the work and the roles that it assigns the clergy, should always keep in the foreground its desire that they continue to function effectively as members of the fundamental priesthood of the whole people.

All this becomes difficult in practice, partly because the church wants so many things of its ordained persons. It wants not only sacramental rites and an icon of the universal priesthood; it also wants church leaders, business managers, experts in public relations, competent

---

167. Another good way of making this distinction is that of Steve Charleston who insists, from the perspective of Native America, that the emphasis ought to be more on "being" than on "doing." "The job or function of the holy person is secondary. The nature of that person is primary" (review of *On Being a Bishop,* edited by J. Robert Wright, in *Episcopal Life,* August 1993, p. 22). Since this is clearly true of the fundamental priesthood, it ought also to be a part of the sacramental modeling of it.

counselors, teachers, missioners, people skilled in facilitating the work of volunteers, spiritual directors (in the professional sense), and so forth. Any of these skills may, of course, be useful. But they are secondary in comparison with the great central desideratum. If we keep focusing primarily on the peripheral skills demanded by one era or another, if we load the seminary curriculum up with things to learn rather than with the central desideratum of growth in priesthood, the danger then arises that the center comes to be lost in the maze of added material. Our problem today is how to locate the center anew and reaffirm its centrality.

The church, of course, can assign functional responsibilities in a variety of ways, both to lay people and to clergy; but, given the investment the church makes in choosing and educating candidates for ordination, it seems likely that, for the foreseeable future, the churches of the West will want the clergy to take on a substantial proportion of these roles. How, amid the welter of competing tasks and demands, do we identify what is central and help both the clergy and the larger church retain a sense of where that center lies? If we want to refocus our understanding of the ordained on this issue of shared priesthood, fundamental and sacramental, how do we go about finding this center?

I should like to take these questions up by beginning, as it were, from the beginning—with the laity. I do this for several reasons. First, no change in our understanding of the ordained priesthood will mean anything unless it goes hand in hand with an equivalent change in our understanding of the laity. Ultimately, we need to dismiss the category of "laity" from our minds. In itself, it is an empty category, defined only by an absence, the absence of ordination. The true meaning of the laity is as the whole people of God. The word therefore embraces the ordained and cannot be defined in opposition to them. If the present situation forces us to keep referring to the "laity," in the conventional sense, we must still make a deliberate practice of preferring phrases such as "the whole people of God" and "the fundamental priesthood." Second, if the clergy are to reunderstand themselves in terms of the fundamental priesthood, that process must begin with a fresh and prior understanding of themselves as Christian and human beings. The journey toward ordination begins while the ordinand is a layperson and ought to emerge out of the person's self-understanding in terms of the fundamental priesthood and the community's perception of the person as priest. Third, it will never be enough for the clergy alone to find a new understanding of their role and purpose. If the laity expect and demand a different set of things from them, the laity are likely to prevail, despite the clergy's opportunity, through preaching and teaching, to specify the terms of discussion.

I begin, then, with a question fundamental to *all* priesthood—the question of vocation. It is something that all Christians (indeed, I think all human beings) experience and it is a basic aspect of our priestly lives. It is the often surprising and, ultimately, always grace-filled recognition that we have a priestly task to perform. The term "vocation" is often used as if it applied only to those who hope to be ordained—as if the only true vocation were a calling to the sacramental priesthood. But that is a serious misunderstanding. Every human being is called to exercise the fundamental priesthood in particular ways, at particular moments and places, with particular people. Our lives are all vocation.

Perhaps we experience vocation most acutely when it calls us away from whatever we are doing at the moment and toward some new and as yet uncertain priestly ministry. And yet, vocation may be at work just as certainly and powerfully in the most familiar and everyday parts of our lives. We may be called to where we are and to what we are already doing. We may, in fact, be where we are, doing what we are, because of that vocation, which perhaps acted on us before we were conscious of it as a calling from the HOLY, before we had words or images to embody such a thought.

How are we led? How do we recognize a calling from GOD? There is no simple answer to that question, since GOD's call to us is as complex and multifaceted as our lives. The call may come to us in the form of a *longing*—a sense of being drawn to a certain place or a certain work, an internal conviction that we belong in this place, doing this task. It may come in the form of our *gifts*—gifts that delight us and lead us in a certain direction as we explore and cultivate them, gifts that make us useful to others and so shape our lives in the communities where we live. Sometimes the call comes through the voice of other people. When they tell us, "You have these gifts and we have this *need*; please help us," we may hear the voice of the HOLY in their voices. Occasionally, GOD may speak to us quite directly, too, though this is the rarest of the ways in which we come to know our vocations.

None of these indications, however, is infallible. Our longings may arise from romanticism or escapism. Our gifts may be intended for ends we never foresaw. The call from other people may be addressed to the wrong person or may emanate from a selfish self-regard on their part and not at all from the mind of the TRUTH. What we take for the voice of GOD may be merely the echo of our own minds, seeking reassurance or confused by mental instability. There is no single, certain indicator of vocation. One can be most confident when there is some convergence among a variety of indicators. The test, above all, is the sense of fittingness, of being where we belong. For the most part, we shall find ourselves able to stick with the priesthood to which we have been called without having to use violence on ourselves to do it; we shall find opportunities in it both to be fed and to feed others; we shall be able to use the gifts we have been given to good purpose; we shall have the concurrence of at least a few people whom we trust to contradict us when they see reason to do so. This is not to say that we find our vocations *easy*. Much of the time, they are anything but easy. But we have a sense that, for better or worse, this is where we should be right now and this is what we should be doing because, in this context, our lives are realizing their priestly potential.

Human beings, of course, vary enormously in temperament and gifts, in hopes and fears. For one person stability is a temptation to become dull and moribund; for another it is the opportunity to grow deep roots and bloom more constantly and reliably. For one person, change is a temptation to distract oneself with new stimuli so as to avoid the need to deal with one's own inconstancy and lack of roots; for another it is the opportunity to peep out from behind the walls of the familiar and so become more open to the possibility of being surprised by grace. There is never any one formula for human beings about how we hear our vocations and pursue them. Indeed, the wise physician of the spirit may give one prescription to one person and its opposite to another: work for one, rest for another; change for one, stability for another.

This brings us back, once again, to the fundamental reality that our priesthood (and therefore all our hearing of GOD's voice) is collegial. It is discerned through honest assessment of our individual gifts and longings and in conversation with one another. The conversation that discerns our vocation is not only a conversation with the HOLY; it is a conversation with one another as well. Vocation is never a purely individual matter, for priesthood always implies that our lives are interconnected and interdependent. Every priest is part of a community of priests.

Discernment of vocation is no less important for the laity than for the clergy or for those setting foot on the track to ordination. Indeed, the process of discernment that ordinands go through is essentially identical to that for the layperson. The questions are the same questions of where and when and how and with whom. And the indicators, too, are the same: the sense of longing, the gifts, the needs, the voice of GOD, and ultimately, the quality of "fittingness." If these indications lead a person toward ordination, that does not make it a vocation of greater importance or seriousness; it only indicates a particular context where one's priesthood is to be lived out. So far from being a superior or heroic vocation, ordination may at times seem almost like a retreat; the cleric may seem to live at one remove from the more intense and demanding world inhabited by the layperson. Still, the alert cleric will find there is a world of deep priesthood to be found even in what may sometimes look like a more sheltered location.

Vocations that lead to exercising one's fundamental priesthood in the context of ordination are not in any way superior to those that lead to its exercise in lay life. The cleric (or ordinand) who imagines otherwise is missing his or her own deepest priesthood. The layperson who imagines otherwise may be avoiding the seriousness of her or his own vocation. There is no vocation higher than that of the fundamental human priesthood, which is Christ's own priesthood. Therefore vocations, including those leading to ordination, always center in the fundamental priesthood and how we are being asked by GOD to fulfill it. This is the process of discernment to which the church should give the highest honor and attention.

This said, what indications might point to ordination as an aspect of a particular person's vocation? Since the distinguishing mark of the sacramental priesthood is its handling of sacred things, the indications of a vocation that includes ordination ought to be directly related to that. What do ordained ministers do in regard to the sacred? They preside at sacraments, they preach, they teach sacred traditions, they hear people's secrets—whether as confessions or as pastoral confidences— they celebrate marriages, they attend on the sick and dying, they minister to the bereaved, they act as sacred representatives for their communities.

A *longing* to fulfill such roles is one indicator. But we have to recognize that such a longing can emerge from a personal sense of insecurity, reaching out after public authority in the hope that external authority will make up for the absence of the internal priestly confidence that is built only through personal authenticity and the grace of LOVE. If so, it does not necessarily mean that this is not a genuine vocation. GOD calls us in all sorts of ways—through our weaknesses and deficiencies as well as through our strengths. Sometimes we grow into the authority that we originally hoped to assume as if it were a garment. Still, those who are helping would-be ordinands discern their calling will do well to take a look at how much they are seeking to escape from painful feelings of insecurity or pursuing a fantasy of public, external authority that fails to find its link with personal authenticity. The process of discerning a vocation is aided, not hindered, by such questions, especially if they are offered in a priestly spirit. Individual longings are subject, in any case, to the discernment of the community. The person who is genuinely called to stand in the pulpit or at the altar should also show some sense of the difficulty of the ordained calling—the way in which it poses a temptation to retreat into the religious sphere. I am most persuaded of the authenticity of the vocation where there is a sense of discomfort with it as well as longing.

The *gifts* that indicate a vocation to the ordained ministry include those related to public liturgical presidency, including not only "voice" and public presence, but also the kind of tactful intelligence that underlies skillful rhetoric, the tact that enables a person to speak difficult things without breaking communion with the hearers. One looks for the gift of listening carefully and respectfully, of conversing rather than commanding. One looks for a courage that does not delight in provocation. One looks for people who are centered in GOD and in their practice of the fundamental priesthood. Being thus centered is a better indicator of long-term stability than the kind of rigidity that presumes to know too much of GOD's will in advance.[168] The person with these gifts will be able to cooperate with the larger community in the discernment of its collective calling from GOD and in examining the movement of the SPIRIT in its life. Such a person will help the community recognize both its gifts and, as need be, those things in it that merit judgment—and will do this not as an outsider set over against the community, but as one who lives in and with and for

---

168. "*Beware of attitudes which try to make God smaller than the God who has revealed himself to us in Jesus.* . . . Whenever exponents of the Christian faith treat it as something which we have to 'defend' like a beleaguered fortress or a fragile structure they are making God to be smaller than he is." Michael Ramsey, *The Christian Priest Today* (New York: Morehouse-Barlow, 1972) 25.

the community, helping it to come to consciousness of its larger priesthood.[169]

The sense of *needs* to be filled will be something the community itself will have to supply. I have already suggested that the community needs a corps of clergy that reflects the diversity of the body of fundamental priests. Indeed, the community needs to go a step beyond mere internal reflection, if possible, so that it can reach out to those who do not yet see themselves as welcome within the circle of GOD's good news or within the church that is its religious model.[170] As far as we can manage, no ethnic or racial group should be without its reflection in the church's sacramental priesthood; neither men nor women should be absent; neither heterosexual nor homosexual; neither single nor married; no group should be excluded because of wealth or poverty, because of education or its lack, because of the precise character of their physical abilities. This is not a call for a politically correct quota system in the clergy. It is a call for celebration of the richness of the humanity created by GOD's love in GOD's image. It is a call for a sacramental priesthood that captures some of the beauty of the fundamental priesthood it serves as icon.

Those bodies in the churches that are specifically charged with reviewing and approving candidates for ordination have a particularly difficult task in the present state of confusion, made more difficult by the fact that we do not take the vocation of the fundamental priesthood seriously enough. What ought to be the criteria for choosing ordinands? How should the church, through its ordaining authorities,

---

169. "Pastoral oversight requires the ability to relate both intimately and broadly to members within a community of faith and, in turn, to articulate their perceptions, concerns, and hopes. Without this capacity to relate to a congregation and therefore represent them, leadership in liturgical worship becomes separated from pastoral oversight. Instead of representing the community in worship, the liturgical leader becomes a performer. Worship then becomes something that happens to the individual worshiper rather than something that worshipers do corporately in expressing and offering their lives to God." Timothy F. Sedgwick, *The Making of Ministry* (Cambridge, Mass.: Cowley Publications, 1993) 61–62.

170. "At the time of my ordination, I happened upon some words of the Brazilian bishop, Helder Camara: 'The bishop belongs to all. Let no one be scandalized if I frequent those who are considered unworthy or sinful. Who is not a sinner? . . . My door, my heart, must be open to everyone, absolutely everyone.'" Frank T. Griswold, "The Bishop as Presider, Teacher, and Person of Prayer: A Personal Reflection," *ATR* 77 (1995): 11.

distinguish the people whose particular gifts and calling point toward ordination as the appropriate context for them to live out their fundamental priesthood? Our concern here, once again, is not with the clergy in their own right, but with the fundamental priesthood that laity and clergy share and with the religious, sacramental contribution that ordained priests make to the living out of that priesthood. How does the church identify people who are more likely to minister sacramentally in and for the priestly people rather than to set themselves over against them?

To begin with, the church itself must abandon its habit of viewing those who present themselves for ordination as candidates for a profession, required to prove their worthiness, or as competitors for advancement, who have to be weeded down to a smaller cohort. These persons are already priests, sharing the priesthood of Christ; there is no better or higher calling for a Christian. They are presenting themselves not for professional or political advancement, but so that they and the church together can discern what are their particular gifts and calling and how they can best share these with the whole priestly community.

A constant temptation for those charged with carrying out the ordination process is to think of their task as choosing the "best" candidates In their efforts to do so, they wind up instituting a competition in purity (or intelligence or orthodoxy or manners or even looks) that is utterly at variance with the identity of the Christian priestly community, laity and clergy alike. The candidates themselves respond by "jumping through the hoops"—trying to look as much like the committee's ideal as they can. In the process, they may disguise, neglect, or even forget their own specific gifts and calling. Both committee and candidates sometimes forget that they are priests of the good news and begin to think of themselves, instead, as the two sides of a personnel dispute. When that happens, the church is harmed in all parties.

What, then, should churches be looking for? Should they just eliminate those who seem to be criminal or delusional and approve everyone else? To do so would hardly be honest either to the candidate or to the community at large. Such a process would evade the real issues of discernment. It would suggest that ordained priesthood has nothing distinctive to contribute to the life of the community. It would evade the church's responsibility for shaping its own life in conversation with GOD. But what is the ordaining authority properly looking for?

Since the church is looking for a person who already displays the characteristics of the fundamental priesthood in ways appropriate to the person's years and experience, it is looking for people of faith, hope, love, and integrity. This is not a competition. The commission is not just looking for people of *exceptional* faith, hope, love, and integrity. The church has reserved the canonization of saints for those who are already dead, and ordination should not be confused with canonization. It is enough that a person gives evidence of being a responsible and trustworthy human being and Christian—and of having been recognized as such within the Christian community.

Above all, the candidate must be a person who is deeply respectful of the priesthood and personhood of others. The candidate should be a person who can be trusted with the confidences, which is to say the souls, of others. No one addicted to gossip ought to be ordained. No one who is known to be hypocritical, either in self-presentation or in judging others, ought to be ordained. No one given to blanket hostility toward any human group can rightly be ordained; racism, sexism, class prejudice, and homophobia all disqualify. No one thought likely to take advantage of a position of trust in order to extract favors from those who might consult a cleric—whether in the form of unusual payments of money, service (for example, sexual favors), or personal reverence—should be ordained. All these considerations arise directly from the nature of Christ's fundamental priesthood in which we share. The church will not, of course, be able to guarantee absolutely that its clergy are free of these faults. But any strong suspicion in these areas should be given careful attention.

The point here is to seek for *congruence* between the fundamental and sacramental priesthoods. The candidate for ordination should show evidence of already fulfilling the fundamental priesthood with seriousness, tact, and reliability. I am not saying that good service at the basic level leads to promotion into higher levels of priesthood. There are no higher levels of priesthood. I am saying only that congruence between sacramental and fundamental priesthoods is the central desideratum. Most clergy will find, in any given congregation, at least one layperson (and very likely more) whose depth of conversion and priestly integrity put their own to shame.[171] That is all to the good. The clergy are

---

171. I remember this as a major point made by Arthur Michael Ramsey in a sermon at The General Theological Seminary, New York, in 1965. It soon proved true in my own experience.

sharers in the common priesthood, not monopolists of it—or even its primary practitioners.

Commissions on ministry will need to distinguish clearly between the signs of priestly responsibility they are looking for and the more visible and measurable evidence of piety and moral rigor. The most pious or rigorous person is often not the best priest.[172] For one thing, exceptional piety and moral rigor, open as they are to public view, can easily lead to a sense of superiority like that of the Pharisee in the Temple, in Jesus' parable (Luke 18:9–14). It was that pious soul's awareness of his own piety that damned him, since he sought refuge in it rather than in GOD's grace. In addition, exceptional piety and moral rigor are sometimes signs that an individual is fleeing from some powerful inner compulsion to do harm—a compulsion that, in some cases, may even be strengthened by being denied in this way rather than by being confronted directly. The recent debacles of certain American television preachers, whose attacks on sexual sin turned out to be products of their own overheated libidos, are a case in point. The church needs responsible but nonetheless *human* beings for ordination, not people trying to persuade themselves and others that they are superhuman. Jesus became a priest by suffering human weakness. He chose most of his intimate followers from the ranks of the most ordinary people, not the particularly pious. Every good priest is cut from the same cloth as the people she or he serves (Hebrews 2:11).

An exceptionally religious person may indeed hear and accept the gospel. Peter, after all, claimed, according to Acts, to have been meticulous about keeping the purity laws, and he was still able to follow the call of the Spirit and to baptize a family of impure Gentiles.[173] Fastidious religiosity, then, is not an absolute counterindication for ordination. Yet it signals the ordaining authority to look for other kinds of rigidity in the candidate—for pride in one's own accomplishments, for habitual derogation of others, for bigotry against other human beings,

---

172. "The human being, when it rejects its own vulnerability, turns against itself, deciding that it can no longer get what it needs . . . to be human and that its only choice is to become superhuman. . . . There is a tendency among us Americans . . . to estimate a person's aptitude for a profession or for a career by listing his strengths. . . . There is a different question, one proper to the priesthood as of its very essence, if not uniquely proper to it: Is this man weak enough to be a priest?" Dwinell, *Fire Bearer,* 77–79.

173. Acts 10–11. Admittedly, Paul was less complimentary about Peter's (Cephas's) commitment to purity (Galatians 2:11–14).

for the inability to entertain new thoughts or rethink old ones, for a disinclination to reach out beyond one's normal circle to aid the needy and to extend welcome to strangers, for a strained effort to avoid confrontation with one's own less innocent self. These are counter to the spirit of the good news itself and will introduce incongruity into the sacramental ministry of the good news.

Finally, commissions will wish to look at those characteristics of the candidate that may tell them something about style of leadership. The "take-charge" person who has neither time nor inclination to listen to others will not be a good colleague and will not encourage collegiality and mutuality in the church. On the other hand, the passive person who wants others to make all decisions and tends to conceal his or her own opinion (or who perhaps does not even have one) is equally inappropriate. What is wanted is the person who can make a contribution to the deliberations of the group and show initiative and responsibility, while still leaving room for others to make their contributions as well—in other words, the person capable of and interested in engaging in genuine conversation as a way toward understanding and appropriate action.[174]

Indeed, the ability to converse well—not just fluently, but with openness and respect both for oneself and for others—may well be the single best indicator of a suitable candidate for leadership in the church, lay or ordained. It is a gift of the SPIRIT with particular relevance for leadership in the church today. If a person with this gift also shows a record of integrity and responsibility in the exercise of the fundamental priesthood and has particular gifts or skills for the work, then such a person would be a very suitable candidate for ordination. The ordinand is chosen not for the sake of some supposed superiority over lay Christians, but because of a perceived ability to represent the priestly life of the whole people.

---

174. "[I have] suggested that prophet, seeker, and leader are inextricably linked. Sometimes two or three are merged in one person. But prophet and leader are seen as seekers first, who later evolve into other roles. What does the seeking role bring to the fusion? Perhaps it is openness, aggressive searching, and good critical judgment—all within the context of the deeply felt attitude that one has not yet found it!" Robert K. Greenleaf, *Seeker and Servant: Reflections on Religious Leadership,* ed. Anne T. Fraker and Larry C. Spears (San Francisco: Jossey-Bass, 1996) 37.

The particular gifts and skills of the candidate and the specific needs of the community are also important, but I do not stress them as strongly as these other elements, because our gifts are not entirely fixed at any point in our lives. When young, we often do not know exactly what gifts we have to share. We learn what they are at least partly by trying out various options and rising to meet unexpected challenges and opportunities. Even in later years, this process is still going on. It will do little good for a commission to decide that the church in a particular area will need ten educators, five youth specialists, seventeen hospital chaplains, etc., and then try to fill those slots by finding specific ordinands for each of them. The people ordained for one purpose may still wind up doing something else. It will be better for the ordaining authorities simply to seek diversity of gifts in the cohort of ordinands and to encourage ordinands to learn what their gifts are, and then to follow and enhance them instead of trying to fit into some all-purpose, generic model of ordained ministry. Paul, after all, suggest that the SPIRIT will give the community the gifts it most profoundly requires (1 Corinthians 12).

If the church seeks out candidates such as these, how may they then best be prepared for the ordained ministry? It is impossible to give a single scenario for the educational process. The existing system of seminaries will have difficulty responding to the needs of, for example, small, isolated Native Alaskan communities. The educational expectations do not match up well enough, the financial support is difficult to sort out, the cultural alienation of displaced students is generally exhausting and often counterproductive. The seminaries serve a genuine need, but they may not be able to serve *every* need. The time has come, in many different contexts, for new experiments in the education of clergy. Some of this is already happening, but too often in response to financial exigencies, without enough imagination in devising new models, and with too low an aim.

The central item to be kept in mind is that the education of priests — all priests, ordained or not — is an education of the whole person. The education of the mind plays a great role, but if such education is divorced from other aspects of learning (as has long been the norm in the modern world), it will fail even of its own purpose. When intellectual education is provided in a way isolated from the spiritual growth of priests, it tends, for most students, to remain in a separate pocket of the mind, never to participate meaningfully in the priestly life of the student, present or future.[175]

The education of the ordained should be seen as education focused in the soul and spirit. Its goal is not simply to fill the head with ideas, but to encourage students to appropriate their intellectual learning as part of who they are. The principal tool of priestly ministry is the self— the self that stands in the presence of the HOLY in conversation with others. Intellectual learning is a significant part of the shaping of this self, but it is not the whole. Indeed, human beings have a certain ability to compartmentalize our lives—an ability that sometimes means we exclude what we know merely with the mind from the arenas of our decision making and our everyday activities. What informs those decisions and actions is what we know "in our bones." Sometimes, that is all to the good; the soul may be wiser than the brain. But what we learn with the intellect may also, at times, be the only way we can break out of the circle of folly, self-conceit, prejudice, and lies that entraps each of us in various ways.[176]

The great tool of priesthood is not any specific knowledge— whether of the Bible or history or theology or newer disciplines such as pastoral counseling or church growth. Any or all of these are of potential value, but the great tool of priesthood is a priestly life, a priestly self. And such a self, as we have been saying, grows and matures by the fact of our living, attentively and in communion with other priests, on the border of the HOLY. It occurs in conversation with GOD and with one another. If students are growing in such priesthood, they will able

---

175. The education of ordinands must be continuous with the education of all priests. Aidan Kavanagh objects that students should already be formed as Christians before they come to seminary: "The seminary's business lies in preparing people of firm faith for ministry to people of faith. The catechumenate's business lies in forming those of initial conversion in faith for initiation into communities of firm faith. Conflating the two processes weakens both and is ultimately damaging both to individuals and churches" ("Christian Ministry and Ministries," *ATR* Supplementary Series 9, 47). The point is well-taken, but the two processes cannot be completely disentangled. Conversion is a process that lasts throughout life.

176. Failure to integrate theological education spiritually leads to the dilemma noted by Michael Dwinell: "I had been trained to be a pastor, a teacher, an administrator, a professional, a preacher, even sometimes a prophet; but I had no idea what it was to be priest" (*Fire Bearer*, 1).

to incorporate their intellectual learning into the process—and probably retain more of it as a result.

What will it take for seminaries to foster this sort of education—education as priestly conversation? It will call for focusing not only on *what* the student is assimilating, but on *how*. How, over all, is the academic learning of seminary contributing to the student's understanding of the HIDDEN HOLY? How is it enhancing the ability to share in giving and receiving priestly ministry in its presence? What is central to priestly ministry is precisely what seminaries often fail to address directly.

For a long time, academic learning has been kept on one track and the student's life of faith or spirituality on another. Classroom and chapel, academic subjects and the life of prayer, might interact politely on occasion, for example in faculty preaching, but seldom at great depth or in any pervasive way. Seminaries have often undercut the interaction of the two in a variety of ways. One way is to enforce a single, strictly defined model of faith and spirituality; this excludes true personal involvement, since individual engagement and creativity carry with them the danger that someone will break the prescribed mold. Alternatively, seminaries may evade responsibility for the interaction of mind and spirit by leaving students entirely to their own devices in this regard— under the rubric of respecting their individual responsibility. The likely result is that the students will assume the integrative process is of no real importance to the seminary.

Much of the difficulty, of course, stems from the history of the faculty themselves, whose own seminary education and subsequent academic preparation have confirmed these patterns. Even if we think of our own calling as priestly (as many of us do), we have little experience of integrating faith with our intellectual pursuits in explicit and public ways. In this, we are like the communities to which we answer—the church as a whole and the academy—and we help to perpetuate patterns pervasive in the world around us.

I do not mean in any way to suggest that intellectual learning is unimportant to priestly education. Quite the contrary, it is vital. It will not, by itself, make a good priest, and people may become priests of real profundity and power with no formal education at all. Still, our priesthood will profit greatly by learning what others have discovered in the presence of the HOLY. Formal education makes available to us a far larger pool of priestly colleagues, enriches us with the hard-won

tradition of Christian faith—constructed over many lifetimes in the border country—and instills in us habits of honesty, clarity, and coherence
in reflection. It can enable us to see a broader picture of the HOLY at
work in human existence and to be more self-critical in our own pursuit of priestly ministry.

I am convinced that Christians, clergy and laity alike, need above
all to learn our tradition, from the Bible on down.[177] Only a knowledge of our tradition can save us from being completely trapped in the
unthinking assumptions of our particular time and place. The tradition
in question is not a simple set of doctrines and rules. Any time tradition is represented as univocal and decisive in that way, it is being mis-
represented. Learning the Christian tradition means learning its tensions
and uncertainties, its weaknesses, and even its failures as well as its
beauties and profundities and moments of glad grace. It is a matter of
learning the priesthood that we share.

What is *not* helpful is to learn some system that affects to answer
all relevant questions. Indeed, the mere notion that such a system can
exist is itself an act of idolatry and to be shunned. Only GOD can hold
all reality in a single, coherent moment of understanding. No human
being ever has or ever will succeed in doing so. A systematic disposition of mind is helpful in ensuring a certain degree of coherence in our
explorations and reflections. But it cannot achieve the end of summing
up all knowledge, theological or otherwise, and we should be wary of
its attempting to do so. The virtue of the tradition is not to give us all
the answers in advance, but to provide us with a mode of inquiry and
with the companionship of those who have gone along this path before
us. The purpose of the tradition is simply to enlarge the company of
the fundamental priesthood beyond our narrow confines of time and
space, so that we share others' experience with the HOLY as we engage
in our own labor of priestly interpretation.

Insofar as we succeed in teaching the tradition as a mode of priestly
and spiritual inquiry, we shall also find that we are loosening its cultural restrictions. Not that European American teachers, like myself,
will be able simply to step outside our cultural realities and to impart
a gospel that is free of cultural limitations—that is completely unimag-

---

177. Only a knowledge of the past can deliver us from becoming trapped in the
provincial certainties of the present, as I argued some years ago in *Biblical Authority or Biblical Tyranny? Scripture and the Christian Pilgrimage,* rev. ed. (Valley
Forge, Pa.: Trinity Press International, 1994).

inable—but that we can hope to encourage a sense of common inquiry into the shared experience of GOD's grace. The growing breadth of the priestly community will eventually enrich the tradition in ways that no one culture can hope to achieve.[178] There is no handing on of tradition, in our era or in any other, that is not also a continuing construction and reconstruction (and, one hopes, enrichment and enlargement) of that tradition. This is as true on the conservative side as on the liberal.[179] Education in the tradition, then, is never simply a matter of absorbing the past. It always involves taking up our responsibility for the ongoing life of this organism that is the Christian community, for creating the tradition that the future will inherit on the basis of the tradition that has come to us.

This means that theological education is not simply a matter of mastering the content of a variety of separate subject areas. It is also, and more especially, a matter of learning to work with these subjects and to think with them and to bring them into conversation with each other and with the world around us.[180] Priesthood is always a matter of dialogue, of both listening and speaking. It is a matter of learning what others can tell us about our own experience and of handing on what we can usefully contribute to others. The Bible, church history, the traditions of intellectual theology and mystical theology, the ethical reflections of past and present, the liturgical tradition—all these interact with one another and, above all, with our lived experience of GRACE, to create the present and future of our faith.

---

178. The presence of such a priestly diversity within the seminary community contributes directly to the education of priestly people. As one professor found in interviewing graduates, "Classroom diversity is another factor that seemed to play a significant role. . . . Conversion was regularly identified as happening because of the great challenge of diversity in the classroom." Kathleen Hughes, "Conversion of Mind and Heart in Theological Education," *Theological Education* 33/2 (Spring 1997): 9.

179. The conservatives who have taken control of the Southern Baptist Convention, for example, are making at least as significant a change in Baptist tradition as they accuse their opponents of making, since they have abandoned the historic Baptist witness to the authority of the individual reader of scripture and to congregational autonomy in favor of doctrinal tests.

180. "Information that is not digested, not shaped by the human mind, is generally of very little use. But in this welter of information that we get, what people *do* need is to hear thoughtful, educated human voices." Brent Staples, "A World in Black and White," interviewed by Joel Levine, *University of Chicago Magazine* 86/3 (February 1994): 27.

Furthermore, the education of the ordained needs to be seen as part of a larger project of educating the whole priestly people of GOD. The idea that clerical education will trickle down to the laity has proven to be largely inaccurate in our own day, at least partly because too much of it strikes the lay audience as irrelevant. The culprit here is precisely the lack of integration in the education of the ordained. The academic side of their education has remained in a sterile compartment, pure of contact with ordinary life, and therefore proves uninteresting to most of those who do not need it in order to get ordained. In this respect, seminary education too often mimics its secular counterpart in the universities, which winds up encouraging scholars and thinkers to talk with narrower and narrower circles about more and more abstruse topics.[181]

If there is to be priestly education for the whole people of GOD, it will need to make its connections with the practice of the fundamental priesthood abundantly clear. Whereas the academic students of Bible, history, theology, and the rest have often tended, at most, to hint at the implications of our studies for the common priesthood, we must now take the risk of becoming more explicit, however clumsily we may do that at first. The pursuit of purely intellectual knowledge is not wrong. In fact, it is necessary. One cannot say in advance what bit of knowledge will prove useful in understanding the past and present or in constructing the future. But this pursuit of knowledge belongs in the larger priestly context so that the two are open to what they can receive from one another.[182]

---

181. The church might well aim to set an example of a more serious and accessible public discourse along the lines suggested by Jack Miles: "When the desire arises . . . to share these prodigies [of research] with a public outside the discipline, what must come first is not teaching but learning; not a pedagogically astute simplification of the research but a psychologically difficult recovery on the part of the researcher. Rather than suppose that the first step to be taken is a step downward, the learned writer for a lay audience must think first of steps outward in several directions." "The Common Reader and the Adjunct Professor: A Meditation on the Lives of the Mind," *Religious Studies News*, May 1998, 6.

182. "My training leads me to stress the content of Christian ethics when I teach. I want them to get it right so that they will know how to preach and teach and counsel. How can anyone attempt to teach Gospel vision or Christian character? Yet, in the final analysis, these more radical gifts alone will equip them for ministry. . . . Theology may help with the words, but the breath to articulate them in a life-giving way can only come from the Spirit of the living God." William C. Spohn, "Academic Theology and the Gospel of Jesus Christ," in *Theological Education for the Future*, ed. Guy Fitch Lytle (Cincinnati: Forward Movement, n.d.) 75.

This may mean giving up some of the sense of security that we gain from the sharing of specialized knowledge with a small academic elite. We will indeed continue to possess such knowledge, but as we begin to trace its connections with our common human and Christian priesthood, we shall find that, as priests, we are on a level with everyone else—or perhaps even below some of our less-educated colleagues. The integration of mind and priestly life will take us as long as anyone else.

I am not asking for abandonment or dilution of the various academic disciplines of theology. I am asking that we bring their traditions of honesty and responsibility, of accuracy and analysis, to the living of our common life of priesthood. It is time for more biblical scholars to begin saying what our studies mean for the life of faith, for more historians to say how our work informs and transforms our own understanding of tradition and of who we are here and now, for more theologians to augment our abstruse conversations with an effort to say what difference those conversations make in ordinary human terms. The general diffusion of secular education in the twentieth century has not always been matched within the churches, which still seem to think that knowledge must be hoarded or, at best, certified and doled out in predigested bites by an elite, whether of church hierarchs or academics. Then we are surprised if people tell us they are not interested!

My point is that, if the ordained are to serve as useful icons of our common priesthood, they should be continually growing in the exercise of that priesthood. That implies a process of personal deepening and transformation that needs to begin before seminary and be explicitly encouraged in the seminary or other educational context. Perhaps the knowledge of the mind is enough to make a capable surgeon or attorney (though I wonder, even in these cases), but it is not enough to make a good priest. Knowledge that has not entered into the process of shaping the self is simply not available for the purposes of priestly ministry. Integration, then, is the key—and integration not merely on the intellectual level, but on that of the soul and spirit.[183]

---

183. For Anglicans, this means, to some degree, a return to our own earlier tradition. "Instead of being primarily focussed on the education of the clerical practitioner, . . . Anglican education has been more vaguely defined in terms of the assimilation of an ethos, the ownership of a tradition and the development of a pattern of being. Furthermore, it has traditionally been rooted in the praying life of a religious community rather than in the purely intellectual atmosphere of the academic community." Mark D. Chapman, "Scripture, Tradition, and Criticism: A Brief Proposal for Theological Education," *ATR* 78 (1996):263.

Education of the clergy, then, under whatever circumstances, needs to be part of a larger vision of how knowledge can benefit the whole people in their exercise of the fundamental priesthood. And it needs to center in the education not just of mind, but of soul and spirit. Superficially, this may sound like a return to the time when biblical studies and the other theological disciplines were merely handmaidens of the ecclesiastical status quo, dutifully explaining to the world the perfections of their sponsoring denomination and offering nothing independent of it. In other words, it may sound like a return to institutional idolatry. It could become that, of course, if the focus does not remain clearly on the fundamental priesthood. This will be the great danger of such a project. But the true purpose is not to shore up the orthodoxies of the moment, but to encourage openness toward the experience of the HOLY and the growth of humble ministry in its presence. I do not want theology to become once again the handmaid of the church, but rather the handmaid of the SPIRIT.[184]

Once the church has identified, prepared, and ordained persons for sacramental ministry, what is their work? Above all, it is the religious, sacramental task of serving as an icon of our fundamental human and Christian priesthood in the rites of the Christian religion. Despite the venerable habit of belittling Sunday service as an hour divorced from the world of "real" life, even perhaps as a refuge from the moral demands of the "real" world, in actual fact the Sunday service and other occasions of common worship are times of great importance in Christian living. They remind us of where we truly live, of the depths under the surface of our daily lives, of our shared priesthood.

In a small congregation I know, composed largely of people who have a history of negative experience with the church and who, in some cases, have found this congregation almost as a last resort, members were asked why they came. By far the dominant response was "for the

---

184. "In order to avoid this danger of *paideia* becoming little more than a conservative form of indoctrination there seems, firstly, to be a vital need to ensure that the particularity of the tradition through which one comes to the Gospel, that is a *particular* mode of ecclesial existence, is not mistaken for the Gospel itself. Secondly, there must always be room within any ecclesial tradition for the critical encounter to take place, a latent suspicion of all attempts to control the Gospel: the Gospel, as ultimate judge, thus stands *over against* any form of ecclesial existence." Chapman, "Scripture, Tradition, and Criticism," 267–68.

Sunday service." When asked to explain that, people said things like: "It shapes the rest of the week." "It lifts up what is of real importance." "It helps me remember who I am." The fact that Sunday worship takes only an hour or so does not mean that it is unimportant. It means that it compresses into a brief, concentrated form things that might otherwise be lost to consciousness. It means that it functions sacramentally.

The nearest all the Christian traditions come to agreement regarding the ordained ministry is in assigning to the ordained some prominent role in the church's worship. Whether that role focuses on preaching, on prayer, or on ceremonial varies; but in any of these traditions, it is still an act of sacramental priesthood at a sacred time and place, reflecting the priesthood of the whole people in the presence of the HOLY. It follows that Sunday worship and the role of the clergy in it can be a powerful experience either for good or for ill.

If some reject or minimize the liturgical context of ordained ministry as trivial or insignificant, these objections testify, I am convinced, not to any intrinsic irrelevance but to a certain tendency of religion to remain attached to a past that no longer exists. We want our religious rites to seem venerable and unchanging, since these are characteristics we associate with the HOLY. But whereas we think of the HOLY as stable and enduring in its own right, we find it always mobile and elusive in our approach to it. When religion tries to model only the enduringness of GOD, it risks becoming torpid and stagnant. The HOLY is capable of surprising us. The HOLY is at work in the midst of ordinary life, where it raises questions and proposes new opportunities of enlightenment and repentance, new ways to rediscover the age-old Truth of death and resurrection. If our worship is to function well as sacrament, it must use its ancient rites in ways that are transparent to the SPIRIT's new and renewing work among us.[185]

---

185. "We must also clearly recognize as makers of the future, that as the Church has its special dangers of conservatism, cosiness, intolerance, a checking of initiative, the domestic tendency to enclose itself and shirk reality; so the cultus has also its special dangers, of which the chief are perhaps formalism, magic, and spiritual sloth. . . . A most delicate discrimination is therefore demanded from us: the striking of a balance between the rightful conservatism of the cultus and the rightful independence of the soul." Underhill, *The Life of the Spirit and the Life of Today*, 140–41.

The central business of the ordained is to foster the worship of the church, the sacramental life of religion that reminds us, week by week, to look for the deeper layers of REALITY, to expect GOD in our midst.[186] We need the ordained priest to function in the pulpit and at the altar in ways that will remind us that all human life is priestly. This means that we want clergy to be at home with the sacred institutions, just as we hope, more and more, to find ourselves at home in the presence of the ONE WHO IS. We want clergy to help make our approach to sacred rites focused and attentive, just as we hope to become focused and attentive throughout our lives in the presence of the HOLY. Clergy today, like clergy throughout human history, are first and foremost sacramental servants of the rites of religion. It is their job to perform these rites in ways that let the rite itself and the sacred emblems at its heart speak, rather than magnifying themselves. In this way, they help make the rite transparent to that encounter with the HOLY toward which it gestures, instead of its becoming an end in itself. The rite can send us back into the profane world prepared, with Jesus, to encounter GOD in the most unlikely places.[187]

If clergy, instead, give way to idolatry of the sacred or if they use the rites, as they sometimes have, to buttress a crumbling status quo or to sanctify some appalling, inhuman, demonic arrogance—slavery, the Inquisition, the Nazi regime—then they stand guilty of a great evil

---

186. "Some years ago, . . . the following question was posed to the assembly of scholars and liturgists: What is essential to an act of liturgical prayer? The answer they gave was that liturgical prayer required a presider capable of calling the community to prayer out of the authenticity of his or her own prayer. In other words, one's own prayerfulness, one's own willingness to be a person of prayer, is a prerequisite for being able to preside at liturgical celebrations. And what is prayer other than a 'quality of attention'. . . ?" Griswold, "The Bishop as Presider," 8.

187. "Something happened at Mass one day that summed up a little of [the] interplay of forces at work in the living-out of chastity. I was watching a priest celebrate the Eucharist at fairly close quarters. He celebrated with such an unconscious beauty, with such deftness and sureness, tenderness and strength that the thought—not a fantasy or temptation or anything of that nature—just the words crossed my mind, as naturally and ordinarily as any other reflection: 'I wonder if he makes love like that?' Blasphemy? No. What is the Eucharist if not love-making in its largest sense; and what is love-making, in its greatest sense, if not Eucharist?" Maggie Ross, *The Fire of Your Life: A Solitude Shared* (New York: Paulist Press, 1983) 72–73.

and earn a just condemnation. If they focus the worship of the community in such way as to make themselves the center of attention, they commit a personal idolatry that undermines their priesthood. If they merely make the worship of the church boring and irrelevant, their judgment may be less severe, but it is still a betrayal. In all these ways, they betray the fundamental priesthood by betraying the sacramental priesthood.

The central task, then, is the custody and maintenance of the sacred places, times, and rites. The other tasks assigned to the ordained clergy should also reflect the church's fundamental priestly identity. If they are assigned to foster and facilitate the life of a community, that is because the community has its whole reason for being in its exercise of fundamental priesthood. Since the fundamental priesthood has its own life and rationale, independent of the clergy, the church's leadership will serve effectively only when it follows the pattern set by the fundamental priesthood of Christ, of which it is part. That pattern is one of mutuality, of ministering and being ministered to. Church leadership must follow a similar pattern, neither dictating to the whole people of GOD nor simply following in the train of popular movements, but entering into a profound and priestly conversation with GOD and with the church as a whole about Christian life and ministry.[188]

This requirement arises from the nature of priestly experience itself. The border country is the realm in which human existence finds its meaning. The border itself is the indispensable condition for this. If you could slip over entirely into the HIDDEN HOLY, you would no longer be in touch with the basic materials and experiences of human life. If you try to slip over entirely into the everyday world, then actions and experiences merely follow each other in succession without forming

---

188. "I have found that the traditional roles of the bishop as shepherd of the flock, teacher of the faith, and focus of unity tend to coalesce in the light of experience and of prayer, and find some focus in my growing awareness of the bishop as 'spiritual director' for the diocese; that is through prayer, and making rigorous links between prayer and practice, the bishop lifts the church into the heart of God." Penny Jamieson, "The Distaff of God: Some Reflections on a New Episcopate," in *Episcopacy: Views from the Antipodes,* ed. by Alan H. Cadwallader (North Adelaide, Australia: Anglican Board of Christian Education, 1994) 349.

a larger whole. The priestly thing is to remain at the border, in active conversation with both.[189]

This priesthood is like the garden, which exists only in and through a "conversation" between human initiative and the given properties of the physical and botanical materials. The gardener must allow each side of the conversation its due. This conversational quality pervades all of human life when life is being lived well. Through a life lived well, the Hidden becomes visible in the everyday world by consenting to speak the language of our conditional, finite reality. The garden that emerges from this conversation may then become, in its own right, an image and reminder of this life on the border.[190]

Priesthood lives in this sort of conversation with both God and the neighbor. In our perennial, faithless longing for simplicity and certainty in this world, we often try to resolve the tensions in the conversation by giving one side of it complete dominance. We want either a humanity that can force its way into the Hidden Holy or a humanity that can only wait and be passive in the presence of God. In the church, we project these absolutist wishes onto the sacramental plane. We want to think either in terms of a clergy that gives orders or of a clergy that takes them. The church, however, is not an army, but rather the commonalty, the society, the community of those sharing in Jesus' priesthood. Even Paul, who believed himself commissioned directly by the risen Jesus as an apostolic founder of churches, was cautious about giving orders to other Christians. He expressed his ideas and hopes and

---

189. For emphasizing the importance of conversation as model of human life and priesthood, I am indebted to the Rev. Joseph L. McInerney. In a way, the model is equivalent to the more common theological use of "dialectic" or "dialogue." I find it superior, however, in a number of ways: it is a less academic term and does not have the same connotation of an encounter between opposed points of view. There is an art of conversation, which can be learned and developed; and it is at home in everyday settings where "dialogue" would sound pretentious. Moreover, the adjective "dialectical" has been appropriated by a modern theological tradition that is anything but conversational in its pronouncements.

190. "I see these objects in my garden as fragments that the garden viewers must string together in their own minds to create some narrative. The objects are like some background chant, ancestral voices guiding our reverie. So the garden visit becomes a journey, linking what is physically in front of you with the imagination of what might have been before. When successful, it removes you from your everyday reality." Roger Raiche, "Shining Prospects: A Conversation," interview with George Waters, *Pacific Horticulture* 58/3 (Fall 1997):34.

expectations very freely and often in strong terms, but he gave orders very rarely. He sought, instead, in ways shaped by the rhetorical traditions of his time, to persuade his fellow believers of the appropriateness of his position.[191]

The conversational model of leadership demands as a norm that the church's leaders, lay and ordained, be faithful in their attendance on the HOLY and open and persuasive with the community about what they see as important.[192] If they consolidate power in their own hands and disenfranchise those who disagree with them, they will violate their own reason for existence. This model should govern not only the leaders' interaction with the church's other members, but also their interaction with one another. Christian leadership is by nature priestly and therefore collegial, and it was institutionalized in collegial ways from early times.

From the earliest documents on, leaders of local churches are spoken of in the plural as "elders" (or presbyters) or as "overseers" (or bishops) and "servants" (deacons).[193] Over a century or two, this

---

191. "In a curious little verse in Philemon, Paul parades a theoretical apostolic authority unmatched elsewhere in his letters. We say theoretical because Paul mentions what he *could* do, but does not do it; 'Wherefore, although I am bold enough in Christ to command you to do what is required (v. 8), yet for love's sake I prefer to appeal to you. . . .' (v. 9). . . . This appeal to love as the proper motive for and limit to exercising one's will is a firm part of Paul's exhortation to the communities. 'Knowledge puffs up, but love builds up' (1 Cor. 8:1). We shall see that where Paul speaks directly of his own ἐξουσία [authority], its purpose also is οἰκοδομεῖν [to build up, edify]." John Howard Schütz, *Paul and the Anatomy of Apostolic Authority*, Society for New Testament Studies Monograph Series 26 (Cambridge: Cambridge University Press, 1975) 221–24.

192. This is of the essence of leadership. "Foresight is the 'lead' that the leader has. Once one loses this lead and events start to force his or her hand, one is leader in name only. . . . Required is that one live a sort of schizoid life. One is always at two levels of consciousness: one is in the real world—concerned, responsible, effective, value oriented. One is also detached, rising above it, seeing today's events, and oneself deeply involved in today's events, in the perspective of a long sweep of history and projected into the indefinite future. Such a split enables one better to foresee the unforeseeable." Greenleaf, *Seeker and Servant*, 22. This is not a new-age guru speaking, but a sober AT&T executive.

193. E.g., Philippians 1:1; 1 Timothy 3:1–13; Titus 1:5–9. There is a diversity of English terminology in this area, depending on whether one translates the Greek words by using their own derivatives or by using more ordinary English equivalents. Thus *presbyteros* is either "presbyter" or "elder," *episkopos* either "bishop" or "overseer," *diakonos* either "deacon" or "servant."

structure developed, on an ecumenical scale, into the classic model of ordained ministry, in which the church in each city had a bishop, a college of presbyters, and a group of deacons. The bishop was a "monarch," in the sense that there was only one bishop in the full sense of the term in each local church, so that the bishop would serve as a focus of unity. Yet this "monarchical" bishop was never an isolated individual leader, but worked in the context of his council of advice (the presbyters) and the group of ministers charged with carrying out the work of the church (the deacons). He consulted the laity, too, on controversial issues.[194] He also consulted with the bishops of other cities and maintained communion with them. It is probably safe to say that no ancient bishop ever needed (or had the opportunity) to make a major decision entirely by himself.

In addition, the clergy in this classic model were drawn from the local church. Accordingly, the clergy were not like modern professionals who are expected to avoid personal connections with their clients. The ancient clergy were members of the communities they served. In this respect, they were more like lay officers in modern churches than modern clergy. They could not readily see themselves as set outside or over against the congregation as a whole. They were members of the community assigned to tasks of leadership.

This picture contrasts sharply with modern practice, even in those churches which retain the classic three orders of ministry. For the most part, modern Western clergy are conceived as only temporarily attached to their particular cures or charges. They are nonlocalized professionals who have embarked on careers[195] and can expect to move a number of times before ending up in some position that will represent the peak of a professional life. Moreover, to a very great extent, they are isolated professionals, in accordance with the common model of one principal clergyperson to one congregation. Even in congregations large enough to have a staff of professional church workers, the staff members are often employed directly by the chief pastor and seen more as that person's agents than as colleagues in the leadership of the church.

---

194. Faivre, *The Emergence of the Laity in the Early Church*, 120–28.

195. The career model, to be sure, was already beginning to appear in the fourth century (Faivre, *The Emergence of the Laity in the Early Church*, 152–53).

Such a structure has very little to do with the mutual and conversational model of ministry established by our fundamental priesthood. As a result, it is not particularly supportive of the fundamental priesthood. This social structure expects the sacramental priest to behave like an "outside expert" rather than an ongoing member of the community. It focuses on the ordained person's knowledge and purity. It emphasizes how the ordained person is different from the laity.

The local Christian community, in the process, becomes a client. It serves as the source of problems which can be brought to the priest-professional for solutions. The cleric remains outside the community, though friendly with it, to be sure. The cleric is always able or even expecting to move on in pursuit of an individual career. In itself, this mobility is not wholly inappropriate in American society. Indeed, one could argue that imposing clerical stability in a culture that assumes mobility as normal would only be another way of cutting the clergy off from other people. What is disastrous is that there is so little provision, in the matrix where individual clergy live and move, to reaffirm their unity with the fundamental priesthood. The combination of a professional career model with the presupposition of a fundamentally one-to-one relationship between pastor and congregation produces, for the ordained person, a minimum of identification either with the ongoing congregation or with other clergy. This, in turn, produces discontinuity in the experience of sacramental ministry for laity and clergy alike.

More collegial models of church leadership can be recovered in a variety of ways. One possibility, for larger congregations, is to reenvision team ministries so that they are not merely extensions of the rector or chief pastor, but are brought together by the congregation with a view to the maintenance of its ongoing community life. There would be a presupposition against the automatic dismissal of the existing staff to make way for a new one whenever a new principal pastor arrives. A new principal minister would enter an ongoing community of ministry, clerical and lay, and would play an important, but limited, role, not creating a new clerical bureaucracy from the ground up but helping to focus the priesthood of the whole congregation in the new ways that this particular pastor's gifts make uniquely possible.

In some areas, particularly urban areas and university settings, smaller churches may often benefit by the presence of nonstipendiary clergy of proven gifts who worship with the congregation.[196] Such congregations can create pastoral councils that will give the principal clergyperson a collegium of ordained persons that can serve, along with the lay leaders, as a council of advice when difficult or strategic decisions have to be made. If the rota for preaching and teaching includes both clergy and laity with appropriate gifts, this will help break down the sense of opposition between the two. This practice, in turn, will serve the whole congregation by bringing a variety of voices to theological reflection in open and respectful conversation with one another. This conversation will be heard not only in preaching and teaching, but in parish and committee meetings where issues of faith are brought to bear on both the life of the congregation and that of the "profane" world, and in personal conversation. The existence of an open and ongoing theological exchange among the theologically trained can also make it easier for those without formal training to enter into the conversation as genuine participants. All alike can increasingly see that this discussion involves real life in the border country, in which they too have experience, and not just doctrinal abstractions.

For churches preserving the classical three orders of ministry, the principal clergyperson of a congregation might suitably be a deacon. The diaconate is oriented particularly toward serving rather than toward presiding or otherwise occupying center stage. This is precisely its strength for Christian leadership. The cleric with a truly diaconal vocation, when functioning as the principal minister of a congregation, will see her or his purpose as facilitating the life of the whole priestly community, not dominating, directing, or authorizing it. The deacon will not be a passive agent of others' initiatives, either, being not so much servant of the church as servant of GOD and the gospel in the church.[197] The business of a principal minister is to maintain a sense

---

196. "I regard the contemporary development of a priesthood which combines a ministry of word and sacrament with employment in a secular profession not as a modern fad but as a recovery of something indubitably apostolic and primitive." Ramsey, *The Christian Priest Today*, 4.

197. I have seen this pattern in use, over a number of years, at Good Shepherd Episcopal Church in Berkeley, California, with Rev. Dr. Kathleen Van Sickle as Vicar, and it has helped produce a Christian community of exceptional theological and spiritual vitality.

of the whole life of the congregation and how it may be served and enriched in its priesthood by the cooperation of all, laity and clergy alike.[198]

In settings where nonstipendiary clergy are not so readily available, the best recourse is probably to group churches and clergy so that a collegium of clergy is jointly responsible for sacramental roles in a group of congregations. In this way, a collegial band of clergy mirrors the expectation that the fundamental priesthood will also function collegially. The disadvantage to them of having to spend more time in consultation and coordination should be more than counterbalanced by having richer resources in both the cadre of ordained persons and in the community of fundamental priests. Ideally, this coordination will be combined with a process of encouraging the full membership of the local congregations to undertake primary responsibility for the priestly mission of each church.

The Episcopal Church has seen important progress along these lines, especially in rural areas, by recognizing the interdependence of lay and ordained ministries under the rubric of "mutual ministry" or "total ministry." This recognition offers a new spirit for the work and life of churches that have been isolated, underfunded, and often depressed. It relieves the isolation of the clergy while also reaffirming the priesthood of the whole people.[199] Needless to say, these arrangements will work only when education of the fundamental priesthood is

---

198. Compare Maestro Herbert Blomstedt's remarks on orchestral conducting: "A conductor must know the score and must know what to listen for. The moment he doesn't listen completely to what's going on, he cannot possibly conduct. Conductors often say, Follow me! Very often this shows that the conductor is not listening to what the orchestra is playing. . . . The conductor is the one who hears everything. He can transmit what he hears from one part of the orchestra to the other, so that everything happens at the right time. The importance of listening can never be stressed enough." (Interview in San Francisco *Symphony* 5/2 (Winter 1994): 3.)

199. "Priests do not have a territory where only they can absolve, bless, and consecrate. Priests are not raised up or set apart or separated from the community. Separation, isolation is and has been corrosive and destructive to priests and their families. Separation, isolation, solitary confinement is how we punish one another." Thomas K. Ray, "The Small Church: Radical Reformation and Renewal of Ministry," *ATR* 78 (1996): 623.

taken very seriously.[200] The leadership taken by rural dioceses in this respect shows that this project does not require a superabundance of material resources. It depends rather on taking our common priesthood seriously. Such models of leadership can sustain the life of the fundamental Christian priesthood more adequately.

Apart from the liturgical roles which are integral to the sacramental priesthood and which every cleric should be able to fulfill with decent competence, the members of such collegial groups of clergy can specialize somewhat—to the enrichment of the churches. This sharing of duties will also reduce the danger of burnout, which arises largely from the ordained person's being subjected to an enormous variety of demands—for some of which she or he will inevitably be ill-suited—in isolation from collegial support and mutuality. No one person can be equally competent at all the tasks expected of the modern cleric. Collegial groups can bring together a variety of skills and gifts and share them more broadly. They should be able to respond more effectively to a broad range of demands while actually reducing the drain on individual members. In the process, they will become a sacramental model for the same kind of sharing throughout the fundamental priesthood.

This practice is both theologically and practically sound. Paul's doctrine of gifts makes it clear that no one person has all the gifts necessary to the life of a congregation. The needed gifts are broadly distributed through the whole membership. If clerics persistently force themselves to do all the work of the fundamental priesthood, they will not only be trying to share gifts that they have not received (and therefore doing poorly at it), they will also be blocking some other person's exercise of exactly the gifts in question. Conversely, a corps of clergy that can acknowledge both the importance and the limits of their individual gifts will encourage the lay member of the congregation to offer the gifts that they alone can give.

---

200. Wesley Frensdorff's basic principles for total ministry in the Diocese of Nevada included: "(1) Each congregation is to be a 'ministering community' rather than a community gathered around a minister. . . . (2) Each member of the church will have the opportunity to serve our Lord in church and world. . . . (3) Seminary-trained clergy and laity will increasingly be trainers, enablers, supervisors and pastors of trainees. . . . (4) The diocese, as the primary unit of interdependence in the life of the church, is the support system." Josephine Borgeson and James A. Kelsey, "Emerging Issues: A Dialogue," in *Reshaping Ministry: Essays in Memory of Wesley Frensdorff*, ed. by Josephine Borgeson & Lynne Wilson (Arvada, CO: Jethro Publications, 1990) 198.

Respecting gifts means learning both which gifts you have been given and which ones you have not. Hankering after the gifts of others or being embarrassed at the limitations of one's own gifts merely produces confusion and an apparent shortage of gifts in the community as a whole. As clergy learn to understand and respect their own gifts better, they will be freer to encourage all members of the congregation in the sharing of their gifts. They will help the community know its needs and help individuals to discover how their particular gifts serve the community. Instead of trying to supply all needs out of their own meager resources, they will look for ways to ensure that all the gifts given by the SPIRIT for the life of the community are being welcomed.

As a result, the clergy will find they are being freed to a degree from the seemingly endless series of demands by "clients," a problem created by the professional model and by the church's having projected too much of its common priesthood onto the clergy. They will then have more freedom to look outside the immediate congregation and to ask how the community of faith can offer the good news of Jesus to people previously excluded. Evangelism still means what it meant in Acts 10–15 —overcoming the purity barriers that we, as Christians, have set up around ourselves and inviting persons unlike us to share in the celebration of GOD's grace and the exercise of Christ's priesthood. A clergy no longer exhausted by demands from within the congregation will be free to pay attention to such evangelism. With others, they will look to see whether the church is being appropriately supportive of the needy and welcoming to strangers. They will pay attention to the environing community, as signs of a fundamental priesthood that is always looking outward toward the others whom we can benefit and from whom we can learn.

None of these tasks are the ordained to do by themselves. Each one will indeed bring some special gifts and skills to these tasks, but their job is not to do everything for the community. As icons of our common priesthood, their use of diverse gifts affirms the legitimacy of the gifts of others as well. Accordingly, their active work in the community is to be aware of the overall life of the congregation, to call needs, resources, and opportunities to the attention of the congregation as a whole, to help individuals discover their gifts and share them, to enter into conversation with the people of GOD in a way that helps the congregation make sound and wise decisions about its life.

Ordained leadership, when it understands both its gifts and its limitations, will encourage all of us in the exercise of our fundamental priesthood. It will reflect the mutuality and collegiality of that priesthood sacramentally. It will help to clarify both gifts and challenges. It will encourage serious and reflective participation by all in the life of the church. And it will do so not by setting itself apart from or over against the rest of the church, but by understanding that it has a particular role to play *in* the church for the benefit of the whole. The ordained ministry—like every form of church leadership—has, as its central functional role, to foster and lead a community in which fundamental priesthood is held up to view and fostered. This is simply the practical equivalent of the ordained priesthood's sacramental reason for existence.

The sacramental priesthood is a mirror to the fundamental priesthood. Ordained priests must not abandon their participation in the fundamental priesthood of Christ, but find ways to let it emerge in their work as clergy. They will do this by continuing to engage in serious conversation with the HOLY and with their priestly colleagues, lay and ordained, by sharing their own gifts and respecting the gifts of others, by moving away from professional preconceptions of their role with the accompanying pretense of omnicompetence and toward more mutual, collegial models of ministry.

Those priests who are not ordained will contribute to a change of mind and heart in the church as a whole by justly valuing the priesthood they have been given by GOD. They must not discount their own experience in the borderlands, their insight into the arcana, their knowledge of GOD, or their ability to share their wisdom with others. The laity need to remember that the priestly work of the whole people is primary—and remind the clergy of it. In a loving, collegial, and priestly way, they can help the clergy see these realities afresh and change the clergy's self-understanding accordingly, so that all can minister together as priests to the full extent of the wisdom and insight granted to each.

The church as a whole will encourage these developments by structuring the work of the ordained in more collegial ways, by choosing candidates for ordination who have good reputations as fundamental priests and proven respect for those with whom they work, and by emphasizing the spiritual preparation of all Christians to discern and serve in our various priestly vocations. Such people will be able to take both their own gifts and those of others with seriousness. They will work to ensure that all have an opportunity to share their gifts with the church and the world. And when they stand in the pulpit or at the font or altar, we shall all see a reflection of our priesthood, which is Christ's priesthood, in the sacramental role they bear.

Part III

Priestly Spirituality

8

Being Priests

Priestly life is nothing more nor less than the fulfilling of our deepest longings, rooted in our capacity for being human. The great purpose of human existence is to enjoy communion with GOD and with GOD's creation—not least with that part of the creation in which we are most intimately involved, namely with one another. Jesus summed this up in the form of two great principles that he drew from the Torah: "You shall love the LORD your GOD with all your heart and with all your life and with all your understanding and with all your strength" and "You shall love your neighbor as yourself" (Mark 12:28–31). These are not merely commandments or rules, but a portrayal of the richest and most joyous kind of human life, the existence we were made for from the beginning.

This priestly existence, however, is not automatic. Like every human excellence, we have to practice it, reflect on it, and grow into it. This process is what we call "spirituality." It is the process of becoming more aware of who and where we really are and of learning to look for the HIDDEN HOLY in and under the busyness of everyday existence. Much of this process, of course, goes on without our conscious involvement. It is like every other kind of human growth in that respect. Because it is natural to us, we do not have to make it happen or be in full control of it; in fact, even if we want to, such control proves to be impossible. What we can do, however, is make ourselves open and available for the conversation with the TRANSCENDENT and with one another. In fact, such engagement on our part is necessary for our priesthood to come to full fruition, for, in the long run, we cannot grow into our full humanity without our own consent.

To enter upon this journey requires an increasingly strong sense of self—not some grasping, self-made self, a narcissistic or solipsistic self that pretends to reside at the center of reality and control it, but a self that springs from GOD's creative grace and is sustained by GOD's continuing goodness. Only such a self can participate in the loving exchange of gifts, the profound conversation that lies at the heart of what it means to be human. To see myself as a gift of GOD is not to belittle myself as something derivative or secondary, but rather to know myself as an

object of GOD's love, a love so great that it grants me my own freedom, accepting the risk of rejection in the hope that I may come freely
to return the love that created me. I have, therefore, a gift to share
with others—with the ONE who gave it to me and with anyone else.

To know myself as gift and as self, I must admit that the same is
true of every other human being. In every other man or woman there
lies at least the same depth of richness and mystery, the same liberty
and power of selfhood, that I find in myself—and probably the same
depth of uncertainty and even fear in the face of that mystery and that
liberty. When Jesus tells us to love our neighbor as ourselves, he is
telling us that we cannot really love either without loving both. We are
all in the same position before the transcendent reality of GOD, utterly
derivative from GOD's grace and yet free to build with that grace something distinctive and personal. This is the situation in which we all live,
and this is the situation in which we minister to one another as priests.

Reality is a long, rich conversation, and conversations depend on
honesty, engagement, generosity, and exchange. We can ruin our conversations by dominating them and so denying the reality of our partners in the conversation. Or we can ruin them by a certain passivity
and disconnectedness, by remaining outside them, by never letting our
real selves become engaged, by saying only what we think we are supposed to say or what we assume the others in the conversation may
want. The art of conversation lies in the balance, the practical recognition that there are real people involved here, of whom each is an "I,"
though only one is *my* "I." I am benefited by the richness of the conversation itself, not only by what I say, but by what I hear, not only by
my positive contribution, but by leaving room for what others may contribute. In this way, what each of us has sought and found at the border with the HOLY becomes available to the rest. This is the practice
of priesthood.

The cleric and the layperson are in precisely the same position as
regards this fundamental priesthood. Their differences, however substantial they may look on a Sunday morning, are relatively superficial.
The whole priestly people can benefit from the icon of priesthood found
in the ordained. Reminded by the icons, all of us can become more
aware of our own priesthood, the truth that is represented for us in the
sacramental image. But no one has ever or will ever enter into the secret
counsel of GOD's wisdom by being ordained. No one can be made a

true priest, in the fundamental sense, simply by ordination. No one discovers the integrity of faithful life simply by ordination. No one learns the love of GOD or of neighbor or of self simply by ordination. All these things come to all of us in the same way: through our living in GOD's presence on the borderlands where the everyday and the HOLY meet and interpenetrate.

The challenge for every human being in the exercise of our priesthood is to discern where this borderland crosses through our own lives and the lives of those among whom we live. There are no prefabricated answers to this question. The answers are as diverse as we ourselves are. All we can do is to be attentive. We discern our own answers, with the priestly aid of others, by considering the gifts we have received from GOD, the challenges and needs that life puts in our way, and our particular sense of being called onward into our priesthood. For each of us, a priesthood unique in its precise contours emerges from the particulars of our selves and our lives. The counsel of other priests is vital to me in discerning this priesthood; and yet, no one else can define it for me, for it is unique to the life that has been given to me and emerges, finally, only in conversation with the GIVER.

This path of discernment and growth begins where we are and, for most of us, leads through territory close to home—territory long familiar to us, but now revealed in new depth and with new meaning. Those just beginning to take their priesthood seriously may assume that it will demand of them some great act of separation from their previous life. It may, to be sure, particularly if our former life was dedicated to avoiding the encounter with REALITY. But, then again, it may not. We have all been practicing as priests, for good or ill, even before we begin to recognize it. The first objective, for all of us, is not to seek some radically new life, but to pay attention to the life in which we find ourselves.

Once we do this, our priestly quest may indeed take us away from our familiar environment and lead us on a pilgrimage to new places or to new kinds of life where we are to practice our priesthood. It may lead to a new sort of work, to a community hitherto strange to us, or to service to neighbors whose very existence meant nothing to us before. Yet, for most of us, most of the time, our priesthood simply calls us deeper within our present life, not away from it. This calling to priesthood seldom entails a calling to the iconic priesthood of ordination. Nor is that calling particularly important in itself. It is the calling to the fundamental priesthood that is implicit in our lives here and now, in the company of our sister and brother priests, to the priesthood of humanity and of Christ.

The very familiarity of our environment, of course, may make discernment of our priesthood difficult. It is not always easy to see how we ourselves may be growing, or what unrecognized gifts we may have for this familiar situation, or how our priesthood is even needed in a setting that may have had, until just now, the feel of a closed system, sufficient to itself. Normally, we need the priestly help of others to see past the familiar surface to the less familiar depths, whence the possibility of the new and surprising arises. It is not that others necessarily see me or my priesthood more clearly than I do (though that sometimes happens). Rather, a plurality of perspectives helps reveal what was partly hidden from my own single line of sight, and the shared vision of others helps focus what my own particular myopia may have blurred. Each of us, then, needs the priestly ministrations of others—priests whom we find one by one in our lives as one person or another proves to have some gift of enlightenment and understanding to share with us.

In this process of discernment, there are certain main points on which to reflect. These are points indicated by the nature of human priesthood itself and also by the specific way in which Jesus' priesthood interprets our shared priesthood for us. Here are at least a few of them—questions that may be broadly useful in discerning the present and future of our priestly lives. These are not questions for clergy, except in the sense that the ordained priesthood is rooted in and participates in the priesthood of all. These are questions for every priest.

In what ways is the life you are now leading a gift to you? With GOD, everything begins not with duty, but with grace, with gift; and this is where our discernment, too, must begin. The question is not one posed by piety (What *should* you feel grateful for?), but a question of fact (What *do* you, as you reflect on your life, feel grateful for?). What people in your life have bestowed blessings on you? What elements in your world are particularly life-giving for you? What gives you joy? What draws you forward in life with delight? What fires your creative imagination? Such blessings are an essential foundation of our priesthood. GOD can give gifts without having received any, but human beings cannot. It is a common, pious perversion of priesthood to suppose that true religion is about giving and giving and giving while never receiving anything yourself. This is not, in fact, real piety but a worship of foreign gods—in this case, worship of a grandiose notion of oneself. The true priest is a human being and accepts that human beings live by gifts. In the beginning was the *gift*, not the duty.

In what ways are you, in the life you now lead, a gift to others? Again, this is a question not of piety (How *should* you be a gift to others?), but of fact (How *are* you a gift to others?). We hope to avoid, here, the temptation of false humility as well as that of false pride. A predisposition to think well *or* ill of ourselves will only mislead us. True humility means working, with the help of others, toward an accurate assessment of ourselves, one that neither scorns nor flatters. For those who are newly discerning (or re-discerning) their priestly ministry, there is often a temptation to think of priesthood as something *added* to ordinary human existence. We suppose that it means becoming something quite different from what we have been, but it would be more accurate to picture priesthood in terms of plunging deeper into the reality of our life. The changes of perspective that accompany our awakening do not lead us away from who we have been so much as they bring us into a new stage of our ongoing personal history with GOD and with one another. *Metanoia* (conversion), which gives us this new perspective on the world, will indeed challenge us to rethink how we live in it. Still, the future will have some continuity with the past and present. One may often miss the priesthood under one's nose by expecting that everything must now be radically new and different. It is not uncommon to find that you are already exercising gifts that serve others in a priestly way and are in fact central to your priestly calling. GOD is able to work through and with us even when we are resistant to it or ignorant of it. Sometimes the new perspective of *metanoia* simply reveals to us the good that GOD has already been working through us, giving us the opportunity to claim it more intentionally as our priestly vocation.

Where and how, in your life, have you been most aware of meeting the HOLY? I place this question after the questions about gifts for fear that, if we were to take it up first, it might distract us from the awareness of our own giftedness. Our encounter with GOD, after all, can also underscore our sense of finitude, of dependence, of marginality. While the HOLY itself is life-giving, our meeting with it may happen under awe-inspiring, difficult, trying, even terrifying circumstances. That is a part of our human reality, part of our being finite, uncertain, growing, changing creatures. But the sense of vulnerability that accompanies our meeting with the HOLY must not be allowed to erase our awareness of gifts received, for the giving of gifts is, in fact, the real reason why GOD approaches us. The gifts are the foundation of our priesthood, placed in our hands and on our lips by WISDOM herself.

Still, the circumstances of our meeting with GOD are a part of our priesthood. How did you and do you become aware of the true dimensions of your own existence? Where do you encounter the HOLY and receive life from it? When does your experience of the everyday world become transparent to the TRANSCENDENT TRUTH that sustains it? Your answers to these questions are integral to your experience in the borderlands. They form a large part of what we have to share with others—sometimes simply by telling our own stories, perhaps even more often by listening perceptively and with understanding to the comparable (though never identical) stories of others.

The exact circumstances of our own lives in the border country do not provide a prefabricated plan for us to hand on to others: "Do what I did, and you'll have the same experience of GOD I had." GOD is not to be manipulated in such ways.[201] Your exact experience may seem to find a close parallel with one person or another, but it will not prove to be universal. Instead of a road map, our experience gives us trail-blazing skills. It gives us a sense of the geology of the borderlands: where springs are likely to be found, where gentle slopes may give way to dangerous cliffs, which passes may offer a thoroughfare and which are likely to be dead ends. The errors and troubles by which we gain this insight form part of the insight itself.

The particular gifts we have each received from the HOLY and the particular ways in which we have each met the HOLY are the foundation of our priestly life and service. It is useful to be aware of the particulars of both the gifts and the circumstances of meeting, since they provide each person's priesthood with characteristics and power unique

---

201. "We will not leave church knowing just what we ought to do. If we come away from hearing a sermon and know exactly what to do, then it is possible that the sermon missed the point, because that sermon would have structured our lives. The sermon in which the Gospel is preached gives no rules and regulations about how to live our lives, but points to a great vision. I am always happiest when the preacher says, 'This is how I see it; this is what I am called to do,' and then I can decide that I want to march with that person; or I can decide that I am not called in that way. Even the person who knows 'This is what I must do' knows it only for that moment. I may be called to do that on Monday, and may *not* be called to do that on Tuesday. We are called to freedom, and the awfulness of decision." Dozier, *The Authority of the Laity,* 28.

to it. Whether you encounter GOD in music or in nature, in the intimacy of prayer or in the complete surprise of unexpected grace or anywhere else, your specific encounters with the TRANSCENDENT bring a particular power to your priestly growth that spurs and shapes it.

Our growth as priests in the following of Christ is shaped by three particular qualities of Christian life—qualities already identified as significant in the first days of the Christian community. They are faith, hope, and love. These qualities connect us with Jesus and with the HOLY and enable us to go on living in the border country at times when that proves hard to do. They help us interpret what happens to us there, even when it seems meaningless. They give us the ability to share our hard-won experiential knowledge with others in ways that are respectful and accessible and genuinely priestly.

Faith is the foundation of our participation in Christ's priesthood because it witnesses not to our desires, hopes, or expectations, but to our *experience*. Faith is an act of the whole Christian community, as it celebrates creation and GOD's adoption of Israel and all the many gifts that culminate in the gift of Christ. It reaches its full priestly power and authority when we each come to see our individual stories as part of the common story. When we recognize that GOD has created not only the universe but our own lives, when we accept that GOD has forgiven not only the sins of the world but our own sins, when we discover that GOD not only gives gifts to apostles and prophets and sages and other exceptional persons but gives gifts to us in our very ordinariness and littleness—then faith begins to permeate and sustain our lives.

The priest must minister not only from what scripture or tradition says (that is to say, from what others have told us), but from lived experience. This is not to belittle the tradition or deny its importance. Faith, typically, first reaches us through the example and witness of others. Through the tradition, we enjoy the company of a vast array of witnesses and fellow pilgrims, even as we discover GOD at work in new ways in our own lives. In John's Gospel, Jesus' astonishing conversation with the Samaritan woman at the well of Sychar caused her to go and tell the people of her town, "Come see someone who told me everything I ever did! Can this be the Anointed?" After the other townsfolk had met Jesus for themselves, their faith was based on their own hearing, and they told the woman, "We no longer believe on account of what you said, for we have heard, ourselves, and we know that this is really the savior of the world" (John 4:29, 41–42). Her faith gave theirs its opportunity; then, without any belittling of her contribution, theirs began to stand on its own experience.

Faith that is truly our own can take shape only in the borderlands. Here, God meets us with the surprises of grace, the moments of insight when the world changes for us, the moments of opportunity when our lives open out in new directions, even the moments of failure or seeming rejection that make our finitude painfully apparent to us. In John's Gospel (chap. 9), Jesus meets a man born blind. His blindness, Jesus says, is so that God's glory may be revealed. (Perhaps the blind man himself had thought of it in more personal and negative terms.) Jesus spits on the ground and makes mud; he smears it on the man's eyes and tells him to go wash it off at a pool far across town. The man, taking the moment seriously as an opportunity for grace, accepts the risk and goes. This, in itself, is faith—this willingness to be open to God, to take risks in pursuing the gifts of life.

Once he has washed and gained his sight, from then on faith is central to his life. He is a person radically defined by a gift received, by an encounter with the Hidden Holy that proved life-giving. His inner transformation is more radical even than his outer one. The Holy has shown itself an immediate, formative factor in his life. His world is different. He is prepared to live boldly and to take risks—in order to remain true to his experience. When questioned about what happened to him, he, an uneducated man, answers his powerful interrogators with words they do not want to hear, with an honest account of his experience with the healing power of the Holy. Faith is the element in us that has seen God at work with us and recognizes that nothing can ever seem quite the same again. It is the acknowledgment that we have been living on the border with the Hidden all along, even when we may not have been fully aware of it.

Faith is not a matter of believing a list of doctrines. Christian doctrine, as a kind of distillate of centuries of priestly experience, is a valuable aid to Christian thought and reflection. But faith is a matter of having seen the Holy at work in your own life. Christian faith is a matter of recognizing that the God at work in your life is the same as the God of Jesus—the creative, self-giving, generous, demanding, forgiving, loving God who dared to become human in Jesus and to serve as our priest. Until we have seen this God at work in the realities of our ordinary existence, we do not yet have a faith of our own. This is not a challenge to try harder or to believe with grimmer determination. It is a challenge to pay closer attention, to find out what is already there in our lives, how the HOLY has been at work with us all along. It is a challenge to live attentively where we already are—in the border country.

Our "religious" life is not even the primary issue. We may think and feel a great deal, religiously, and yet make no connections between that feeling and our daily life. The strength of religion is that it looks to the HOLY and provides an accessible model of it in the sacred; and that is also its weakness. Religion easily degencrates into a kind of spiritual titillation: emotions enjoyed for their own sake, rites performed to satisfy obsessive needs, a moralism that reassures us that we who are religious are better than the unclean people outside. In such cases, religion, despite its positive potential, becomes a dead end. Our encounter with the sacred may well prove helpful to us; but it is never enough—certainly not enough to make a priest. Religion is helpful only when it sends us back into our daily existence looking for the gifts of GOD that make us who we are: gifts of creation, forgiveness, and the rest. The gifts themselves and our daily living with them are what make us priests.

"Faith" that is mere repetition of what others have said or mere attachment to religion may be worse than unhelpful. It can become positively dangerous if unchecked. It is possible for a person to gain a certain kind of credibility merely by repeating what has long been said—by being an expert in the tradition. This is a counterfeit faith, which is not only worthless in itself, but debases the legitimate currency. Because it knows nothing beyond religion, it overvalues religion and encourages the tendency of the religious to become exclusive and arrogant. It is of little help in the real quandaries and crises of everyday life, because it only knows and believes in a god of religion, not in the HOLY that undergirds the real lives of people. In short, a purely secondhand faith is destined to become idolatrous and, finally, helpless.

True faith, on the other hand, is a gift received in conversation with the HOLY. It therefore knows its own weakness and incompleteness and gains strength from that knowledge. It expects GOD to do surprising things. It expects the HOLY to be involved in the lives of every sort of person, from the greatest to the least, from the purest to the most unclean, from the most religious to the least. It expects GOD to reach out for us and to us in every possible situation. True faith does not try to retreat into some sacred preserve where it might be safe from the vagaries of everyday life. It keeps remembering, with surprise and gratitude, all that GOD has accomplished in its own experience and it finds, in the unlimited generosity of Jesus' GOD, the explanation of these surprising graces.

Since faith evolves through living at the border, it shapes our priesthood and teaches us how to further the pilgrimage of others. Faith gives us the courage to act as priests, however diffidently, because we know that there is indeed some experience in our own lives by which we have been brought close to GOD. We have seen the HOLY and lived and brought back a tale to tell. We discover that we are people of experience. We have held converse with the HIDDEN, and we believe—indeed, we take it for granted—that the HOLY is at work both with us and with our neighbor.

With this confidence—a confidence in GOD rather than in ourselves—we can listen to the stories of others and join in the conversation between them and GOD, as they discern the HOLY at work in their lives. We shall not try to force some preconceived interpretation on our neighbors' experience. We will not make our personal experience the exclusive standard. Instead, we will look, in their experience, for the self-revelation of the HIDDEN ONE, however surprisingly manifested. Our goal, as priests, is not to impose our interpretation, but to elicit the way in which TRUTH is taking visible form in the other's life. Perhaps we can also give some reassurance, in difficult moments, that GOD's giving and forgiving love endures. None of this will come only from a book or a tradition, valuable though they can be, but from something more immediate and authoritative—our experience of life on the border. True faith arises in no other way.

Faith is not a way of pretending harsh realities away or of sweetening bitter pills. Human life is full of things we would rather not face. This was as true in Jesus' life as in any other. Real faith neither ignores the threatening aspects of life nor avoids them. What it can do is face them as they are, without despairing over them, because it has seen GOD at work in the midst of such troubles before. In this way, faith becomes the foundation block of hope, and hope is the engine bolted to that foundation, imparting to us the energy by which we can live boldly in the world without having to tell ourselves sugared lies.

For *hope* is not optimism. It is not a happy accident of temperament or a habit of looking on the bright side. Nor is it a way to deny the realities of the world in which we live, a refusal to see problems or a willful insistence on expecting improbable sorts of rescue. Christian hope does not depend on our being attended by the standard variety of miracles—rescued from sickness, failure, grief, loss, distress, death itself. We give thanks for these miracles when they come; but what we hope for is not that GOD will spare us the harder realities of life in a finite world, but rather that GOD will continue to be the same GOD we have come to know through the experience that grounds our faith. What GOD has been for us, GOD will never cease to be: one who loves and sustains and shares our lives in intimate conversation.

Hope is a kind of courage in the midst of the unknown. In the words of an able theologian and preacher: "Gospel expectancy means living without fear and with great hope. It means we live on the edge of things where things are not completely settled or well-ordered, nor are we certain how exactly they will be settled. So it's where we can think imaginatively, act creatively, and love boldly because we don't have to be afraid that GOD is watching us to make sure we're getting it right. The only way we couldn't get it right is not to act at all. . . . Certainly, we're going to make mistakes. . . . But the freedom of the Gospel is the freedom to live without fear, and that means taking risks."[202]

Hope animates the smallest of our human and priestly acts—and the greatest. Hope animates the small kindnesses that enrich our lives and connect us to one another. The same hope animates the challenge of true martyrs who, when there is no sanity left in their world, can at least stand up and say, "This is insane"—if need be, at the cost of their lives. Hope animates our every expedition into the unknown, which is to say that it animates life itself. For any truly human life is involved in growth, and all growth is an adventure of change and learning, of choices and repentance, of new vision and new departures. Any kind of change can be frightening—most of all, those changes which touch us most deeply. Only an authentic hope, based not on fantasy or a sanguine temperament, but on our experience of the HIDDEN at work in our lives, can sustain us as we move forward. The alternatives—the effort to gain complete control of our lives, the effort to gain control of GOD, the effort to escape into intoxication of body, soul, or spirit— these are all subterfuges that are doomed to fail.

If hope is essential to human life, it is equally so to human and Christian priesthood. We rely even more heavily, I think, on our priests' hope than on our priests' faith. The Samaritan woman not only told

---

202. Jay E. Johnson, sermon preached at Good Shepherd Episcopal Church, Berkeley, California, November 14, 1993.

her fellow townsfolk what had happened to her. She enticed them to come with her and encounter Jesus for themselves: "Come see some- one who told me everything I ever did! Can this be the Anointed?" In this way, she opened for them future possibilities they had not at all expected. She not only shared her faith—the surprising experience of GOD's meeting her at the border in her life. She also aroused an expec- tation that others would find GOD at work in their own future.

The border country where we encounter GOD at the limits of our everyday experience is a frightening place. It has about it an element of death—death, at least, to the ordinary and predictable, if not always death in the most literal sense. When we find ourselves on this bound- ary, we are in a place of decision and danger. Even if we believe that GOD is a GOD who has loved us and given us gifts, who has reached out to us across whatever separates us, it is still a challenge to look toward the future, to let go of our anxieties, and to live actively in the assurance that GOD, when all is said and done, will continue to love and commune and work with us. The HIDDEN HOLY is neither against us nor aloof from us, but *for* us (Romans 8:31).

Even if things do not go as we wish, even if circumstances appear to be against us, even if GOD seems to have abandoned us (as Jesus also felt on the cross), hope keeps us looking forward and expecting some surprising grace. This expectation is not just a matter of passive waiting, though there may be moments when that is all anyone can do. It is a matter of living expectantly and therefore of framing a life that keeps looking forward. Even under adverse circumstances, the Christ- ian stands up straight in the knowledge of being loved and chosen and lives as honest an existence as possible, showing respect both for self and for neighbor.[203] That is what it means to live in hope.

All this would make alarming demands on an isolated person. Tor- turers typically resort to isolating their victims because the isolated per- son gives up more readily in the face of uncertainty and distress. The person who wants to stand up straight needs a strong sense of the shared humanity that binds us to one another in giving and receiving. Amid the realities of daily existence, we draw hopeful courage for the future from one another. This is, above all, why priests are so important to us. We resort to them not only because they know something about the border country, but because they have found the hope and courage

---

203. The image of standing up straight and holding one's head up is used in Luke 21:28 as a summary of Christian ethics under stress.

to go on living there. When we draw near to the boundary, we find the land already inhabited by people who love us.

It is *love* that permits us to accept the services of others as our priests. We can trust others as priests only if we are persuaded that they have a genuine reverence for us and care more for us and our well-being than for their own authority. The priest who is mainly interested in a fee of some kind is not a true priest. The fee in question may be material, or it may be emotional or spiritual. The priest may want to get rich, for example, or to gain intimate power over the lives of others, to get and hold a reputation for being always right or to be praised as superhumanly supportive. There is a multitude of such temptations in the path of the priest, and the priest who loves the fee rather than the neighbor has failed an essential test of priesthood.[204]

Love demands its own integrity. If I speak of holy things to another solely in order to benefit the other, the other person is reasonably safe, even if my advice should be, for one reason or another, wrong. The integrity of the relationship is protected. My neighbor's well-being was my goal. If my advice is not entirely correct, I have already implicitly endorsed the principle that my neighbor's spiritual well-being, as goal, takes precedence over following my own advice. If, however, my real aim is to get a fee of whatever sort—whether of money, personal service, respect, compliments, or a prominent reputation—I will turn my counsel to that end rather than to the good of my neighbor. I will try to control the other person. I will seek to attach her or him to myself rather than to GOD. I will lie, if need be, to achieve that. And once I have lied, I will try to keep others in the dark so that my deceit will not be discovered and my client lost to me.

Priesthood requires that priests have a profound respect—one might legitimately say "reverence"—both for their own integrity and for that of their neighbors. This is a big part of what Paul means by

---

204. I do not mean to say that fees given to our spiritual guides are invariably wrong. The person who, for good reason—perhaps at the behest of others—devotes herself or himself full-time to the exercise of the fundamental priesthood still has to eat. In such cases, the fees should be clearly defined as the custom of the culture demands; and there should be some provision for the poor who cannot pay on the normal scale. Perhaps it is best if the fees are material and quantifiable, so that the priest is not deluded by receiving too much reverence. Under such circumstances, one can pay or receive such fees without guilt. A problem arises only when the fee becomes the goal. This is especially dangerous with fees of "respect," which can easily turn the priest away from GOD towards him or herself. The desire for such respect has been the downfall of many priests, well-known and little-known.

love (1 Corinthians 13). "Love" is a difficult word because it means so many different things, some of which are not useful and may even do harm. The love required in priesthood (and indeed in all faithful and hopeful living) is not an isolated emotion. It is not sentimentality. It is not infatuation or obsession. It does not grasp or try to control. It does not lie in order to preserve a good image of itself or of the beloved. It does not "protect" people from the truth any more than it belabors them with it. It does not treat grown people as children who are incapable of taking responsibility for themselves. It does not aim at possessing those whom we love, but at sharing life with them.

Love implies reverence for one another. In every person, ourselves included, we see one whom GOD has created, chosen, loved, forgiven, welcomed, and celebrated. We therefore see each person as a complex and beautiful mystery, worthy of all this outpouring of GOD's gifts. It may be that, in one case, this beautiful mystery is concealed by extreme diffidence or stunted, for the time being, by fear. In another, the mystery may be disfigured by violence or greed or some other evil. Real love does not ignore these calamities, but it sees that there is more— that the mystery is there, both in myself and in the other person. The mystery is to be honored in both of us. Love is the honoring of it.[205]

The beauty of this mystery, unique in each person, draws us to one another. It inspires our love, and our love allows us, even if just briefly, to transcend the distance between us. It can do this work, however, only in the presence of honesty. Hypocrisy or pretense destroys priesthood because it means we are either avoiding our own true self or avoiding the truth of the other. Such behavior is not love, then, since it does not really desire to be initiated into the mystery of the other. It is a pseudolove, seeking to build false connections between pseudopersons, with the goal of escaping from reality and warding off the HOLY. Hypocrisy cannot do good. It can do great harm, especially to

---

205. This love acknowledges, among other things, that at any moment our neighbor may prove priest to us. Robert Coles's remarks on his conversations with children form a model of priestly conversation: "Prolonged encounters with children are the essence of the clinical work I learned to do in hospitals and of the work I do in the homes and schools I visit. Each child becomes an authority, and all the meetings become occasions for a teacher—the child—to offer, gradually, a lesson. My job is to listen, of course. . . . My job, also, is to put in enough time to enable a child . . . to have her say—to reveal a side of herself not easily tapped even by good schoolteachers. . . " (*The Spiritual Life of Children*, 27).

those whose pilgrimage in the border country is still relatively new or uncertain.

Love is the strength that flows from hope. We have confidence that our life, our priesthood, our ongoing conversation with GOD at the border will continue, and we see that GOD woos every person with the same deep and persistent affection. So we begin to understand that we are, all alike, being woven together into a single fabric of honor and delight. Like the lovers who address each other in the Song of Songs, we are all equals, all beautiful, all desired and desirable, all reaching out to touch each other with joy and reverence. That is what happens when LOVE is truly having its way with us. None of us is, as yet, fully practiced in love; but, bit by bit, as the HOLY grants us power and opportunity, we grow into it. We learn love as we grow in faith and in hope.

The great measure of our priesthood, then, is how much we love, how much we esteem the beautiful possibilities in every person's conversation with GOD, how much we esteem and revere the other's unique experience in the borderland. As our love becomes more and more genuine, it sheds the need for lies. It drains away the desire to assert our own priority. It frees us from the need to possess and control, the need to claim unique authority for our own interpretation of the HOLY.[206] It makes us free to delight in one another's mystery, to share one another's life on the boundary. True love, ultimately, is the living out of our human priesthood in long, rich conversation with one another and with GOD.[207]

Priesthood relies on the faith of the priest, gained through our collective and individual experience, confirmed and illuminated by the good news of Jesus. It requires hope, by which priests share their own hard-won reliance on the goodness of the HOLY with the neighbors who are new to the borderland or perhaps shaken by their experience of it. It requires, above all, love—the affection and reverence we have

---

206. ". . . it is love and not fear that inclines us to repentance." Thompsett, *We Are Theologians*, 86.

207. The pianist Artur Schnabel once said, with regard to the study of the great piano literature, "As far as my knowledge goes, nothing in the world has ever grown from the exterior to the interior. . . . Love has to be the starting point. . . . It is one of my strongest convictions that love always produces some knowledge, while knowledge only rarely produces something similar to love" (quoted by David Blum, "Artur Schnabel, 1882–1951," *BBC Music,* July 1997, 35).

for one another by virtue of the mystery each of us is found to incorporate in our conversation with GOD. These qualities will give the priest something to share and the willingness to share it, and enough respect for the neighbor to share it in a way that the other can afford to accept and acknowledge.

The priesthood of Jesus was the same as ours. It differed only in the completeness with which it filled his life and the fullness with which he—or GOD in him—brought it to its goal. The priesthood of the Christian people, as I have been describing it, *is* the priesthood of Jesus, carried out in widening circles by those whom his priesthood has touched. It is also continuous with the fundamental priesthood bestowed in creation on all humanity. Christians need not be surprised to receive the most profound of priestly ministrations from people who have no conscious or intentional relation to Jesus at all. Jesus, John's Gospel tells us, is TRUTH (John 14:6). Jesus is the WORD of creation (John 1). Jesus is the point of origin for all priesthood. He did not, then, replace the fundamental human priesthood that he himself created, but interpreted it with new clarity and brought it to culmination in ministering it.

As Christians, we live by GOD's gifts, relying on Jesus' priesthood and that of one another, celebrating what GOD has done for us in the past, looking forward to what GOD will do in the future, welcoming one another into the border country with the kind of reverence and delight that can only be evoked by the sight of those whom we love. When we do these things, we are living as priests. Our lives will grow in the wisdom and insight, the clarity and realism that allow others to recognize us as priests. Even with all our inadequacies, our uncertainty and fear, we shall, by the grace of the HOLY, find ourselves being true priests to one another and receiving the priestly ministrations of one another. There is no more profound experience of being Christian or of being human.

Finally, all priesthood is dependent on growth in *integrity*. This, of course, is a great challenge, for our lack of integrity will want to protect itself from discovery and will blind us, if possible, to the presence of hypocrisy in us. Probably none of us can become fully truthful all at once. Yet we can, at times, notice the loose edges of the camouflage our hypocrisy has drawn over itself, the places where it does not quite match its surroundings, where a certain trouble of conscience reminds us that we are being less than truthful with ourselves and others. Then

we may, with humility and priestly assistance, be able to roll that edge
back a little so that more of our truth is exposed to the light.

This is a disturbing process and often painful as well. But it is vital
to our life and work as priests. The best priest is not the invulnerable
and faultless person. Even the Son, according to Hebrews, could not
serve as priest without experiencing weakness and suffering. The best
priests are people who have suffered and, by suffering, moved toward
wholeness. The whole person is a truthful person, a person of integrity.
By developing, bit by bit, in truthfulness and by losing some of our
pretentiousness, we find ourselves beginning to accept our weaknesses
along with our gifts. And far from what we may have expected, our
priesthood is not dimmed or clouded by these imperfections. Indeed,
as they are acknowledged and repented, they make our priesthood the
more transparent, so that God and our neighbor can meet one another
through it.

We may still ask, of course, whether we are situated where we belong
or whether God may be calling us to some new and unexpected context for our ministry. I began this chapter by suggesting that, in most
cases, our priesthood happens right where we are. Yet it would be wrong
to make an absolute ideal of stability. Our God has long been a God
of nomads and pilgrims, and God may at times call us in our priesthood to new places, people, or tasks. There is no easy way to be sure
when this is happening, but if we remain open to the possibility, the
conviction of such a call will validate itself through discernment in the
company of other priests.

The good news of Jesus has always been spread by people who discover, sometimes in unexpected and unwelcome ways, that they have
been given the vocation and gift of ministering to people unlike them.
When Paul was struck down on the road to Damascus, Jesus promised
to send him to speak to the Gentiles (Acts 22:6–21). Poor Paul! The
champion of purity and persecutor of the new way would now go off
and preach the good news of Jesus to a lot of filthy outsiders! It was
not a priesthood he could have chosen for himself—or even imagined.
But it proved to be full of power for the future. It is not always a direct
voice from the Holy that sends one out on such a mission. Sometimes
it is an accident of our own lives that throws us among people we would
not have expected even to know. Sometimes it is the voice of the other
people, the people unlike us, that we hear making a claim on us. We

ask, then, whether this is indeed GOD's call to us, a call to let our human priesthood cross whatever gaps now keep us from the priestly exchange of gifts with others.[208]

Such a priesthood, a priesthood that lives among and serves strangers and outsiders, may look like a daunting prospect at first. But it will be lived out on the same boundary with the HOLY as all other manifestations of our common and fundamental priesthood. As messengers of the good news we do not merely bear that news with us, but also seek it in the place to which we go. However strange and distant that place, the SPIRIT has always come there ahead of us.[209] What sustains and enables our priesthood is not some fixed resolve of our own, triumphing over every challenge, but rather the gifts we receive as we go. This priesthood takes place at the confluence of GOD's love for us and humanity's urge toward the HIDDEN REALITY. It takes shape in the lives of specific people, who live on this boundary and help interpret it for the neighbors who come to it in new ways or with unanswered questions.

Such priesthood, willing to adventure into the unknown and uncertain, is particularly important in our time. There is so much crossing of boundaries to be done between human groups. We have crossed those boundaries often enough, in past centuries, in war; now we must learn to cross them in peace, with the kind of reverence and respect for one another that alone makes true priesthood possible. It is not only our boundaries with other humans that call for priestly ministry. The relation of human beings to the rest of the created order is in a state of crisis, too. The prophets and other priests who have made us aware of this reality are still too few in number. It will take many such priests to discover and to tell us all how to live in greater harmony and humility with the rest of our world, created and loved by the HOLY as much as we. If most of our priesthoods are lived out at home, many

---

208. "Jesus ate with outcasts; Paul and Luke took strong stands on behalf of those relegated to the position of second-class citizens in the church. They did so . . . because they knew that God *by nature* recruits outsiders to be partners in providence, makes a home among them, and through them enriches the world. We miss out on this fullness of life when we limit our partnerships to those who most resemble ourselves." Koenig, *New Testament Hospitality,* 126.

209. "Even at its best, . . . our inner space cannot itself provide a home for the external stranger. God will grant that to the stranger, while calling upon us to help in building up the spiritual and material environments that make it possible." Koenig, *New Testament Hospitality,* 126.

of us will also find ourselves called to an adventuring priesthood, a priesthood that moves outward and forward. There has never been a time when such priesthood was more important.

All of the above applies equally to all priests, laity and clergy alike. But there are a few things that might well be said specifically to each group:

To the clergy, I would say: *Take your priesthood more seriously than your ordination.* Nothing can surpass the gifts bestowed on you in birth and interpreted through baptism. By this priesthood, we live the truly human life in human community, giving and receiving the gifts that make us human. GOD will always be more interested in how you have practiced your fundamental priesthood than how you have served in your sacramental one. You will need the priesthood of others, and they are as likely to be members of the laity as of the clergy. Nothing should seem to you more attractive and desirable than to participate in that beautiful interchange of gifts.

In practicing your sacramental priesthood, then, remember the greater priesthood of which you are an icon. *You practice the sacramental priesthood best when you are most transparent to the more fundamental priesthood to which it points.* Handle the sacred rites with a respect that looks beyond them to the human encounter with the HIDDEN HOLY, toward which, as signs, they direct us. Look through the water of baptism to the ongoing rebirth and resurrection of all people, through the bread and wine to the body of Christ nourishing the world, through the Gospel book to the joyful message of new life that it signifies. Bear the sacramental priesthood with a reverence that is transparent to the glory of the fundamental priesthood in, with, and under it. Live and work as colleagues in and with the whole priestly people, remembering the traditions of the fundamental priesthood and sustaining its life. Enrich it with whatever gifts you are given while also welcoming the gifts that only others can bring. Build your life and help others build theirs not merely on the church, not just on foundations of religion or the sacred, but on the one unshakable foundation, laid deep in the heart of reality, the HOLY itself.

Live out your priesthood, fundamental and sacramental, with a large—indeed, a divine—generosity. You are ordained within a particular Christian community, but the priesthood of which you are sacrament recognizes no human boundaries. When we limit our ministry to our own narrow group, ignoring those outside, we are, in effect, denying the fundamental priesthood we serve. For the true priest, every person is a neighbor—not a mere category.

Give up the heroic impression. Priesthood belongs, as a gift, to all who live. You will not create it or claim it as your own or become deserving of it by your labors. If you wish to exemplify it well, you will do so by seeking a deeper understanding of the everyday world in which you live, not by seeking out feats of heroism. If the occasion and call for heroism do befall you, respond; but wear your distinction lightly, as Jesus did when he tried to suppress reports of his miracles.[210]

Finally, *do not take advantage of your ordained status.* Since you will be perceived as a visible representative not just of the sacred, but of the HOLY, you will have the power to do much harm. You will probably do some harm inadvertently, in any case, but you can avoid the deliberate infliction of it if you seek your chief joys in the exercise of the fundamental priesthood, in the mutual care that makes us all equal in the borderland with the HOLY, not in the pursuit of power or prestige.

To the whole people of GOD, I would say: *Think of the sacramental priest only as a reminder of who and what you yourselves most truly are.* The point is to look through them rather than at them, to find them a glass transparent to the fundamental priesthood, not an opaque object of fascination in their own right. When you look through them, you will see that they are simply an icon of the whole people of GOD. In the community of the baptized, we encounter GOD's loving affirmation of the priesthood of all humanity. It is a community given life by the sharing of the gifts each has been given to share, gifts that will give new life to the spirits of all. It is a community that is being fed by GOD's own life, sacramentally in the Eucharist and in the ongoing experience of grace. It is a community that brings humanity and GOD together, forming and reforming their mutual love in the border country. In this community, we need no longer be divided by fear and deceit, but are bound together by faith, hope, and love.

The altar of the HOLY is in the midst of the world. The sacred rites of the church are sacraments of the common and fundamental priesthood that we live out every day in innumerable ways and in the most diverse settings. Our deeper priestly service takes place over tables when people share food and something of themselves. It takes place at sales counters and in offices when people allow themselves even a moment's

---

210. E.g., Mark 1:43–44; 5:43; 8:26.

acknowledgment of the other person's humanness. It takes place between lovers in bed. It takes place when neighbors help each other, when parents encourage their children, when students and teachers join in learning. It takes place in moments of joy, when we lose ourselves in delight. It takes place in moments of deep distress, which reveal us anew to ourselves and open us to one another. It takes place in studios where artists bring something of the HIDDEN to expression and in studies where writers attempt to do the same. It takes place in counsel, in reading, in singing and all making of music. It takes place in the garden. It takes place in the giving of gifts and in the receiving of them. It takes place in every moment of human communion, direct or indirect, with the HOLY and with one another.

In all things, we are priests. The degree to which faith, hope, and love permeate us with integrity determines how effective we are as priests, but to be no priest at all is impossible. There is no hierarchy in our priesthood. A saint like Francis whose work has influenced millions of people over many centuries is no more nor less a priest than the dying laywoman who many years ago introduced me to the mutual priesthood of GOD's people. I was a very young and green cleric, and she was one of the first people I ever visited in severe illness. She was not a regular churchgoer. I had not met her before and saw her only once or twice afterward. At this point in my life, I no longer know her name. I came into her room, introduced myself, and asked her how she was. She replied, with some effort, "I think I'm dying." In my youth and inexperience, I was struck completely dumb. She saw my difficulty and said to me, "How are you?"

In that moment, many of my assumptions about ministry were reversed and what seems to me a truer order of things began to make itself felt. It is the order I have tried to point toward in this book. My ministrations as a sacramental priest at that bedside were not unwelcome, but they were not central, either. They were only an image—a sustaining one, I hope—of the truer and deeper priesthood in which she was at that moment (and perhaps always) more gifted than I. We are all likely to be humbled by this priesthood, by living on the border with the HOLY and with one another. But we also rejoice in gifts received and in gifts shared, we sustain one another in faith and hope and love, we grow in integrity and reverence, we become true citizens of the borderlands where human life is richest and freest and closest to its origins and its goals. We become friends of GOD and of one another. There is no higher vocation for any human life.

Acknowledgments

The origins of this book date back to the 1960s, and it gestated for two decades in the form of private reflections on priesthood, spurred by my own ordination as presbyter in the Episcopal Church in 1965 and my experiences as an ordained priest in parish and academic settings. One result of the long and rather meditative development of my thinking is that I can no longer identify all the influences that helped me, whether by suggesting ideas or by forcing me to reflect on things that I did not understand. I sometimes fear I have learned as much from my own mistakes as from any other one source, but I regret that I cannot list all those who have contributed to my reflections over the years. Perhaps I owe most to the congregations that have been priests to me in my sometimes perplexed and distracted service to them as an ordained person.

In the decade or so I have spent writing this volume, I have become increasingly aware of the formative influence exercised on me by the writings of Evelyn Underhill. I remember being asked on a graduate-school application form in the late 1960s which twentieth-century theologians had made the greatest impression on me. I could not then name any that I wanted to acknowledge that kind of debt to, since I had always been more interested in ancient Christian writers than in modern ones. Over the years, I have come to realize that I do in fact owe a profound debt to Underhill for her example of clarity and sanity, for her insistence on writing in real English rather than the argot of academic cliques, for her refusal to let theology occupy a hermetically sealed compartment, and, above all, for a sense of the limits of human language, especially the variety commonly called "expository prose," as a tool for expressing the deeper realities of human experience. Underhill set the standard for any later writer who wants to write about theology, other academic disciplines, and actual human *life* in a way that acknowledges their interdependence.

Biblical quotations in this book come from my own translations for the New Testament and from the New Revised Standard Version for the scriptures of Israel. The footnotes represent some of the other voices with whom I have been in conversation for longer or shorter amounts of time. Rather than use the notes to validate an argument, in the usual scholarly style, I have for the most part taken them as an opportunity to share some of the writers who have "struck sparks" for me.

Still other voices in my ongoing priestly conversation are the friends who have reflected on this subject with me and, in some cases, read various earlier versions of the present work. That list includes, without pretending to be exhaustive: Clayton Crawley; Blake Franklin (who introduced me to the work of Edward Schillebeeckx); Joseph Lee Mc-Inerney (to whom I owe the beauty and tranquillity of my Berkeley garden); Donn Morgan; Shunji Nishi; Juan Cabrero Oliver; Paul Michalenko; Thomas Schultz, OHC; Elizabeth Smith; Paul Strid; Catherine Miles Wallace; and Michael Wyatt. I am also indebted to various groups to whom I have presented some of these ideas and who have given me invaluable criticisms and encouragement, among them clergy groups in the Puget Sound area, in Indianapolis, and at Pajaro Dunes, California; the annual meeting of the Lesbian and Gay Christian Movement in London and the annual gay men's spiritual retreat at the Kirkridge Conference Center in Pennsylvania; and church audiences in La Jolla, Santa Barbara, and elsewhere. Sabbaticals from The Church Divinity School of the Pacific helped to provide writing time.

I thank Hal Rast of Trinity Press International for his priestly patience in waiting on a work that took so much longer than anticipated. He kept telling me, "You'll know when it's ready," even during the times when I thought it might never be and he may well have wondered. Thanks also to Debra Farrington at Morehouse for her enthusiasm and encouragement when the manuscript came under her care.

Last of all, I thank the spell-check program in my computer software, which repeatedly urged me to replace the word "layperson" with the word "leper," thereby reminding me of the reasons for writing this book.

Bibliography

Adams, Doug. "De Staebler *Winged Figure* Installed at G.T.U. Library." *Arts* 6/3 (Summer 1994): 4–7.

Attridge, Harold W. *The Epistle to the Hebrews*. Hermeneia. Philadelphia: Fortress Press, 1989.

Aulén, Gustaf. *Christus Victor: An Historical Study of the Three Main Types of the Idea of the Atonement*. Trans. A. G. Hebert. London: SPCK, 1953.

Bahn, Paul G. "Treasure of the Sierra Atapuerca." *Archaeology* 49/1 (January/February 1996): 45–48.

Bare, Judith E. "A Gospel of Her Own: The Apostolic Secession of Emily Dickinson." Ph.D. diss., Stanford University, 1993.

Barrett, C. K. *Church, Ministry, and Sacraments in the New Testament*. Grand Rapids, Mich.: William B. Eerdmans, 1985.

Bartlett, David L. *Ministry in the New Testament*. Minneapolis: Fortress Press, 1993.

Bede, Belinda. "A 'kinder, gentler' Anglican Church: The Novels of Barbara Pym." *Anglican Theological Review* 75 (1993): 387–98.

Blomquist, Jean M. "Barefoot Basics: Yearning and Learning to Stand on holy Ground." *Weavings* 8/5 (September/October 1992): 6–15.

Blomstedt, Herbert. Interview in San Francisco *Symphony* 5/2 (Winter 1994).

Blum, David. "Artur Schnabel, 1882–1951." *BBC Music*, July 1997, 32–35.

Boff, Leonardo. *Trinity and Society*. Trans. Paul Burns. Maryknoll, N.Y.: Orbis Books, 1988.

Borgeson, Josephine, and James A. Kelsey. "Emerging Issues: A Dialogue." In *Reshaping Ministry: Essays in Memory of Wesley Frensdorff*. Ed. Josephine Borgeson and Lynne Wilson. Arvada, Colo.: Jethro Publications, 1990. Pp. 197–219.

Bradshaw, Paul. *Liturgical Presidency in the Early Church*. Bramcote, Notts, England: Grove Books, 1983.

Buckingham, Warren W., III. Opening plenary address for National Episcopal AIDS Coalition "Hope and Healing" Conference, Santa Monica, Calif., February 3, 1994.

Chapman, Mark D. "Scripture, Tradition, and Criticism: A Brief Proposal for Theological Education." *Anglican Theological Review* 78 (1996):258–74.

Coles, Robert. *The Spiritual Life of Children*. Boston: Houghton Mifflin, 1990.

Collins, John N. *Diakonia: Re-interpreting the Ancient Sources*. New York and Oxford: Oxford University Press, 1990.

Commins, Gary. "Death and the Circus: The Theology of William Stringfellow." *Anglican Theological Review* 79 (1997):122–62.

Countryman, Louis William. *Biblical Authority or Biblical Tyranny? Scripture and the Christian Pilgrimage*. Rev. ed. Valley Forge, Pa.: Trinity Press International, 1994.

————. *Dirt, Greed, and Sex: Sexual Ethics in the New Testament and Their Implications for Today*. Philadelphia: Fortress Press, 1988.

————. *Forgiven and Forgiving*. Harrisburg, Pa.: Morehouse Publishing, 1998.

————. *The Language of Ordination: Ministry in an Ecumenical Context*. Philadelphia: Trinity Press International, 1992.

————. *The Rich Christian in the Church of the Early Empire: Contradictions and Accommodations*. New York and Toronto: Edwin Mellen Press, 1980.

Culbertson, Philip. "Pastoral Theology and Multiculturalism." *Anglican Theological Review* 79 (1997):163–91.

Cummings, Charles. *The Mystery of the Ordinary*. San Francisco: Harper & Row, 1982.

Dickinson, Emily. *The Complete Poems of Emily Dickinson*. Ed. Thomas H. Johnson. Boston: Little, Brown & Co., n.d.

Dillard, Annie. *Holy the Firm*. New York: Harper & Row, 1977.

Doss, Joe Morris. "The Unified Symbol of Ministry: Sacramental Orders." *Anglican Theological Review* 72 (1980):20–36.

Dozier, Verna J., with Celia A. Hahn. *The Authority of the Laity*. Washington: Alban Institute, 1982.

Dwinell, Michael. *Fire Bearer: Evoking a Priestly Humanity*. Liguori, Mo.: Triumph Books, 1993.

Edgar, Cornelius H. *The Curse of Canaan Rightly Interpreted, and Kindred Topics*. New York: Baker & Godwin, 1862.

Faivre, Alexandre. *The Emergence of the Laity in the Early Church*. Trans. David Smith. New York: Paulist Press, 1990.

Ferry, James. *In the Courts of the Lord: A Gay Priest's Story*. New York: Crossroad, 1993.

Frensdorff, Wesley. "The Captivity of Sacraments." *The Witness* 75/5 (May 1992): 5–6.

————. "Ministry and Orders: A Tangled Skein." In *Reshaping Ministry: Essays in Memory of Wesley Frensdorff*. Ed. Josephine Borgeson and Lynne Wilson. Arvada, Colo.: Jethro Publications, 1990. Pp. 17–41.

Giles, Kevin. *Patterns of Ministry among the First Christians*. Melbourne: Collins Dove, 1989.

Gomes, Peter J. *The Good Book: Reading the Bible with Mind and Heart*. New York: William Morrow, 1996.

Goss, Robert. *Jesus Acted Up: A Gay and Lesbian Manifesto*. San Francisco: Harper, 1993.

Grant, Robert M. *A Historical Introduction to the New Testament*. New York and Evanston, Ill.: Harper & Row, 1963.

Greenleaf, Robert K. *Seeker and Servant: Reflections on Religious Leadership*. Ed. Anne T. Fraker and Larry C. Spears. San Francisco: Jossey-Bass, 1996.

Gregory of Nyssa. *The Life of Moses*. Trans. Abraham J. Malherbe and Everett Ferguson. New York: Paulist Press, 1978.

Griffiss, James. *Naming the Mystery: How Our Words Shape Prayer and Belief*. Cambridge, Mass.: Cowley Publications, 1990.

Griswold, Frank T. "The Bishop as Presider, Teacher, and Person of Prayer: A Personal Reflection." *Anglican Theological Review* 77 (1995): 5–13.

Haldane, Jean. "Private Faith and Public Responsibility." In *Reshaping Ministry: Essays in Memory of Wesley Frensdorff*. Ed. Josephine Borgeson and Lynne Wilson. Arvada, Colo.: Jethro Publications, 1990. Pp. 179–96.

Hardy, Richard P. *Knowing the God of Compassion: Spirituality and Persons Living with AIDS.* Ottawa: Novalis, 1993.

Harper, Ralph. *On Presence: Variations and Reflections.* Philadelphia: Trinity Press International, 1991.

Hellwig, Monika K. *The Eucharist and the Hunger of the World.* New York: Paulist Press, 1976.

―――. *Whose Experience Counts in Theological Reflection?* Milwaukee: Marquette University Press, 1982.

Hopkins, Alberta Pualani. "The Challenge of the Future: Creating a Place Called Home." In *The Challenges of the Past, The Challenges of the Future.* Ed. John L. Kater, Jr. Berkeley, Calif.: Church Divinity School of the Pacific, 1994. Pp. 73–80.

Hughes, Kathleen. "Conversion of Mind and Heart in Theological Education." *Theological Education* 33/2 (Spring 1997): 1–10.

James, E. O. *From Cave to Cathedral: Temples and Shrines of Prehistoric, Classical, and Early Christian Times.* London: Thames and Hudson, 1965.

Jamieson, Penny. "The Distaff of God: Some Reflections on a New Episcopate." In *Episcopacy: Views from the Antipodes.* Ed. Alan H. Cadwallader. North Adelaide, Australia: Anglican Board of Christian Education, 1994. Pp. 343–55.

Kavanagh, Aidan. "Christian Ministry and Ministries." *Anglican Theological Review* Supplementary Series 9 (1984): 36–48.

Kitagawa, Joseph. "Priesthood in the History of Religions." In *To Be a Priest: Perspectives on Vocation and Ordination.* Ed. Robert E. Terwilliger and Urban T. Holmes, III. New York: Seabury Press, 1976.

Koenig, John. *New Testament Hospitality: Partnership with Strangers as Promise and Mission.* Philadelphia: Fortress Press, 1985.

Lawler, Michael G. *Symbol and Sacrament: A Contemporary Sacramental Theology.* New York: Paulist Press, 1987.

Leech, Kenneth. *Soul Friends: The Practice of Christian Spirituality.* San Francisco: Harper & Row, 1977.

McFague, Sallie. *Models of God: Theology for an Ecological, Nuclear Age.* Philadelphia: Fortress Press, 1987.

Mead, Loren B. et al. *Excellence in Ministry: Study Document: Personal and Professional Needs of the Clergy of the Episcopal Church.* New York: Episcopal Church Foundation, 1988.

Miles, Jack. "The Common Reader and the Adjunct Professor: A Meditation on the Lives of the Mind." *Religious Studies News,* May 1998, 6.

Miles, Margaret R. *Practicing Christianity: Critical Perspectives for an Embodied Spirituality.* New York: Crossroad, 1990.

Moore, Charles W., William J. Mitchell, and William Turnbull, Jr. *The Poetics of Gardens.* Cambridge, Mass.: MIT Press, 1993.

Morse, Christopher. *Not Every Spirit: A Dogmatics of Christian Disbelief.* Valley Forge, Pa.: Trinity Press International, 1994.

Nelson, Richard D. *Raising up a Faithful Priest: Community and Priesthood in Biblical Theology.* Louisville: Westminster/John Knox Press, 1993.

Neusner, Jacob. *First-Century Judaism in Crisis: Yohanan ben Zakkai and the Renaissance of Torah.* Nashville and New York: Abingdon Press, 1975.

Norris, Richard A., Jr. "The Beginnings of Christian Priesthood." *Anglican Theological Review* Supplementary Series No. 9 (1984): 18–32.

Nouwen, Henri. *The Wounded Healer: Ministry in Contemporary Society.* Garden City, N.Y.: Doubleday, 1972.

Otto, Rudolf. *The Idea of the Holy: An Inquiry into the Non-rational Factor in the Idea of the Divine and Its Relation to the Rational.* Trans. John W. Harvey. New York: Oxford University Press, 1958.

Parent, Rémi. *A Church of the Baptized: Overcoming Tension between the Clergy and the Laity.* Trans. Stephen W. Arndt. New York: Paulist Press, 1987.

Raiche, Roger. "Shining Prospects: A Conversation." Interview with George Waters. *Pacific Horticulture* 58/3 (Fall 1997): 25–34.

Ramsey, Michael. *The Christian Priest Today.* New York: Morehouse-Barlow, 1972.

Ray, Thomas K. "The Small Church: Radical Reformation and Renewal of Ministry." *Anglican Theological Review* 78 (1996):615–27.

Ross, Maggie. *The Fire of Your Life: A Solitude Shared.* New York: Paulist Press, 1983.

Scarfe, Janet. "A Pastoral Charge to the Episcopate in the New Order Which Has Already Begun." In *Episcopacy: Views from the Antipodes.*

Ed. Alan H. Cadwallader. North Adelaide, Australia: Anglican Board of Christian Education, 1994. Pp. 201–11.

Schillebeeckx, Edward. *Church: The Human Story of God.* Trans. John Bowden. New York: Crossroad, 1990.

Schütz, John Howard. *Paul and the Anatomy of Apostolic Authority.* Society for New Testament Studies Monograph Series 26. Cambridge: Cambridge University Press, 1975.

Sedgwick, Timothy F. *The Making of Ministry.* Cambridge, Mass.: Cowley Publications, 1993.

Shove, Fredegond. *Poems.* Cambridge: Cambridge University Press, 1956.

Smith, Jonathan Z. *Map Is Not Territory: Studies in the History of Religions.* Leiden: E. J. Brill, 1978.

————. *To Take Place: Toward Theory in Ritual.* Chicago and London: University of Chicago Press, 1987.

Smith, Martin, ed. *Benson of Cowley.* Cambridge, Mass.: Cowley Publications, 1983.

Spohn, William C. "Academic Theology and the Gospel of Jesus Christ." In *Theological Education for the Future.* Ed. Guy Fitch Lytle. Cincinnati: Forward Movement, n.d. Pp. 73–75.

Staples, Brent. "A World in Black and White." Interview by Joel Levine. *University of Chicago Magazine* 86/3 (February 1994). Pp. 25–30.

Stelmach, Harlan. "The Post-Laity Movement." *Laity Exchange* (Winter/Spring 1992): 8–9.

Stringfellow, William. *Instead of Death.* New York: Seabury Press, 1963.

————. "Resisting Babel: Preserving Sanity and Conscience." Excerpt from *An Ethic for Christians and Other Aliens in a Strange Land* (1973). *The Witness,* 78/9 (September 1995):16–19.

Swartley, Willard M. *Slavery, Sabbath, War, and Women: Case Issues in Biblical Interpretation.* Scottsdale, Pa., and Waterloo, Ont.: Herald Press, 1983.

Thompsett, Fredrica Harris. *We Are Theologians: Strengthening the People of the Episcopal Church.* Cambridge, Mass.: Cowley Publications, 1989.

Thurman, Howard. *The Luminous Darkness: A Personal Interpretation of the Anatomy of Segregation and the Ground of Hope.* New York: Harper & Row, 1965.

Underhill, Evelyn. *The Life of the Spirit and the Life of Today.* San Francisco: Harper & Row, 1986. [Originally published in 1922.]

———. *Worship.* New York: Harper Torchbooks, 1957. [Originally published in 1937.]

Weil, Simone. *The Simone Weil Reader.* Ed. George A. Panichas. Mt. Kisco, N.Y.: Moyer Bell, 1977.

———. *Waiting for God.* Trans. Emma Craufurd. New York: Putnam, 1951.

Williams, Rowan. *Christian Spirituality: A Theological History from the New Testament to Luther and St. John of the Cross.* Atlanta: John Knox Press, 1979.

Wright, Robert J., ed. *Prayer Book Spirituality: A Devotional Companion to the Book of Common Prayer Compiled from Classical Anglican Sources.* New York: Church Hymnal Corporation, 1989.

Yerkes, Royden Keith. *Sacrifice in Greek and Roman Religions and Early Judaism.* The Hale Lectures. New York: Scribner, 1951.